(Continued from front flap)

been implemented. This book does more than merely explicate and bemoan the disasters in our society. It calls for more "Anna Krosses" and for direct action from the citizenry *now*:

"If voters can't find the force at the polls, and use it; if politicians can't find the money, and it's there, Democracy has to go under. And it should. There aren't any more options. Democracy's successor is peering in on us now, at every aspect of our daily lives and nightly agonies, quietly waiting while we complete arrangements for our own exit.

"In your own lifetime, whatever your age, doesn't this moment seem closer now?"

Photo by Ken Torrington

MAX WYLIE has written many books, among them *Go Home and Tell Your Mother*, *Trouble in the Flesh*, and *Assignment: Churchill*.

400 Miles from Harlem

ALSO BY MAX WYLIE

NOVELS
Hindu Heaven
Never the Twain
Go Home and Tell Your Mother
Trouble in the Flesh (life of Eugene O'Neill)

NONFICTION
Textbooks
Radio Writing
Radio and Television Writing
Writing for Television

Biographies
The Gift of Janice
Assignment: Churchill (with Inspector Walter H. Thompson)

Anthologies
Best Broadcasts (annual collections)

Social Studies
Career Girl, Watch Your Step
Delinquency Can Be Stopped (with Judge Lester H. Loble)
Clear Channels

PLAYS
The Greatest of These
Everywhere a Chick-Chick (with Milton Geiger)
The Time of the Comet (with Milton Geiger)
Present Danger (with Milton Geiger)
The Flying Nun (for television)

400 Miles from Harlem

COURTS, CRIME, AND CORRECTION

MAX WYLIE

THE MACMILLAN COMPANY, NEW YORK, NEW YORK
COLLIER-MACMILLAN LIMITED, LONDON

Names of persons mentioned in verbatim testimony of included court cases are fictitious.

The Macmillan Company
866 Third Avenue, New York, N.Y. 10022
Collier-Macmillan Canada Ltd., Toronto, Ontario

Library of Congress Catalog Card Number: 72-80908

First Printing

Printed in the United States of America

For the excellent name of Sydnor, wherever it lives and works; for its achievements as historians, artists, writers, musicians, statesmen; and more particularly the Sydnor family of
  Dr. James Rawlings S., theologian, organist, hymnologist
  Margaret Wylie S., singer, teacher, civic leader
  Susan Barksdale S., cellist extraordinary
  Evelyn Sackett S., child therapist and great healer
  Wilmina Kiskaddon S., philosopher, military strategist, these
pages, most of them written in their home, are lovingly dedicated.

Richmond, Virginia
April, 1972

Contents

Introduction

FOR ALMOST THE FIRST TIME in the history of America's prisons, a woman and not a man was appointed to the top spot—Commissioner of Correction—in a major American city. The woman was Anna Moskowitz Kross. The city was New York. And 1954 was the year.

Anna Kross—you've seen the name—held this impossible job for twelve years.

What she found and did, what she tried to do and failed at, is a useful miniature of this nation's big blow-up—San Quentin to Attica—an instructive microcosm of the general agony and the large disgrace that confronts us now.

She lived and worked in an atmosphere of tempest, of tough men (Tammany was part of it), and of a few effective women, surprising for their time. Because the work of Anna Kross was so thorough, what she saw and went through deserves current inspection; deserves it because we do not have today in any city, and won't be having, any new brawls or civic thunderings, any new rushings about or emergency improvisations, that weren't here before.

You name it, she had it.

She inherited a bad press, something this country's jailers can count on, and as she moved through the disinfected cloacas that were her avenues, this same bad press was her most faithful companion. She raised a lot of hell, she shoved people around, and those who needed it most were of course those who disliked it most and who retaliated.

She also inherited the stingiest of priorities to run her prisons with, the same baleful compromise the public has to deal with right now; the same emergency dike-patching, with the public's thumb nervously bobbing from one leakage to another, whether Attica, child-abuse, detention, or the Tombs.

To some of this, because she complained so hard, there was an unusual consequence: Anna Kross was the only woman in our penal history ever to be investigated by three separate committees at the same time.

She was fiery, loving, incautious, vulnerable. She was a quick and disturbing sum-upper. For example, her first view of the charnel-house that was Raymond Street Jail, an antebellum horror-chamber in Brooklyn, provoked only two sentences: "This is a horrid place. I'm going to close it." And only one sentence when notified one midnight that the girls in the Women's House of Detention were rioting: "I don't blame them a bit."

This book is not her biography. It is, rather, a long odyssey, somewhat personal, which I felt compelled to undertake, partly due to the sudden challenge of her unexpected proposal ("Why don't you go down to the Tombs, Mr. Wylie, and speak to the prisoners?") and partly due to my own knowledge that little was being done for a large company of men and women who, whatever crimes they'd committed, were seeing the very worst of America, having the worst of times in the worst of chances.

If this book is not her biography, enough of her story is here to introduce the reader to a sharp recognition of the actual climate for that kind of work, that kind of life; and of what kind of person it is who would even want it, or seek it, or try to survive in it.

Anna Kross never wanted to be a warden. She wanted to be a judge in the Children's Court.

Though I'd been in many prisons in the '40s and '50s to make documentary films, Anna Kross opened new doors for me, doors closed to the public: of Family Court, Children's Court, Probation, the psychiatric and alcoholic clinics, the prison ward at Bellevue, and (most pitiable of all) the children's wards in city hospitals, where youngsters, from six months' old to ten years were (and are now) trying to find their way back after the beatings and burnings and smotherings of sadistic parents. These are the homes many of our murderers come from, not the offending parents but the whipped and mutilated children. If they live, they grow up to pay off the old scores.

I began seeing much of Anna Kross in 1954. In that year, at

her invitation, I joined a volunteer group called the Friendly Visitors, men and women who were willing to give some of their time to talk to and listen to prisoners; prisoners of every type, stripe, color, need. Many were, and are now, redeemable. Many were irretrievably vicious and are now. And will remain so. But all were astonished that someone—anyone—from outside would take time to look in on their cramp and their unrelieved monotony. It was something judges never did. Nor legislators. And precious few clergymen.

One day I wanted to see her famous Home Term Court in action. Everyone knew of it—perhaps her most unique innovation —but no one (except a committee of four) was allowed to attend hearings there. But she opened this door, too, and I went. It was quite a surprise to me, and will be to you.

Home Term Court did not look like a courtroom. And it was not supposed to. No jury-box (no jury), no flags, no audience, no picture of Washington or Old Abe. The judge sat at a small unraised desk. He wore a business suit, not a robe. When I came in, he was quietly turning over some papers his clerk had given him.

A badly battered white woman of 25 stood near the judge's desk, her husband beside her. It was a familiar enough assault case. The plaintiff was nervous, but she was firm. You could tell that by the way she stood, a real but trembling resolution. She'd had all the physical abuse she planned to take. For now, anyhow.

The husband? Uncomfortable, arrogant, he was trying to manage a superior unconcern for the whole proceeding, impersonal detachment, a hint of scorn.

"I've seen you two before," the judge said, looking up. The woman nodded. "I think you better see a doctor before we talk this over." Then to the man: "Bring your wife back here in an hour, Mr. Gifford."

Mr. Gifford, the wife-beater, tensed slightly.

"She can come back in an hour if she wants to but I won't be here."

Now the judge also tensed slightly: "What do you mean you won't be here?"

"I mean it's my wife's affair. She can come back if she feels like it but I won't be here. Period!" Here Mr. Gifford's jaw thrust out as if to add: "So there!"

"You'll be here. In just one hour."

"I *won't* be here! And you don't look like any judge to me!"

"Perhaps I don't look like a judge," the bench conceded evenly, "but I am a judge. This complaint indicates you've not learned anything from two previous appearances here in Home Term Court. And your deportment suggests that common courtesy has no meaning for you at all. That you're something quite special. Well, you're right about not coming back here in an hour. You're going to jail now. For thirty days. Right now. Right from this room."

"But Your Honor! Your Honor! It was just a family squabble. I mean—please! I didn't mean—"

"Thirty days! Rikers Island. Take him out, officer."

The court officer, built like a bailiff and powerful in the chest, put the arm on Mr. Gifford, who blinked his eyes, showed a flash of strong teeth, then stamped out.

I realized I was in the presence of something altogether remarkable.

Here was a process that by-passed all the judicial detritus that had carried millions of cases for many hours or days—weeks even—beyond their need. Here was justice, raw and quick and effective. Anna Kross had been fighting for this kind of court for many years. The tortuosities and blind trails she had to blaze or cut through to get even this far are a big part of her character and her history, a story whose main elements, so far as I know, have never been set down before in one place.

I want the reader to take this journey with me.

The subject of prisoners, especially the young man and the phenomenon of his bleak return to one prison after another, has interested me for a long time. In this connection I read a story some years ago of the success a western judge was having in stopping an almost unstoppable rash of juvenile delinquency in his territory. This was Federal Judge Lester Loble. I did not believe the story, so I flew out to see him and to inspect the operation there, spending several days with this benevolent but tough-minded jurist. Though retired now, he was and still is quite a dynamo.

At about this same time I read of another man, Judge D. A. Yergey of the Juvenile Court in Orlando, Florida, who was practicing the same technique in that city that Judge Loble had initiated in Montana. I flew down to see him as well. The system works there, too. These two judges have done it. It was all true and I wrote Judge Loble's book for him: *Delinquency Can Be Stopped.* Other judges have caught hold of this idea, Judge Leo Weinstein, to mention one more. He is judge of the Juvenile and Domestic Relations Court in Monmouth County, New Jersey.

In widely scattered pieces of American geography, these men have brought an end to the muggings, gang-bangs, rapes, knifings, filling-station holdups, and car thefts that were terrifying entire counties and that are probably terrifying your own now, wherever you live.

Their secret was and is quite simple. Judge Loble came upon it when, upon being sworn, he discovered he had inherited such an epidemic of teenage crime that Helena, the capital of his huge state, was known throughout the west as "Little Chicago." He discovered that juvenile crime could be stopped by *reversing* the ancient custom of shielding young offenders from public examination; that crime among the young where it most flourishes could be stopped by *turning on the floodlight of publicity.*

In Judge Loble's court the young felon's parents sit in the front row. So does the press. The parents see it all. The press reports it all. No aspect of the offender's life is left uncovered.

In its way it was as innovative as the Anna Kross invention of Home Term Court—blunt, honest, quick, disenchanted. Being innovative, it was fought and is being fought by powerful groups, the National Council on Crime and Delinquency primarily, a well-financed organization operating in eighteen of our states; a publicity structure made up of some of our finest citizens whose character is in no way impugned; whose idealism, however unreal, is based upon a true benevolence, but whose pragmatism is so barren as to constitute a treason against the young in this country.

The philosophy of concealment does not diminish crime. It perpetuates it.

It is claimed and it is popularly accepted that publicity scars a young person for life; that it immobilizes the rehabilitative services we already have; that to expose young people to public gaze is cruel. By those fighting the Loble-Yergey-Weinstein salient, it is claimed that what obtains in a western city of 25,000 or in a southern city somewhat larger doesn't relate to Detroit or Philadelphia; that young felons in New York or Boston are anonymous and lost in the huge populations of such invisible multitudes.

I believe this to be altogether untrue. And for these reasons: the city boy knows his own block brick by brick. It's marked off and jealously guarded. It's his Helena. It's his turf. He lives in a great city but is unaware of this. He moves and operates within an ethnic microcosm of known and restricted boundaries, speaks the language, assumes the walk, the clothes, the passwords. Here he is known. And knowing. Here he goes to school. Or truants. Here he steals, shoots up, marries, begets, abandons. It is in this compressed enclave where his vanity (what else is there for him?) is gratified, threatened, and defended. And where his ego starves.

In the matter of juvenile crime, whatever the reader may think of the late J. Edgar Hoover, he did author what I consider one of the most compelling sentences in our language: "Anyone old enough to commit a felony is an adult."

We excuse it all. We hide it all. So we keep getting it.

In today's angry criss-cross, for example, of who killed George Jackson—the society who produced him or the tower guards who shot him—it can be persuasively argued that had his first hearing been held in the presence of his parents and the press, the ensuing years might have been different. There is very good reason why the head-on philosophy of Judge Loble for dealing with young criminals hasn't worked in large cities. It has never been tried in them.

Of course it can be argued, and is being, that George Jackson was a born criminal and that all his actions as a teenager, from jailbreak to stickup, were gun-toting actions destined to end in some sort of shoot-out. But that is not the point here. The point is that correction did no correcting.

It almost never does.

The young addict who knifed my daughter to death had had fourteen arrests, beginning at age fifteen. And two incarcerations before he was twenty. What did society do to rehabilitate him after the first arrest? After the fifth? The tenth?

These thoughts come back now to recall with some embarrassment my own delinquency. It was not so destructive as some but it had serious beginnings: truancy (much of it), forged excuses, car-stealing. The truancy, to see the world; car-stealing to see girls. And the forged excuses to escape punishment. The forger in our group was more diligent than gifted and we were caught cold, all five of us. And quickly and appropriately punished: three hours a day in a silent study-hall for seventeen weeks. I missed the track team that spring. I had much time to consider this simple question: "What am I doing in here when I could be *out there*?"

Rather suddenly I began to grow up. I was sixteen. Sixteen is a dangerous, a critical age for any American male. For any male, any race, any color. It is in the teens that you go one way or the other.

By what close margins we all escape! And you, more daring, may have come closer than I.

We've had a depressing tonnage of articles about rehabilitation, too many of them written by reformers whose typewriter ribbons seem snarled in the ivy, never dipped in the black ink of the cell. To me there seems a good reason we seldom see an article or a study on why it doesn't work. Rehabilitation does not exist. It is my finding that rehabilitation in any practical sense or degree does not exist at all, and I say this after appearing before inmates in many states over the past 22 years and *looking* at the process that converts the offender into a recidivist.

If the thinkers and theorists, the howlers and bleeders would do something besides a Letter-to-Editor, let them go into a prison on their own time and their own money and teach prisoners their own skills, whether typesetting, muffler-installation, or hairdressing.

Social workers push hard at their burdens but they never get the money they need. Nor does Probation. Nor do the psychiatric clinics. So the overload keeps building and the probationer finds his way to Attica—which is 400 miles from Harlem—or Raiford, where the pre-release services are never the hard cash of sincerity but the tin tokens of society's aimless benevolence. ("I gave at the office.")

In every city in America today our best minds, our best edi-

torials are whacking away at the same problem that defeated
Anna Kross. And they are getting the headlines and getting the
mike. But they are piling up just where she did; and just where her
successor did. No money.

So things go on as before: Mayors blaming courts for judicial
drag, courts blaming police, police unwearyingly pointing out that
nothing happens when they bring in a felon, D.A.s saying it wasn't
a "good" arrest. It is openly conceded that houses of correction
correct nothing; that they are "colleges of crime." We know all
this. And agree with it all. But we never act.

Public exasperation has now become very large. So has public
fear. Private fear is deeper still and more fermenting, having no
vent. In a stray sentence buried in their more urgent paragraphs,
all our analysts and editorialists wish there was more money. Yet
none says how the money can be got. One would suppose if they
knew they'd say.

Thus the focus in this inquiry—better to call it an odyssey, for
in these past decades I've been to over a hundred facilities, both
prisons and mental hospitals, and spoken to inmates in 56 of
them—is on the hard rock of there being no money.

To pick a single whimsical example, it explains why there is no
such thing as rehabilitation. So don't wait for it, for you won't see
it. Nor will this nation's inmates see it. Planned, legislated reform
has been on the drafting-board for fifty years. And is there now in
all fifty states. And for fifty years has stayed there. And will. The
money is always recommended. Then the hose is bent. Nothing
comes out the nozzle. We set up treatment centers for addicts and
celebrate our civic goodness. Then we look at the bill and close
them down. We do the same for alcoholics. Yet there is no man in
prison who is untouched by one or the other.

Viewing this wretched parade of foot-draggers and stumbling
pass-receivers, the public sees itself as a defenseless victim. The
fact may be quite different. The fact may be that the public is not
the victim at all but the villain. "We have met the enemy and it is
us." Could it not in truth be you and I? You and I who so nobly
disapprove the whole show, you and I who tolerate all of it?

The fact is—or so it appears to me—that no American *really*
wants to get into the act of courts-crime-correction. What he
really wants is to hear about it, read about it, see it on television,

gasp, and discuss it. Americans are great discussers. We will discuss anything with anybody provided we don't have to do anything or fix anything or get up. If this booming apathy had applied to maritime enterprise, we'd still be a British colony.

It does apply to something no less visible than steam and sail. It applies to the inner rot of Democracy. We really don't want to have to deal with crime, its origins, its perpetrators, nor deal very much with its poultice-applicators. What we really want to do is to walk away from it all. So we do.

And here we are altogether contemptible.

It may be inevitable as well; inevitable in any society that can put a Lieutenant William Calley on a pedestal and a Sergeant David Durk in the pillory. We have become a society that no longer deplores the departure of decency from American life. We don't seem to know it's gone. Nor what it was. So how can we miss it?

If voters can't find the force at the polls, and use it; if politicians can't find the money, and it's there, Democracy has to go under. And it should. There aren't any more options. Democracy's successor—you name him—is peering in on us now, at every aspect of our daily lives and nightly agonies, quietly waiting while we complete arrangements for our own exit.

In your own lifetime, whatever your age, doesn't this moment seem closer now?

Historically we've ignored our Cassandras, wilfully at first, pitiably soon after. So with Anna Kross who spelled it all out for all who could read, think, hear, or care. Her assessment, her predictions, too, are with us now, every one of them. So also is the funereal similarity between the city she served and every U.S. city now. And she didn't throw in the sponge till 1965, at age seventy-three

Because what she found and reported and gave her life to repair (and largely failed at); because the evil eutrophication of the swamps she pushed her horses through; because this identical terrain is now ours, I have run many a weary mile and done so for one reason only: that this special and perceptive modern-day Cassandra can now be heard and heeded. We're still clattering about in the same fens and baileys where she was unhorsed. If we have a chance to remount, we should take it. No fresh horses are on the way.

In this study the primary focus, as I've said, is on money. The secondary focus is on the American-family-in-trouble and an examination of the social matrices that seek to bind such families together when they come unstuck. Without the preservation of the family, as a working and viable unit, without the enduring basis of stabilized families, we have nothing and we cannot survive, Alvin Toffler's unsettling prediction of future family-structure notwithstanding.

It has been suggested that at the core of our private convictions about the etiology of crime and the care and feeding of our criminals, we really don't give a damn. This may be true. The conscience and the vanity of most of us is so easily served in sudden flares of personal protest, sudden articles, or fiery appearances on television as to exempt us from action. We "told them off" and, in doing so, dispersed the pressures of our own fears and furies. But this exemption is false. It is also both epidemic and durably American. If it isn't our most popular response to crisis, it is our most weatherbeaten, and it shows its gray mosses, in black type, in every city's paper every day.

I should like to give special thanks to Judge Florence M. Kelley, Administrator of the New York Family Court, by whose authority I have been able, during these past years, to attend a large number of hearings, trials, and conferences that are by law and tradition closed to the public. And given permission by her to publish what I saw and heard.

There are some great energies at work on the huge problems of our courts and prisons and correction services. It is possible we are coming to the end of our blindness. If this does not turn out to be true, then I must join the other Jeremiahs and agree that we have come to the end of our rope.

Don't expect prison reform in your lifetime because you're not going to see it. You'll hear a lot about reform—you're hearing it now—but all you'll see is a reshuffle of the same old numbers.

Society is indeed responsible for society's mess, each waiting for another to act. No one acts. It is society—which is to say it is you, it is I—who go on maintaining this horror; maintaining it by going on talking; by feeling but not thinking; by reading something about prisons or prison guards and reacting sharply to it, then going to the movies.

It is not a facetious challenge that you offer your skills to a prison or a jail. In most prisons you'd be very welcome. Wardens have only what you give them, his guards only the pay you allow. If you want to see a warden drop dead from shock—happy shock —knock on his office door:

"I'm a choir director. I want to teach your inmates to sing."

But bring your own stuff. He won't have much.

This book is about some of the people who knocked on the door.

PART ONE

The World of Anna Kross

THERE WILL ALWAYS BE PROSTITUTES

IN NEW YORK, as elsewhere throughout the western world, it was rare that a financially successful prostitute or a flush madam was ever apprehended. They could "pay to stay." It was always the poverty-stricken, illiterate street-walker who took the knock. Very often these sad women—most of them young—had been driven to prostitution because they didn't have enough to eat. No training either, and no skills. And no job openings.

In 1907 a law was passed that created a "night court." This law had a good idea behind it: to offer an immediate hearing and a proper trial for both males and females who had had the bad luck to be arrested after the regular courts had closed. But in three years this new court was so overcrowded as to be functionless.

One day in the early 1940s the late Mayor La Guardia, in one of his Sunday afternoon radio talks with the kids and family, reminisced, bringing back some of his own memories of that early court. He'd spent a year there making money as an interpreter (in four languages). He spoke of the old "jail judges" and of the "fining judges" who sat there.

When a "fining judge" was sitting, La Guardia recalled, a great wave of cases swept in. Money for everybody. And police could maintain a good arrest record. Bail bondsmen got rich. The traffic through that court was so cynical, even the press was shocked. Through the efforts of Senator Alfred R. Page this court was later split into two sections, separating the men and the women. The men went to East 57th Street, the women to Jefferson Market. This occurred in 1910.

Jefferson Market concentrated on cases of prostitution. There was a small percentage of shop-lifters, but for the most part, and right through its bleak and bleary existence, its specialty was the $2-a-trick girls. With the pin-spot right on them, night after night,

15

year after year, it gradually got through to the public that what
was going on down there wasn't making much sense. And wasn't
helping either the city or the girls.

The true conditions in the lives and backgrounds of many of
these lost and giddy creatures was from time to time poked into by
an independent crusader or reporter. And right after World War I
there were the beginnings of an awakening of public conscience:
first acknowledgements of guilt, stupidity, civic responsibility. Not
much, but some.

A Preacher Takes Off His Coat

Among those whose conscience had been stirred were several
members of the Protestant Episcopal Church of the Ascension,
geographically quite close to the court in question. This church
was, and is, a fine old specimen of Victorian Gothic and is often
visited by tourists coming to admire the John LaFarge mural, the
Ascension of Christ. But the main spark was the rector, a young
bachelor—Percy Stickney Grant. Reverend Grant represented
something long vanished from the American pulpit and only half
seen by the vision of today's seminarians: a bold willingness to
wade into something unusually dirty and try to clean it up.

This man, still well remembered by many old-time New Yorkers, never did anything just for show. He wanted action, not approval. His pulpiteering had little fire and no exhorting, yet he was
overwhelmingly convincing. The warmth and genuineness of his
appeal was irresistible. He made sense, hard sense, about all he
did, all the time. He opened the doors of his church to the poor,
the underprivileged, the homeless, somewhat as Norman Vincent
Peale is today providing free counsel and relief for the psychiatri-
cally damaged.

Of course, the fact that Percy Stickney Grant was a good-look-
ing bachelor in his mid-thirties probably gave him added persuasiveness with the ladies, but he used this well, too. And he was
practical.

He started a forum at the Church of the Ascension that met
every week to have open discussion of any of the serious social
problems afflicting the city at that time. And not merely to "discuss" them. They met to *deal* with them.

Deal with them how? In the case of jailed prostitutes, deal with them by visiting them in prison; bringing them clothes to come home in, books to read, yarn to knit, or carfare so relatives could visit.

It made a permanent impression on almost any young prostitute when a well-dressed, well-spoken, well-heeled woman came to pay her a visit, bring her something good to eat, and did it without any tsk-tsking whatever. It was a brand new experience. But where had the good lady heard about all this?

Anna Kross, the Jewess, Meets Some WASPS

Active in the forum was Bertha Rembaugh, who knew Anna Kross and had heard her talk of the true situation as it then obtained at Jefferson Market Court. As a lawyer, Anna Kross had stood at the shoulder of many hundreds of these wronged and machine-processed young whores and had represented them before the various circulating magistrates who spun through the old hall on the rotation system then prevailing.

She wanted people to know what was going on, so she accepted the invitation to appear at the church, and there described a typical session of the Night Court for Women:

"A policeman is sworn. He seats himself as a witness. 'I saw the accused loitering,' he relates, naming a location on the West Side. 'It was about 1:30 A.M. She accosted a man. She said something to him. The man shook his head and went on. She stopped two other men. I asked the last man: 'Is that your wife?' He said, 'No, she asked me if I'd go with her for a good time.' So I arrested her.

" 'Did you personally hear what the defendant said?' asks the lawyer. 'No, I did not,' says the policeman. Now the lawyer for the girl objects to what the man or woman is supposed to have said. 'Your Honor, that is hearsay,' he points out. Invariably from the bench is the same response: 'Objection overruled.'

"The defendant now takes the stand. She protests her innocence but says she has been drinking. 'That's our case, Your Honor,' says her lawyer. 'She had a few drinks but she was not drunk. And she did not solicit.'

"Nonetheless the judge finds her guilty. First she is fingerprinted, then held for probation investigation. Now may I point out to this forum that there is no law against drinking, not in the whole state. Nor for that matter is there a law against fornication. There *is* a law against adultery but I've never seen it invoked."

A Committee That Didn't Talk but Acted

A committee of fifteen was created, with Anna Kross as chairman. It went right to work. Its chief job was to protect indigent girls from shysters and bail-bond thieves; from being conned by pimps and procuresses who hung about every night, partly on the lookout for new talent for their own stables, partly to familiarize themselves with the faces of the Vice Squad plainclothesmen. The group from the Church of the Ascension wanted to handle only one aspect of a bigger problem: to see that the girls in this nightly show got a fair break.

Prior to the existence of this committee, there of course had been a public "attitude." It proceeded on the theory that if the prostitutes, once caught, were found to be diseased, they would be cured. If sent to a reformatory, they would emerge reformed. The small matter of justice was shunted to one side by "good intentions." We still have this.

But the Ascension group was special. Reverend Grant's committee was on the job, every night for years, acting as or providing counsel. There was at least one committee member present every night for the rest of the year Night Court was open.

Since it was an open court, Jefferson Market had an audience about as refined as a floor show. Night after night the prurient hung about, ogling and gaping, sniggering, enjoying their peculiar browsings. The huge room, bare as a warehouse, was crowded with pimps, tired cops, dope sellers. Here the magistrate was judge and jury. Cases spun by with slot-machine speed. The vans pulled up, the girls were loaded in, and rolled off in predawn darkness. I saw it twice. It was part of my neighborhood when I was a young man, and it shook me.

It made Anna Kross mad. In addition to the Legal Committee, a Prison Committee was soon developed. Its members would go into the jails and detention pens and talk to prisoners; see what help they needed; register their complaints; report their findings to the Legal Committee.

This kind of community intervention, of practical intercession —invasion if you wish—has pretty much disappeared from the court and prison structures of most American cities, but the work done through that church, that man, and his workers is, in some of its ramifications, still going on. Today's organization—the Friendly Visitors—had its origin in this earlier reaching-out of nearly fifty years ago. It was a new thing: the "saved" talking to the "lost" with no trace of patronage. New York's best women were going into every jail to listen to "true-life" stories of physical and social anguish beyond bearing.

It took time and it took courage, but there were some great women about at the time (1910–1930) who had both: Mrs. Fitz-hugh John Porter, Mrs. William S. Dessar, Alice Menken come to mind. You didn't have to be an Episcopalian to get into the act. You just had to believe in the work and be willing to get dirty. Alice Menken, for example, belonged to the Spanish-Portuguese Synagogue and took care of the Jewish inmates' problems.

The Other Side of Frank Harris

The stench and the injustice and the pure quality of cynicism that hung about the Jefferson Market facility was so fixed that other services were called on. The impact of the Federation of Women's Clubs was thrown behind these earlier phalanxes. They presently made it the big issue in their activities.

So also, for a time, did the famous-infamous rake and ravisher, Frank Harris.

His bedroom acrobatics, internationally celebrated, have been allowed to obscure other enthusiasms that were properly his, and out of which he made his money. It is true that he spent so much time in bed it is a wonder he was ever seen, dressed, on a London street. But whatever else he was, he had a lot of raw courage. He was a believer in causes, an accepter of challenges, an angry recti-fier of injustice, a garish though accurate reporter. He was a man afraid of no contest, standing or lying down. When not in bed with an interesting companion, he was in bed with a pad and pencil. It's where he wrote.

He was in New York now. Anna Kross read about it and went to see him. He had a large unconcealed scorn for "Jew lawyers"— his term—but Mrs. Kross had come for something well beyond personal concerns. She wanted him to see the mess at Jefferson Market and write an article about it in *Pearson's Magazine*. She was a great believer in the effectiveness of the pointed finger.

She was not impressed with the Frank Harris reputation, his waxed moustache nor his wavy hair. She was impressed with the power of his vocabulary, the colorful spurt in his phrase-making, the sting of his fury. And she knew this priapic flaneur wasn't quite through as a journalist; that though suspect in some areas, ostracized and broke, he still had a robust Quentin Reynolds punch or two and she wanted it struck where it would count.

When Anna Kross got through talking to Frank Harris, he agreed to go down and see for himself. And he did so. He was outraged, fascinated, aflame. And presently went to work. Nine articles appeared, not just one, six of them in the latter half of 1916.

He was a tough man to shock but what he saw and heard shocked him thoroughly. He got beneath the surface of this whole grisly show: the framing of the girls, the unwarranted arrests that were pretexts for mulcting the girls, postponements of trials for the purpose of extracting bail money. Corruption everywhere; cruelty, heartlessness, judicial idiocy.

For this labor, Harris earned the hostility of the court's advocates and the wrath of John F. Sumner, head of the Society for the Suppression of Vice. Sumner outdistanced his predecessor, Anthony Comstock, for being the most cloth-headed package of stilted self-righteousness this nation has brought forth up to now. Sumner had actually brought a court action against *Pearson's Magazine* to try to prevent the printing of verbatim testimony given in court! (Sumner, the purist, lived into today's "porno" age but it was just too much for him, and he died in 1971, aged ninety.)

Early Police Scandal

The case that had Frank Harris foaming was this: Michel Guilbert, an industrious Alsatian and an immigrant with a good job in

Hoboken, was successful and happy. He was thirty. His wife, Marte, was three months' pregnant. The Guilberts had enough money to provide an occasional "hired girl" to help Mrs. Guilbert with the cleaning and with meal preparations. One Saturday afternoon in the summer, before Michel had come back to Manhattan on the Barclay Street ferry, an elderly acquaintance of the Guilberts stopped by. Mrs. Guilbert had been to the A&P, getting the weekend groceries. The change from a $10 bill lay on the kitchen table. Mrs. Guilbert excused herself for a moment, changed into a light housedress and returned to show the hired girl where the utensils were for cleaning the stove.

A man knocked at the door; he said he was a traveler and was tired. He was admitted, offered a chair, and given a cup of tea and a biscuit. The hired girl, finishing with the stove, left. A few moments later, the stranger also left. Almost at once he was back, however, and this time with a detective who arrested Mrs. Guilbert for prostitution, claiming that a $2 bill on the table was marked and had belonged to him.

Speechless with astonishment, rage, and fright (her English was not secure), Mrs. Guilbert was taken to Jefferson Market court and tossed into the detention pen.

After frantic inquiries and wild chasing about, Michel, the husband, finally found her there, but in such hysterical shape she had not been able to answer the judge's questions. So she had been imprisoned. Monday morning she was brought into court again. It was then that Anna Kross, as chairman of the Legal Committee operating out of the Fifth Avenue church, moved in on the terrified creature and offered to help. She noted at once that the "weak" part of the case was the presence in the Guilbert's kitchen of the elderly acquaintance. She instructed Mr. Guilbert to bring this person, as well as the hired girl, to court as witnesses. They appeared the next morning.

All three testified to the woman's absolute honesty, fine character, unblemished neighborhood reputation. But she was pronounced guilty nonetheless and sent back to prison for two more days, when she was released on three months' probation. But the ordeal was too much for her and in seventeen days she was dead.

The whole case rested on the testimony of the detective.

Pearson's Magazine gives a full account of this traumatizing foul-up and it set the tone for the many articles which followed. (These can be seen in the Microfilm Service of the New York Public Library.)

Once more Anna Kross had levelled a finger at this ash-pit of civic shame; once more moved a bit closer to its abolition.

Her own committees and those she worked with were unlike any committees ever seen: they accomplished things. They didn't meet; they acted. They raised the devil. They shook and stirred people.

By this time the New York City Federation of Women's Clubs had rolled up its sleeves and were as militantly ready as the two earlier committees that came into being through Percy Stickney Grant. They banged away at the Albany legislature. They rented Town Hall and Webster Hall. They irritated the Wigwam. Eventually, in 1919, they won a big break-through. They got Albany to change the infamous Vagrancy Law (Section 887 of the Code of Criminal Procedure, Subdivision 4). The law—unchanged since 1829!—had come to apply only to "females." The drive of the committees secured the changing of this word to "persons," thus removing the stigma of sex from the statute.

It's still not a good statute and it's badly administered, but the victory pleased the committees, and especially pleased Anna Kross. Her whole remembered childhood had been spent half a block from the Allen Street brothels, and her earliest rages had their origins over the penalty system that always branded the woman but never mentioned her sexual partner. But a chance soon came.

Anna Kross in Action

One night on Eighth Street this ancient rage of hers boiled over. She was on her way home from Night Court. It was two in the morning. As she stood waiting for the Eighth Street trolley, a man sidled up to her and offered his company for the rest of the night.

"Sure," said Anna, hiding her fury. "Let's have a good time."

She walked along with him till they met a policeman. Then her grip tightened on the man's wrist.

"Officer," she directed, "arrest this man! He solicited me!"

The policeman gave her a queer look. But the lady lawyer

insisted he go back to the Night Court with her so she could be identified for sure. This done, they had to walk to the Mercer Street precinct, ten blocks away, so the masher could be booked. At the station-house there was poor cooperation. Nothing like this had ever happened—a *woman* arresting a *man* for *soliciting*! It was nowhere in the book.

She then made the policeman escort her back to Eighth Street and wait there with her till her trolley came. That wasn't all:

"If I can get up in the morning to appear against that masher, I guess you can. I have your shield number. You better see you're there."

The next morning she appeared as both complaining witness and lawyer against the amazed defendant. Today, her comment about what happened is brief and sour:

But it was really her victory and she knew it.

"He was fined ten dollars. A woman would have been sent to jail."

Another Scandal—A Big One

Very soon after this the papers got hold of another story, one that carried such a wallop that the whole city was shaken. In the case of Anna Kross bringing in a man for soliciting *her*, she had surprised and delighted New York with the bright logic of such an unexpected turnaround. It had a neat heroine touch to it. It was something that had never been done before; its obvious fairness could face down any challenge.

But the case of New York against Emily Hoffman for prostitution was such an outrageous rig, a case so instantly seen through and so quickly castigated by the whistling lash of a fine judge (Wadhams), that you can still hear it hit and feel the sting of it. It made headlines all over America. Here is some of it:

Court of General Sessions of the Peace in and for the County of New York, Part I—
The People of the State of New York, on the Complaint of Gilbert Wheelwright, against Emily Hoffman.
Charge: Vagrancy. Prostitution in a Tenement House.
New York, Wednesday, Sept. 11, 1920

Appearances: James E. Smith, Esq., Assistant District Attorney for the People, Paul D. DeFrere, Esq., for the Defendant.

JUDGE WADHAMS:—

"The defendant appeals from a judgment convicting her of Vagrancy, in that she violated Section 150 of the Consolidated Laws, being a Section of the Tenement House Act, the charge being that the defendant offered to commit prostitution.

"Without examining the evidence of the defendant, it appears from the testimony of Gilbert Wheelwright, the complaining witness, that he is a police officer attached to the Headquarters Division, and that on the night in question, November 26th, 1919, he called the apartment of the defendant on the telephone. The object of this call was to make an appointment to call upon the defendant.

"Thereafter, and about an hour later, the telephone call having taken place at 11 o'clock, at about midnight the complaining witness arrived at the premises with another officer and was admitted. What subsequently happened, in the words of the police officer, is as follows:

" 'We sat down in the front room and waited until they got on their hats and coats. We went out about 12:30 in a taxicab and went to Healy's at 66th Street. We entered Healy's and had beer for drinks. After having beer for drinks at Healy's we left about 3 A.M. We went back to the premises, went into the apartment of the defendant where we remained for a short time.'

"And then," interposes Judge Wadhams, interrupting his own reading of the transcript, "the officer alleged that the defendant committed the act of which he complains." Being asked what took place at Healy's the officer answers: 'We danced and we laughed and we drank.' "Question: 'You ate, of course, in addition to drinking?'

"Answer: 'No, didn't have anything to eat; just drank and danced.'

"It further appears that the officers then returned with the defendant and the companion in a taxicab to the premises.

"Question: 'And you returned to the apartment at what hour?'

"Answer: 'I should judge it was about 3:30. That is to say, three thirty in the morning.' "

JUDGE WADHAMS:

"It is unnecessary to pursue this evidence further. It appears from the evidence that instead of the defendant being on trial, the officer should be on trial. It is the officer who solicited the defendant, by calling her on the telephone, by taking her to Healy's, by there plying her with drinks until 3:30 in the morning.

"The District Attorney of this County is directed to inquire by what authority the city's money is being used to hire taxicabs and paying for dancing and drinking in a public resort until three o'clock in the morning.

"This method of proceeding is known as provocation. The court has already, on previous occasions in writing opinions, pointed out the distinction between the legitimate trap and a provocation of crime. In the case of a legitimate trap, the police, learning that a crime is about to be committed, arrange that witnesses shall be present in order that the evidence may be obtained to convict on the commission of the crime by the defendant, independently of any inducement on the part of the police.

"This is not such a case. In this case, the crime is induced, procured, and provoked by the police who deliberately undertake to effect the commission of the crime, to lead the defendant into the commission of the crime.

"The danger of permitting such convictions to stand or tolerating the obtaining of judgments by such methods is obvious. One illustration alone is sufficient to show the danger. Take the case of a man paying alimony to some woman, the step from the procedure in this case to the procedure in such a case is a very short one. The man paying the alimony, in order to get out of paying it, induces a police officer to take a taxi ride or a trip to Healy's or some other restaurant and remain out until three o'clock in the morning with the woman to whom the alimony is being paid, that he may be rid of her.

"Moreover, this method of procedure opens the door wide to blackmail.

"The record before me is a scandalous record. It shocks the sense of decency. We have a body of policemen in this community who are faithfully performing their work, a courageous and diligent body of men. The acts of policemen, as this complainant, bring the whole police force into disrepute. *The first duty of the law is to be lawful and not to procure the violation of the law.*

"It appears from this record that this police officer not only was the initiator and instigator by calling on the telephone and making the appointment, but, having arrived in the premises, he took the defendant in a taxicab, remained out with her until the early hours of the morning, dancing and drinking, and then returned with her in a taxicab.

"I think it is very doubtful upon the record whether the word of such an officer can be accepted. His own conduct is such as to absolutely destroy the credit of this testimony. It is obvious that his conduct makes him unworthy of belief under oath.

"It appears from the evidence of this officer that at a time when there was a war measure in effect prohibiting the sale of intoxicating liquor, this defendant took part in violation of that pro-vision, paying for the drinks with the city's money. *The taxpayers' money is not to be used for violations of the law.*

"This Court will not sustain any judgment of conviction where, from the testimony, it appears that the crime was procured to be committed by the acts of the police.

"On the facts and on the law, the judgment is reversed. The complaint is dismissed. The defendant is discharged.

"The Clerk of this Court is directed to send a copy of this opinion to the Police Commissioner."

This case, and the clean, coherent thrust of thought that made up the opinion, was widely celebrated at the time, and is still referred to. Of course it hit all the papers. For the matter at hand, it was of huge value to Anna Kross and her co-workers in their missionary zeal to set right the degrading conditions and the medieval unfairness of Women's Night Court. Such independent corroboration as the court opinion just seen served dramatically to pull together and to package a number of evils that she, as a lady lawyer, had been firing away at for years. When a male judge banged his gavel after a whithering statement like the above and set free a woman more sinned against than sinning, it had the effect of snatching Joan of Arc from the fire.

But the meretricious smell of Women's Court still had a long time to smoulder.

Then quite suddenly, quite by chance and by chance only, something unusual happened. The impeccably scrupulous Anna Kross wound up at Tammany Hall and joined all the rogues.

Tammany and the Mayors

Tammany Hall, now a hundred and five years old, wasn't such a dirty place to those who had desks there. And it can claim a number (not unlimited) of thoroughly incorruptible men. Anna Kross became a Tammany creature without meaning to. While a member of the Legal Committee of the Church of the Ascension and while putting aside several nights a week to look in on the Women's Night Court, she was making her living as a lawyer specializing in labor union disputes.

Her daily contact with courts and judges began to interest her in other aspects of the law, criminal law especially. She thought she ought to know more about it, as part of her general development as a good barrister. She began attending the juicy routines of the General Sessions Criminal Court, where felony cases were tried before a jury.

In those days—1915–1920—if you wished to be assigned to represent an indigent defendant, you handed your card up to the judge. She handed her card to a judge named Warren Foster, who in turn assigned her to a man doing time in the Tombs. The prisoner was up on a burglary rap and unable to raise bail. Anna Kross visited him many times, prepared the case, and presented it in Judge Foster's court. And lost the case.

When the trial was over (it was quite short), Judge Foster surprised the young lady attorney by inviting her into his chambers and congratulating her on a seriously prepared piece of defense, "forcefully and convincingly delivered."

They chatted for an hour. George B. McClellan's 1916 campaign against John Purroy Mitchel for Mayor of New York was about to start. Judge Foster was running for re-election to the Court of General Sessions. A canon of legal ethics prevents a judge already on the bench from participating in a campaign. Foster asked Anna Kross to speak for him.

She didn't know anything about politics and though she spent her life in its pits and caverns, she never did learn. Not the first thing. (Twenty years after this, Mayor La Guardia was to scream at her: "Anna, you're a *lousy* politician!") But she agreed to help Judge Foster. She was meeting people, getting closer to those who ran things, being "with it."

Judge Foster took her to Tammany Hall. It was then on Fourteenth Street and Irving Place. She equated Tammany with corruption and had done so since her Lower East Side upbringing, where Jews, in fear of being dispossessed or unable to put food on the table, never thought of Tammany. "Go to Eighth Street" was their solution. There was a Jewish philanthropic office on Eighth Street.

She still had not realized that if she appeared on platforms for a Tammany man, she would herself be connected in the public mind with Tammany. Her first talk for the Judge took place in a huge vacant store, later taken over by Hearn's. There was smoke in the air and sawdust all over the floor. Men's voices, loud laughter, the scrape of chairs, the sounds of hammering, the glare of unshaded light bulbs and the clang-clang of passing trolleys didn't suggest that her talk would be received with cathedral hush. But she was ready. She never used notes; she was too near-sighted. This of course, as any speaker knows, was a valuable plus. It gave freshness and immediacy, the sure sense of direct communication. She did her own rehearsing in her own mind, on subways and trolleys.

Judge Foster pounded a gavel and roared out an introduction. Anna Kross got up and began to talk. She was tiny, but she was vital. She realized she was the only woman in the immense room; realized, too, that this was a bit of a novelty for the men. She had other things going for her: she was a born speaker and she was very sure of her subject. She admired the Judge and said so. Quickly she took her audience through the Foster biography, villains he'd put away, money he'd saved the city, injustices he'd corrected.

It was the first of 44 talks she made for this gentleman, appearing in any spot, for any occasion the campaign committee called her for. But he lost the election.

Her forensic power, her persuasiveness, her easy manner on platforms, her sudden fire, her absolute command of her own legal speciality—all these began to get talked about. Her prejudice about Tammany got smoothed over and sandpapered. She found out the truth of its origins: that it was originally a fraternal group designed to help new immigrants, Irish especially, find their way in a new climate and new culture; to help and protect them. It had come into being soon after the Civil War. If you were in trouble, somebody in Tammany knew it because somebody in Tammany lived in your block. They put coal in your cellar, blankets on your bed; took you to the hospital, brought you home. "We do this for you. All you do is vote for our boy.

(Charles A. Beard, the historian, had a comforting thing to say about it: "It gives relief first and investigates later." He declared it to be the best social agency in the city.)

By this time, Anna Kross had met Al Smith. When he decided to run for Governor from his position as President of the Board of Alderman, she went to see him and to offer her services. He took her to Tammany Hall to talk to Charles F. Murphy, leader of the Democratic Party. It was the beginning of a friendship that lasted through the rest of Murphy's life. Both these men—Murphy at the peak of his powers, Al Smith very much on the way up—began to see, in this slim little brown-headed lawyer, something that was both new and intriguing: the great potential of women in politics.

Woman in a Man's World

Women in New York State had just won the right to vote. They'd heard much of Anna Kross. Her field, labor law, had given her a wide acquaintance with plasterers, bricklayers, roofers, cloth-spongers, lathers, carpenters, hoisters, plumbers. Not only their problems but their special vocabularies became her own. She'd gone to bat for hundreds of these fellows: men fallen from scaffoldings, burned at the rivet forges, crippled by machinery, crushed, dismembered, killed by it. She fought for the widows' pensions when their men were gone. Her voice was clear, her words simple. She had the great gift of instant rapport. And although built like a sparrow, she had presence. As counsel for the Building Trades Compensation Bureau she'd heard and dealt with all the heavy risks and cruelties of New York construction, from subways to skyscrapers. She had developed command and authority. She knew her stuff, the exact formula of mortar, the impact in foot-pounds of a 165-pound man who had fallen 42 feet.

Her meeting at Tammany with Al Smith and Charles ("Commissioner") Murphy was productive. She outlined what she thought: that Al Smith was not well known in upstate New York; that most voters outside of New York City didn't realize Smith was a strong supporter of the Widow's Pension Law, of the 48-hour work week, the St. Lawrence Seaway, Adirondack waterpower, social services for the poor. And for the immediate elimination of every railroad grade-crossing in the state.

Anyone who ever took a trip on the New York Central during the '20s and before will remember the intimate excursion these trains took, nosing their way through Syracuse bedrooms, bathrooms, and corner candy stores. Anna Kross had the insurance figures for the ghastly toll for the whole state. The automobile was very much here by then.

Political Hustings—First Time Out

They decided to send her. She averaged five talks a day for five weeks, reaching Southern Tier counties she'd never heard of, unnamed towns, Granges, colleges, conservatories, fire houses, churches, and private homes. From Plattsburgh to Buffalo, she was a real smash.

When she got back, she could have had anything she asked for. But she didn't ask for anything (a fatal flaw in her make-up, as you will soon see). She was immediately appointed vice-chairman of the Speaker's Bureau of Tammany, a non-paying title that took all her "spare" time.

The campaign was tough. The decimating flu epidemic of 1918 kept many crowds light. The excitement and relief of the ending of the war in Europe, the parades of returning regiments—these interests moved in and out of the political struggle in the state.

Al Smith didn't want the fixed label of Tammany tagging to all he said, nor to all those he was seen with. And in a true sense, though he did not consider Tammany a necessary evil, he exactly knew its depth as a pool of reinforcements that could be tapped at any time; knew it as the principal power center through which candidates got elected. And at that moment, winning was what mattered.

The Anti-Saloon League screamed about Al Smith's being a drinking man. Every Protestant bigot in the state, about half its Protestant population, saw in Al Smith the specter of the Vatican if he got to Albany. Cartoons had him closeted with a cadre of sinister silhouettes—his "advisers"—all bishops and cardinals, to judge by the hats, and all mischievous, to judge by the susurration.

Inevitably, some vapid zealot resuscitated the earlier defamation: Rum, Romanism and Rebellion. So far as anyone could determine, the Pope never sent Al Smith a dime, but he wasn't only a Catholic, he was a self-pronounced *devout* Catholic—the very most dangerous kind! He drank and he approved of it and said so. And he was Tammany, venal, fascinorous, and brash. My, my!

Another Moskowitz Comes In

In addition to Anna Moskowitz Kross, there was another Moskowitz about, no relative of Anna's, a woman who for many years had been a vital factor in settlement work. Her name was Belle. For as many years as her good works were known, she was just as often cited as the most violent anti-Tammany crusader the organization ever had to deal with. She hated it altogether, and everywhere said so. And said why. She had good credentials. Her husband, Henry, at that time head of the Madison Street Settlement House on the Lower East Side, had earlier been Civil Service Commissioner under the outspoken Tammany-hater, Mayor John Purroy Mitchel.

But Belle Moskowitz, after hearing Al Smith speak only once, was determined to meet him. And of all things, to work for him.

She had been completely captured by the depth and constructive import of his social consciousness; his energetic sponsorship of social legislation. She was already working too hard to take on a full-time job. She was helping to support the three children she had had by her first husband, Charles Israels.

Belle Moskowitz had an unattractive personality, bleak, blunt, and barren. And she photographed poorly. But personality wasn't what she was selling. Nor offering. All she wanted was tc help Al Smith peddle his social programs.

The Governor-to-be met her through Abram Elkus chairman of the Al Smith Citizens' Committee. The instant he met her, Smith "bought" her. The Elkus committee was a good organization, with a lot of flex. Its women's branch was headed by Elizabeth Marbury, who brought some style to it, and a little dazzle as well, through trophies she supplied from the current Broadway stage.

Belle Moskowitz was to be the influence to "offset" the Tammany influence. She was a sub-committee of one. She dived right in. With the possible exception of Robert Moses, she was the brainiest of this lot. Soon, as all know, she had become Al Smith's closest adviser, then an indispensable confidante. And she drafted a great many of his finest speeches.

But it was all a bit unusual—the acceptance, then the constant inside promotion, of Belle Moskowitz. It was as if she were to march up Fifth Avenue on St. Patrick's Day with an orange shamrock stuck in a green derby.

The "capture" of Belle Moskowitz confounded the newspapers, puzzled an enormous number of uncommitted voters, but moved many to Smith. Belle herself paid no attention to her own aboutface. Tammany would have to take care of itself. Hell with it. And none of her doing anyhow. What did she care—her man was up and she was putting her best words in his mouth, her own convictions. His too.

She was educated, brilliant, articulate. She could see it and say it and write it. Al Smith was not educated. He was brilliant and brave and human. He could sense it and say it but he couldn't write it. Belle Moskowitz, as his principal speech-writer, made Al Smith sound better than he ever had before.

His victory over the incumbent Charles S. Whitman got some of its boost from independent voters, some from women, much from Tammany, and from the unusual power (this was before the days of sound trucks) provided by the Tammany Speakers' Bureau, and by Belle Moskowitz's typewriter.

There were several "victory" dinners, one of them at Hahn's Restaurant near City Hall that the Governor-elect hosted for the women who had helped him most. These eight especially: Belle Moskowitz, Frances Perkins, Mary Dreier (these two being prominent members of Al Smith's Factory Investigation Commission), Sara Pike, Mrs. William H. Goode, Mary Simkhovitch, Elizabeth Marbury, and Anna Moskowitz Kross.

This little group was the first to hear of the plan that the new Governor had created. In his first message to the Albany legislature, the plan became known to the public as the Reconstruction Commission. Today it still gets a paragraph in many high-schoollevel history books.

It was an immense undertaking: total reorganization of the state's government. The State of New York had grown so big, so fast, much of its governing machinery was no longer operative, much as New York City's is now, and for some of the same reasons. The real architect of this monumental construct was Robert Moses, though in the colorful bloom of his later years this unusual contribution is overlooked. He was as prickly then as now and would go after anything, whether it could be done or not, if it seemed to be needed by the public, or if it excited him.

Anna Kross was a member of the committee, of course. The legal mandate was deceptively simple: "generally to bring the laws of this state, civil and criminal, into harmony with modern conditions."

That was to take some doing. The sentence, and its implied meaning, almost directly relates to most of today's miseries in fiscal, court, and criminal justice mismanagement. Many of the structural weaknesses that existed then read as if they came from today's papers.

For example, it was found that hundreds of towns and hamlets could be under as many as thirty different police jurisdictions, under a dozen taxing powers; that from one county to another in New York's sixty-one, there was little uniformity of law, clarity of interpretation, or consistency of penalty; no uniformity of franchise eligibility, no standards for assessors. (Striking parallels to these weaknesses will be found in the section, "The Dilemma of America's Cities.")

Many judgeships and magistracies were scandalous sinecures. Laws that were two and a half centuries old were still on the books, still invoked. The governments, and the courts as well, were a glacial mass of anachronisms for the whole of the state.

Al Smith served five terms as Governor. This gave him the time—and he needed it all, even with dynamos like Robert Moses and Belle Moskowitz—to bring to its full fruition the bright vision he had of New York State: the concept of Reconstruction. And projections of the same basic plan were now in his mind for application to the entire nation.

Its success led directly to the ascendancy of Al Smith as a national figure.

Temblors Shake Tammany

In April 1924, the sudden death of Tammany's boss, Charles F. Murphy, threw a clangor into the mayoralty situation in New York. His death occurred at a time when James J. ("Jimmy") Walker was preparing to oppose John F. ("Red Mike") Hylan for re-election. Hylan had been a Murphy man. So, to a certain extent, had been Al Smith. But Smith, stung throughout his whole life by the cruel press he got from Hearst, was determined to unseat Hylan, a Hearst protégé. So he supported Jimmy Walker. So did Edward J. Flynn, boss of the Bronx.

George W. Olvaney, formerly a judge of the Court of General Sessions, was elected leader of Tammany. When he joined Flynn in supporting Walker, the nimble Jimmy was sure of two of the five boroughs. But Hylan had a lot going for him: Brooklyn, the Hearst empire, and Queens and Richmond.

Flynn and Olvaney put Joseph V. McKee on the Walker ticket, as candidate for president of the Board of Alderman, Governor Smith's old job. Joe McKee had just been elected a justice of the City Court and was not well known; not yet, even though he'd served in the state legislature. But it was the first time anyone from the Bronx had ever stood for a major city office. And this man sincerely wanted to serve his city.

McKee was well educated, well dressed, and photographically prepossessing. He'd been a high school history teacher before his term in Albany. He was a little stuffy, a little pedantic, and a bit naïve. But he wanted the job and was willing to work hard. In his dealings with people, he was direct. He said to Anna Kross: "I want you to do for me what Belle Moskowitz has been doing for Al Smith."

"I can't write your speeches. I'm too busy having a family."

"Well, never mind the speeches. Just run my campaign for me."

"But the Jimmy Walker team already has a manager." (So it did, Ben Schreiber.)

"Jimmy will get all the Schreiber attention. I need somebody to look out just for *me*."

Anna Kross took the management job. It infuriated Schreiber. He thought he should run the whole show or none of it. Walker agreed. But the decision remained and Anna Kross opened up a campaign office in the Commodore (where Walker's already was).

Herbert Lehman, then treasurer of Tammany, was persuaded to head the committe for McKee, a step that exasperated Schreiber even more.

The primary was dirty and bitter. The Hearst papers attacked Walker's private life, an exercise so easy as hardly to seem sporting. But Hylan made a bad decision in opposing a state appropriation for the elimination of grade crossings, an issue that had been boiling for six years. He was also bothered by a lumbering pomposity. Jimmy Walker was quick of tongue and smile, a great crowd-pleaser and wisecracker, and if his private life was a scandal it was simply delightful to read about. He was a real swinger, never still, and all his girl friends were "lookers."

Things were moving well until a representative of a large Jewish organization walked into the committee office and placed an article before Anna Kross.

Anti-Semitism

The article had been written by Joseph McKee ten years before. It had appeared in one of the leading Roman Catholic magazines.

"What are you showing me this for?" inquired Anna.

"McKee is anti-Semitic."

She read the piece. On the whole it was well written, and fair to the Jews. Though it did state that much of the crime in New York was committed by Jews, it did not seem out of proportion on an ethnic or statistical basis. Other groups were amply represented. But taken out of context, as the enemy most surely would do if they saw it or dug it up, single sentences could be construed as very damaging evidence against McKee.

They had McKee in. He explained that he had written it while teaching history at DeWitt Clinton High School; written it while seeing a great deal of a Jesuit priest who impressed him. The committee decided that the best way to handle the problem, if the article couldn't be kept secret, was to meet it as a youthful indiscretion. McKee himself didn't see it as anti-anything, and there was no streak of anti-Semitism in the man at all.

That night there was to be a dinner at the Lehmans' home for the heads of the various campaign committees. McKee and Anna Kross got there early to discuss the article with Herbert Lehman, lest he, a prominent Jew, should resign as leader of the McKee committee. Lehman agreed that if McKee could convince Louis Marshall, president of the American Jewish Committee, a major society combatting anti-Semitism, then Lehman would remain. Of course McKee agreed. He at once saw Marshall, made an open declaration about the episode, held nothing back, and succeeded in persuading Marshall he was clean and untainted (which was true), and had never been anything else.

This cleared it up for the campaign. In fact, the story did not get out then. (But it rose to haunt McKee nine years later in 1933 when he ran for Mayor against La Guardia, and lost.)

Jimmy Walker's ticket prevailed, as expected, and Joe McKee, as president of the Board of Aldermen, offered Anna Kross the top job in his office, Commissioner of Purchase. She refused it. She was interested in one thing only: a judgeship in the Children's Court.

The Bare Cupboard of Politics

She had been disappointed when nothing came in for her after Al Smith's victory. Now she was offered something she didn't want, and she said no. She was never to learn the most rudimentary law of politics the world over:

The time to take tarts is when they're passing.

Disappointment was to turn quickly to humiliation. The late Charles F. Murphy had promised her an appointment as soon as a vacancy occurred on the bench of Children's Court. Now there was one. She went to George Olvaney to see about it.

"I am under no obligation," Olvaney said, "to honor the promises of my predecessors. And you have been disloyal to the Democratic organization besides."

"In what way?"

"I understand," he said, "that you have been appointed chairman of the committee of the New York County Lawyers' Association to investigate the Magistrates' Courts of New York City. You never advised me of this. And you have not reported your findings to me."

"Let me remind you," she answered, "that the New York County Lawyers' Association represents the legal profession of this city. As chairman of the special investigating committee I have the duty of preparing a report and submitting it *only* to members of the association. The committee is pledged to secrecy. But now that you bring up the subject, the committee has found that the activities of several magistrates are such that it will be only a matter of a few weeks before a serious scandal erupts. Its stench will weaken the Democratic County Organization and might even destroy it."

The next day she noted a small news item in the *World Telegram* to the effect that Mrs. Margaret Ramsy Reese had been appointed vice-chairman of the Tammany Hall Speakers' Bureau, the position to which Murphy had appointed Anna Kross six years earlier.

That was her punishment by Olvaney, the new leader of Tammany Hall.

Perhaps she did learn a little something from it. "I had been politically naïve to divide my allegiance. It was a cardinal sin to be a Manhattan woman and work for a Bronx candidate. My mistake was often to haunt me. Of course it hurt. But in this game you can't cry when you lose. It's part of the gamble."

Olvaney resigned as Tammany's leader in 1929 and John F. Curry, through the influence of Jimmy Hines, got the job. The city was smoking with known but unexposed scandal and the Seabury Investigation was making its deadly preparations to find and name the Most Wanted thieves, then to place them against the wall. Jimmy Walker didn't have much farther to go. He seemed tired. The Irish bounce was mechanical, the jokes a little delayed. The girls were gone. Under interrogation he tried to grin but only grimaced. Odd fragments reached the radio, but whole sections of question-and-answer reached the papers and splattered the front pages. Everybody was a crook. And now they'd been caught. And wasn't it delicious?

Jim Farley

The political scene seemed to change for the whole nation, not just New York. James A. Farley had become the Democratic

Party whip. Sensing that Al Smith could never be elected President, he swung the Democratic Convention that summer (1932) to Roosevelt. Anna Kross, with other members of the Women's Democratic Club, attended the convention. Al Smith literally walked out on the convention. To those watching, he seemed to have turned his back forever on public life.

A strange wind had arisen and blown them all away—the good, the bad, the mighty, and the tattered.

On September 1, 1932, Jimmy Walker resigned as Mayor. Joe McKee, as aldermanic president, automatically became Mayor. His support of Roosevelt in Chicago, his abandonment of Al Smith, would have earned him a stoning by Tammany if the power had been there to throw anything, but there was abundant warning of bad things to come. As one of his first actions, after taking the governorship from Smith, Roosevelt instituted the Seabury Investigation. This put a floodlight, then a sweeper, into every corridor of the Walker regime. There was a lot to look at. McKee, now Mayor pro-tem, resolved to clean house, too, even if his tenure was likely to be short.

As acting Mayor, he offered Anna Kross the Commissioner of Purchase, a job peculiarly loaded with opportunities to improve one's basic salary. He knew she would never pick up a 2¢ stamp she hadn't paid for. In fact, she'd refused the "extras" at Tammany, and in her private practice as a labor law expert she was so firm about money that she was considered naïve, an attribute of small toot in any political horn. But it was this very flat-footed honesty McKee wanted.

"But you know I want to be a Children's Court judge. It's my whole interest. The problems of family."

"Anna, this commissionership will make you the most important woman in the country. Think it over."

She wouldn't commit herself. She voted in Jimmy Hines's district and as district leader she felt Jimmy Hines had a right to know of the McKee offer. She breezed in to him.

"Would you like to congratulate the new Commissioner of Purchase?" she offered jokingly, tentatively.

Hines's face clouded. "I didn't know that was what you wanted, Anna." He was seeking the spot for one of his own captains.

"It isn't what I wanted. You know what I want. The Children's

Court. I've waited years. You promised to help me get it. But you never did."

Hines wasn't comfortable in the presence of this reminder.

"I can't prevent you from accepting," he managed. Then he reminded her that the Court of Appeals had not yet decided whether an election of a new Mayor to succeed Jimmy Walker should be held at once, or whether McKee would be allowed to finish out Walker's term. It had about a year to go. He asked her the blunt question: "What will a job as Commissioner of Purchase mean if McKee isn't re-elected?"

She shrugged her shoulders. He picked up the phone and called John F. Curry, Tammany's leader.

"What shall I tell Anna Kross to do?"

"Tell her not to take the job," Curry said, and hung up.

"If I don't take the commissionership, will you get me the Children's Court judgeship?"

"You know I'm standing by you."

The Court of Appeals ruled that there should be an election, a new one, for Mayor. Most of the newspapers praised McKee, and they should have. But Tammany didn't want a Bronx man in City Hall. It decided to oppose McKee with all the power it could mobilize. McKee lost the Democratic nomination to John P. O'Brien. Even Flynn, McKee's close personal friend and county leader, didn't support him. Flynn was for Roosevelt and now firmly anti-Tammany.

O'Brien was high-principled, not at all colorful; gentle, old, and slow-moving. He was a Surrogate of New York County. He asked Anna Kross to manage his Women's Committee. She did, and O'Brien served New York in a benign sprawl of apopemptics to school children, mispronunciations ("opreatic" for "operatic"), and the belief, stated at a high school commencement in Brooklyn, that Horace, the poet, was a Greek. Things had grown dim in his mind.

The free-for-all regular election in the fall of 1933 found O'Brien standing for a full term, and, surprisingly, McKee, too, though with no organization behind him. He created one, called it the Recovery Party. He thought he would make a good Mayor. Perhaps he would have. And for a splinter-party showing, he did remarkably well. But Anna Kross saw no future in splinter parties, however noble their purposes. She said no to McKee's offer of the fat post of Purchasing. She said yes to O'Brien's appeal for her to manage the women's division of his campaign as the Tammany candidate.

The Count

McKee and O'Brien were opposed by Fiorello La Guardia. Here is how it came out:

La Guardia	858,000
McKee	604,000
O'Brien	586,000

The loss of this election cost Tammany the control of the city. It would not recover until the tall, gloomy figure of Carmine de Sapio appeared.

Anna Kross Speaks for Herself

Anna Kross had worked hard for a lot of big men and never got anything for it or from it. She wouldn't take money. And she'd refused offers that either didn't interest her or were jobs for which her life had provided no training. When nothing came in for her, and with another era about to end, she decided to ask for something, something for *herself*. A judgeship in Children's Court had again eluded her.

The last day of O'Brien's term had arrived. It was the last day of December 1933. The morning passed with no word from him. At noon she got a call in her law office on Broadway. It was Jimmy Hines. He told her there would be no appointment. Somehow, this time she couldn't or wouldn't believe it. She called City Hall and was put through to O'Brien. She told the moribund Mayor she'd just had a call from Jimmy Hines. She asked O'Brien point blank what the score was.

"Why don't you call John Curry?" he suggested.

"That I will not. You call him yourself."

Then she reminded the outgoing Mayor that the press had been hounding her for weeks as to what preferment she was accepting. Surely she was "up" for something. She had to be. "The *World*

Telegram was here in my office this morning. You want me to tell them that Mayor O'Brien's last breath was dictated by Tammany Hall?"

A half hour later her phone rang. It was John O'Brien.

"Anna, come right down to City Hall and get sworn in."

Thus, she became a judge. But it was not Children's Court. It was Magistrates' Court.

She learned, just before being sworn in, that someone else got the place intended for her, a man named Alfred M. Lindau. He was Max Steuer's son-in-law, and Jimmy Hines, who was obligated to Steuer, had forsaken Anna Kross for him. Steuer had been a long-time member of the Tammany Board of Strategy.

Anna Kross felt betrayed by Jimmy Hines and told him so when he came to her office, wanting to "explain" how Lindau got the spot.

"You don't have to. Let the past be forgotten."

She saw him no more. As scandal was soon to break, it was a good thing her appointment had no fingerprints of Jimmy Hines on it. He was darkly, inextricably enmeshed; deeper than any thought, any but the District Attorney, Thomas E. Dewey. He was gunning for Hines. And for many more. He sent Hines to Sing Sing.

Anna Kross, now a judge, had a score to settle with the *World Telegram*. The newspaper had knocked O'Brien sideways for his "eleventh hour appointment." Anna Kross had been singled out as being short of the proper credentials for the job of Magistrate. She got on the subway and went down to Barclay Street to see the paper's editor, Lee Wood. She asked him at once what he knew about her qualifications.

"I know you're Tammany. That's enough to disqualify anyone. I'm surprised that anyone with your intelligence can *be* a Tammanyite."

"Tammany didn't damage the morals of Al Smith or Herbert Lehman."

"They're exceptions."

"So am I. Now, Mr. Wood, you've said some hurting things about me and I'm going to sit right here while you examine my qualifications. And get it straight in your mind just what I am."

She supplied him with ten minutes' worth of reading matter, the most notable entry being the record of her work as chairman of the Committee on Magistrates' Courts of the New York County Lawyers' Association. This experience had given her a comprehensive knowledge of the way these courts functioned. Already she knew more, and cared more, about the Jefferson Market court, for example, than anyone in New York.

There she sat, her little hat primly severe, and her legs, not long enough quite to reach the floor, dangling her inevitable space shoes.

Lee Wood confessed he had been wrong in his judgment.

He didn't know—no one did but her husband—the price she'd paid, in the relentless grind, the savage collisions, the being-a-woman-in-a-man's-world, a lawyer where they weren't expected or wanted, the long waiting, the weariness, her own insufficient money with tons of easy money all about.

She told him of the long struggle of so many woman lawyers, herself among them, to get women admitted to the New York City Bar Association. For years they had debated amending their constitution to admit women. When all else failed, they pointed to the inadequacy of the plumbing!

She and Lee Wood liked each other. They talked for two hours. She told him the story of Olvaney's revenge, the good and the bad of Tammany. Lee Wood didn't know how close she had come to getting no appointment at all.

The *World Telegram* let up on her. *The Times* gave her a fine editorial sendoff.

New York's Chief Magistrate at that time was James E. MacDonald. He asked the new lady Magistrate where she would like to start her judicial career.

"In the same place in which I started my legal career."

So the induction ceremonies were held in the old Jefferson Market court. It was a dazzlingly bright January day. At 10:15 Al Smith and Chief Magistrate MacDonald escorted Judge Kross from chambers into the main courtroom. All rose, clapping at first, then cheering. There was a spirit of joy in the room, he first ever in the history of its bitter memories.

Al Smith loved this gallant little woman and noticeably enjoyed her own enjoyment. He robed her—a handsome new magis rate's robe given to her by the Womens' Civic Organization. Fo   brief moment, another ceremony flashed through her mind and her eyes smarted. She thought of the humiliating day when she couldn't attend her grammar school graduation exercises because the Moskowitzes just didn't have the dollar to rent her the white dress all the other girls would be wearing.

Then Al Smith spoke:

"We should never overlook an opportunity, whenever it is presented, to stress to our people the importance of our minor courts, both criminal and civil. They hold a very important position in our entire judicial system. There are a great many people who got their first, and, in many instances, their only impression of the administration of justice, of fair dealing, in the minor courts. Many of them never see any other court. It will be from such a room as this that they will carry away their idea of American fair play, and what constitutes even-handed and impartial justice. That this may be brought about, there must be a broad understanding on the part of the presiding judge. There must be that order and that decorum in the court that sustains the majesty, dignity, and sovereignty of the law."

Judge Alfred J. Talley, of the Court of General Sessions, said at the ceremonies that the lady's looks belied her twenty years at the Bar. She was in her thirties and the city's batterings had not begun to show.

Her rabbi, David da Sola Pool, reminded her, and the audience, of Anna's heritage:

"You come of a tradition that has ever set justice as the basic principle for its social ethics; for Moses, the great law-giver, on behalf of the children of Israel, appealed for justice, justice at all times. Down through the ages that has been the tradition of your people."

She knew. And she was ready to put it all into practice.

The New Mayor Gives the New Judge a Tough Job

You will recall that George Olvaney, former head of Tammany, had punished Anna Kross when it was revealed to him that she had been making a "secret" investigation of the Magistrate's Court system. Actually it had been secret only in the sense that it had been directed by the New York County Bar Association and was a matter not of secrecy but of confidentiality.

There is a large legal and moral difference. Olvaney was distressed far more from fear of a loss of Tammany power through an expected loss of patronage than he was at her "disloyalty," for he was not naïve. He had to know ugly things would soon surface. His charge of party disloyalty was expedient, glib, and insincere. He was only trying to save face with the men around him, so he clipped her chevrons.

While still trying to abolish Women's Night Court, La Guardia now assigned her, as one of his first directives, the task of investigating the practice, use, and theory of all Magistrates' Courts. She'd already done it, of course. But now, as a magistrate herself, the job had a special piquancy. And this time the findings would be made public.

La Guardia and Anna Kross were very much the same person in all their basic beliefs and their instant chemical reaction to anything dirty or dishonest. Though their methods were different, had their names, jobs, and sexes been reversed, very much the same range of attainments and of change would have occurred (though Anna, much to La Guardia's disgust, stuck up for the gamblers).

Anna Kross Is First to Recognize the "Victimless" Crime

La Guardia was present when she put some blunt questions to a gathering of lawyers in Webster Hall, and it is possible that when he heard these, he knew what to do with her. Certainly no one knew what to do with the questions.

Here are some of them. Once more what she was putting before the public's intelligence sounds as if it was lifted from a big-city newspaper editorial of the 1970s, not the early '30s.

"In this day of psychological insight, is it not obvious that the prostitute is a product of forces beyond her control, rather than a wilful enemy of society? The vagrant or the drunk, arraigned after thirty previous convictions—is he not a victim rather than an antagonist? Answer me: what problems does it solve to give such people a short term in the workhouse, then turn them out again? The penny-ante gambler? A young girl is charged with being a wayward minor. How does the magistrate know if the girl isn't rebelling against the squalor of a horrid home life? What is a magistrate to do with a blind beggar? What if all these wretches and derelicts are of such low mentality that they belong permanently in custodial institutions?

"Today the magistrate's official answer to all these questions has to come to this: 'I don't know'."

In her findings, released six months later, startling anachronisms came to light. Gross inefficiency, too. And much, much that still lingers.

The report was comprehensive, dramatic, widely circulated, apodictic, and celebrated. It was also resented.

In its candor and humanity, most of all in its sense, the report was irresistible. Here was a judge sticking up for her colleagues, sticking up for the law, for the poor, for the "people," pleading only for machinery that would let judges do the work they were paid for, and pleading for the money to get it done.

Why was the City Magistrate System inoperative? For six solid reasons, and most of our cities have them still.

Essence of the Report

1. Magistrates didn't have *time* to give proper attention to the cases before them. Cases rammed through these courts at the rate of one every six minutes.

2. In the event a magistrate felt a certain case warranted a special effort, he could not make it. Reason: magistrates were too peripatetic. They had no permanent headquarters. In fact they had no "quarters" at all. They were shoved and shunted about, all over New York's five boroughs, *every two weeks.*

3. Magistrates had no chambers. Some had space in a cloak-room behind their bench but court attendants kept passing through to use the phone. Why did they have to do this? It was the only phone.

4. Magistrates didn't have a *law clerk.* "Even in the Chief Magistrate's office there is no clerk," complained Kross. And *no law library.* In trying to solve a difficult question, no magistrate had access to any research facility. Thus magistrates solved their own problems independently, leaving the tough ones unsolved or improperly solved.

5. Magistrates had to depend on what was brought to them by

assistant D.A.s, by police, or by court clerks. But due to a magistrate's inability to search thoroughly into fact, many abuses —extortion, fixing, perjury, bail-bond manipulation—could thrive. And did.

6. There was no *continuity* and no *uniformity* of policy. Standard offenses were receiving a great range of different punishments.

"A magistrate's work begins and ends on the bench," Anna Kross complained. "There is no incentive to reserve decision. There is no time. His books and papers he must lug about with him. There is no filing space. No stenographer. No typewriter.

"Thus, magistrates administer what we are calling 'barnyard' equity. They do this not because they don't know the law. They do it because they have no time to *apply* it."

Who resented the Kross report? Certainly not the magistrates. It was resented by the fixed personnel of the courts, the stationary attachés who didn't want anyone rocking the boat. They had a good thing going.

Ironically, the reason for the rapid rotation of magistrates was to *prevent* corruption. It was the feeling that any permanent set-up would make possible a relationship between magistrates and local attorneys through which political influence could affect cases by way of fixing and bribery.

Anna Kross held the opposite view: fixing was a lot easier if the magistrates were being constantly reshuffled but the *court staff* were permanent.

She was right.

Without supervision, and with "new" judges floating in and out every two weeks, complaint clerks could and did draw complaints to read as if the case were milder than the incoming facts warranted by the complainant. Clerks could "chip the cube of truth to make it roll."

The severity of almost any complaint could be reduced. As is common all over America right now, in every city and town, "assault" could become "disorderly conduct." And since the Magistrate's Court—any court, in fact—must rely on the written complaint, here was an easy method of plea-bargaining: to be held for something venial instead of something severe.

Magistrates couldn't stop this. If such a ploy became apparent to a magistrate in the course of a hearing, the bench was helpless. Once a hearing is in progress, a magistrate cannot increase the charge. With new magistrates coming in and out, the evil practice of the bribed clerk was hard to uncover. If caught, he could plead innocent error, then next week resume the old practice with the next incoming judge. With the same magistrate there all the time, he couldn't get away with it.

A large proportion of the magistrates were deeply conscientious men—informed, morally brave, responsive. Sooner or later, through the rotation system, most of them hit the notorious Jefferson Market court, of course, where its evils were visible in a few minutes' time. All saw remedies. All were frustrated. The speed and relentlessness of reassignment stopped them before they got started. Most realized that evil, here, was epidemic. Few realized that evil, through the whole system, was pandemic. The inevitable happened: the Magistrate System had bred a race of automatons, not judges: "Ram it through and go home."

These problems set up such a high profile, they made good copy for the press. The newspapers worked over the terrain with fierce and satisfying regularity, reducing to zero any lingering confidence an occasional taxpayer might have in municipal justice; destroying altogether the few scattered islands of esprit de corps that exceptional magistrates had begun to build.

These courts, and thousands of criminal courts throughout America today, were glutted with the most rubbishy kind of non-criminal debris. The Kross Report had some simple affirmatives for this: for persons receiving a summons for a minor offense, *standardize* the fine and let the defendant *mail* it in. (It's taken 35 years to get around to this, in Traffic Court alone.)

Magistrates' Courts were always crowded with peddlers whose licenses had expired; with sidewalk gypsies selling ties, toys, or bracelets, who didn't have any license at all. You've seen it, whatever your city. Anna Kross had been brought up in a pushcart, street-vendor climate, Christie Street on the Lower East Side. She knew peddlers. She saw them for what they really were: honest men trying to make a living; to stay off relief.

"They are respectable citizens. They are not criminals."

Her recommendation: don't clutter the courts with such.

Having known extreme poverty in her youth, seeing it forever before her in the faces of defendants, it was inevitable she would suggest "free legal aid be given to defendants in Magistrates' Courts, so that any defendant, other than those up for trivial matters, may have a lawyer. The people who appear in them are poor. There should be lawyers for all these poor, to serve without cost to them."

This rearranging of the way things are to what they ought to be was typical of the hard-sense approach Anna Kross brought to all the jobs handed her. Tammany's response to the Kross Report was a bit less than boisterous, as you can guess, since some of the magistrates and many of the clerks were "their boys." But by now they'd learned that the lady judge would never "go along" with anything. "Throw it out!" "Bury it!" "Close it!" "Clean it up!" Though she spent her whole life in it, she never seemed to get the *idea* of politics. Certainly she must be the only Tammany graduate ever to miss her diploma by such a wide margin and still get a degree.

Her bluntness could bring her, more quickly than it does most lawyers, to the gravamen of any problem:

"The proposal for amalgamation of the Magistrates' Courts and the Court of Special Sessions, sponsored by the highest authority, is studiously neglected for political reasons. Similar indifference is revealed with reference to the centralization of the Magistrates' Courts. If persons arrested in all precincts in Manhattan and the Bronx can be taken to one central Night Court, why not to one central Day Court? Because the police justices of a hundred years ago sat in district courts, so, naturally, today's magistrates must do the same. If we decide the time for change has come, why do we not make the change decisively and completely?"

Probation in Magistrates' Courts

Magistrate Kross, secure now and toughened, knew that *all* of the Magistrates' Courts should be abolished, not just her favorite target—the Women's Night Court. She knew, too, that it was going to take a long time. She turned her attention to Probation, not to its practice in other systems but to the use made of it in the system of which she was now a part.

Origin of Probation

It is true that many of the mechanics and principles under which we are judged are quite ancient. It is also true that many of the concomitant assists and services are not only new, but of this century. Magistrate Kross's hopes for an effective application of Probation, in Magistrates' Courts, were pretty much built on earlier praise heaped upon this new instrument of redemption.

Probation was introduced into Magistrates' Courts in 1901. It was, and was so considered, bold and constructive; a sort of motivated behavioral breakthrough that would save lives and communities and reputations before any serious or irreversible deterioration had occurred; that early intervention could reshape individual attitudes and save families.

In 1910 the Page Commission had this to say of it: "We know of no more marked step forward in the administration of criminal jurisprudence than the Probation System."

Equally laudatory, and in the same year, was Chief Magistrate Otto Kempner's statement upon reading the report of his own chief probation officer:

"It is my firm conviction that the Probation System is destined to become the greatest reformatory factor in criminal justice in our time."

In New York it had a quarter of a century of ups and downs, good here, inept or inadequate there. But the potential for good was obvious and acknowledged. The professional attitude toward Probation is well summarized in these two paragraphs from the Crime Commission of 1931:

The system of probation in existence prior to 1928 had fallen into disrepute, and its abolition was being urged by many, even those in position, as the only cure for the evils then existing. The Commission, however, has taken an entirely opposite view. We hold that a properly organized system of probation could do much to remould the outlook of those committed to its care. As a result, a new probation act has been adopted, which as far as possible, guards against repetition of previous errors, and today the probationer has every incentive to reform and go straight.

It is the attitude of this Commission that probation should be extended to the utmost. Proper and sympathetic supervision and guidance of the young offender will salvage boys without number. With this also should go the combined work of the psychiatric clinic and the social worker.

Of course, there is some naïve optimism in the above, and many holes, but Anna Kross saw the undeniable preventive value in any probation system that was really working and spent much of the year 1935 studying its operation in her own and her colleagues' courts.

"The promise of Probation has not been fulfilled," she wrote. "During 1935, 170,000 persons were convicted of offenses and some form of punishment was meted out to them. Yet the Probation department during that year made only 5,800 investigations; 83,000 persons were given suspended sentences but only 3% of these were placed on probation."

Judge Seabury had a good question: "If so many are guilty, why do so few need probationary supervision?"

Was it a failure of theory? No. A failure of personnel: not enough officers, and such as there were weren't good enough. No money, of course, so the pay had to be poor.

Somewhat earlier (1931), Seabury, reporting as referee to the Appellate Division of the Supreme Court, had stated the hard facts as he saw them at that time:

"It is clear to me, from a comparison of the work done by the probation officers in the Magistrates' Courts with that done elsewhere, that the best work in the Probation Department of the Magistrates' Courts is below good probation standards and much of it is even below the standards of volunteer work by untrained persons.

"The review of probation, as conducted in the Magistrates' Courts, shows that a large proportion of the money now being spent on the Probation Department of these courts is wasted."

There was other evidence. Probation service was so bad, it became the subject of a ten-weeks' study (summer of 1936) by the New York State Division of Probation. Two paragraphs will indicate that anything derogatory that had previously been felt, written, or said had not been overstated:

Only nine of the present staff have had previous experience in social work. Among the previous occupations represented in this group of thirty-five officers without previous social work experience are brick-layer, chiropractor, salesman, nurse, stenographer, shipping clerk, jeweler, bookkeeper, prison keeper, teacher, lawyer, housewife, auto mechanic, army, navy, and factory foreman.

With a group of individuals so different in background and experience, with so little homogeneity in professional training or point of view, it is not surprising to find that the probation service in Magistrates' Court is to a large extent probation in name only.

What to do? Being one of the primary complainers about Probation's ineffectiveness in Magistrates' Courts but being a builder, Anna Kross created the Social Service Bureau. It sounds a little stuffy. Not so, not at all. In a sense it was the true genesis of her Home Term Court that would open in 1946, ten years later, a sample of which we saw in the introduction. She never knocked anything down—whether it was Jefferson Market, the Women's House of Detention, or the Raymond Street Jail—just to see the wrecker's ball swing. She knocked it down so something better could go up. In any big city, this is hard. Ask any Mayor. Ask any judge or D.A. Her main objectives had always been simple and easy to state. She was trying to *modernize, humanize,* and *accelerate.* To bring sense out of nonsense, economy out of waste, speed out of drag.

The purpose of the Bureau was simple: "To do something about the tens of thousands of cases which present not criminal but *social* problems."

Immediately after creating the Bureau, Magistrate Kross recommended its being integrated into the grid of the Magistrate System officially, complete with intake bureau, investigative facilities, and three clinics: medical, psychiatric, and alcohol. New York would give her no money for this. So she begged it from foundations and private benefactors. And got it.

It made good sense, especially in view of Probation failure through the whole of that same system. Yet everything Anna Kross ever attempted seems to have been knocked around pretty thoroughly before it was allowed to settle down and deliver its practical benefit to the public.

There follows now the kind of exasperation that all movers and shakers must somehow survive: public punishment of Anna Kross by the same people (the New York State Division of Probation), and in the *same report*, for trying to repair the very thing they themselves had found to be so awful. Here is what they said of her Social Service Bureau:

The Social Service Bureau of Magistrates' Court was established in March 1936 by Magistrate Anna M. Kross. The Bureau, privately financed, consists of a staff of one full-time professional social worker, assisted by a troup of part-time volunteers and two paid clerical assistants. Office space is provided free of charge in the 7th District Court Building at 314 West 54th Street.

The staff operates under the immediate supervision of Magistrate Kross. The professional staff accompanies Judge Kross to any court over which she may preside. At her request they interview parties to a complaint, before conviction, and act in a liaison capacity between Judge Kross and the various social agencies to which she may refer defendants for specialized service. The function of this Bureau is largely of a referral nature. Its work includes interviews with defendants of their relatives, clearance and follow-up with the Social Service Exchange, and referral to whatever agency seems indicated. Interim reports are requested from the agencies used and these are filed in the Social Service Bureau's individual case records.

The Bureau workers undertake no treatment but limit their work to investigation and referral. Two or three other magistrates from time to time have asked the Social Service Bureau for assistance but, as a rule, the work of the Bureau is limited to Judge Kross's cases.

There has been misunderstanding between the Probation Bureau and the Social Service Bureau. The probation officers justly feel that the Social Service Bureau, as unofficial agency, is performing public probation service and claim that the duplication of effort is confusing to the public who find it difficult to discriminate between the two Bureaus.

The Social Service Bureau was established by Judge Kross to provide services which she felt the Probation Bureau was not equipped to render, either because of numerical or professional inadequacy of the staff.

The organization of this privately financed project illustrates the lack of coordination that is possible in Magistrates' Courts. Any judge, when he so desires, may with little difficulty organize his or her own particular investigating body to work independently of the Probation Bureau (the official social agency of the court). This of course tends to decentralize responsibility, and inevitably results in overlapping of services and possible waste motion to the clients, the court, and the community.

The fact that one or more magistrates have the services of such an agency makes for discrimination in the dispensation of justice, and results in inequality of treatment toward defendants appearing before different magistrates. It weakens the probation service, and makes confusion for the defendants, the probation officers, and the community.

There is no valid reason why officially appointed officers should not perform the service now being rendered by the Social Service Bureau. The probation staff should be enlarged and equipped to perform the types of services rendered by this private bureau.

With justifiable sarcasm Judge Kross had a good time answering the celestial mindlessness of the above:

"In other words, the author of the report believes that the probation staff should be *enlarged* and *equipped* to perform the *types of services* rendered by the private bureau, which is condemned because it does the things which the Probation Bureau should do but doesn't."

It marks a high level of forbearance that she didn't put a "bang" at the end of that sentence.

She had a few more things to say:

"Because some defendants have the advantage of the services which now only the Bureau provides—but which all defendants should have—it is claimed that this makes for "inequality" and the Bureau should therefore desist. This is especially ludicrous in view of the fact that hitherto there was inequality before different magistrates because there was *no* Social Service Bureau. Besides, the services of the Magistrates' Courts Social Service Bureau are available to any magistrate who cares to use them."

Of the scores of reports I've examined, this one represents, to me at least, the real and gritty reason why superior people wonder why they ever got into public service at all; the exact sort of frustration that recently (Dec. 31, 1971) engulfed Anna Kross's successor, George McGrath; the exact sort that will now engulf *his* successor, Commissioner Malcolm. It has nothing to do with race, experience, integrity, or color: Anna Kross is Jewish, George Mc-

Grath Irish. The new Commissioner is a black. *It has to do with money and nothing but money.*

But Anna hung on. She was a stayer. And she had friends in high places. Raymond Moley brought strong independent support to the Kross invention. So did Samuel Seabury, the slightly overweight white knight who had brought down Jimmy Walker. Her creation caught on, and ramified.

Her philosophies, too.

Children's Court

How was Probation doing in other courts? Very well indeed.

Most improvements in court practices, whether in philosophy or procedure, are evolutional at best, seldom showing any visible rate of advance. At the same time, an innovation in one area can sometimes excite quick action in another. Something very much like this occurred in Children's Court. The basic idea of having a separate court for children came along, almost simultaneously, with the Probation idea, both ideas having this same root—that people accused of crime should be helped, if possible; helped rather than punished.

As early as 1901 some New York magistrates were empowered to assign a separate part of their courts for cases involving children, "which part may for convenience be called the children's court." The trend toward this kind of thinking took a quick upturn in 1924 when the New York City Children's Court Act became a reality. It set up a Children's Court quite independent of the Magistrates' Court system. In 1933 the new court was integrated into the Domestic Relations Court and in those years—a remarkably short time for anything of real significance or large usefulness to develop in an institution so ponderous and stuffy and tradition-prone as a court edifice—this court had become the most highly "socialized" court in the entire judicial system.

The court had a widely extended probation reach, and it had sophisticated investigators. It had a fine battery of trained social workers with a thorough grounding in family casework. Full investigations of complex family snarls and uproars were known to and understood by a staff of patient but persistent observers. There was a well-planned intake bureau, and for the first time a really respectable facility for both medical and psychiatric service.

All of these forces brought their special informations and their own evaluations of these *before a hearing took place*. Thus, a great deal could be placed before a judge, or made quickly available to him at any time; material that would have taken many days to wring out in a trial. And all of these exploratory exercises were based on the expanding theory of prevention as against correction.

Some intelligence was beginning to find its way in, and in Part Two, present-day Probation is explored in more detail.

Two "experimental" courts were created: courts for young people over sixteen (hence not "children") but under twenty-one. One of these courts was for boys—the Adolescents' Court of Brooklyn—the other for girls—the Wayward Minors' Part of the Women's Court. Both these courts sought to do for adolescent offenders what Children's Court had been doing for offenders under sixteen. The objective, in both courts, was to study offenders as *individuals* and to so work on them as to relax their social (anti-social) problem before their threat to the community had time to harden into something irreversible; that the community, any community, would be best served by the rehabilitation of the offender than by punishment of the offense.

Concerning the motivation behind these two courts, Judge Kross wrote: "It is an attempt to relax the rigid and traditional procedure of the criminal law. Because the personality, experience, and background of a boy or girl is more important in rehabilitation than whether or not he or she performed a specific criminal act, these courts tend to consider evidence which, without the consent of the defendant, would not be strictly legal. And because jailing an adolescent is about the worst way of reforming him.

"A new type of record has been inaugurated," she reported, "so that there is included in the investigators' report information as to the defendant's family background, childhood, adolescent life including school record, social and religious life, mental and physical health history, sex education and history of sexual experience, and work history or vocational training. This report is read by the magistrate *before* the next court appearance of the defendant. The magistrate also consults with the representatives of social agencies who are or may be interested in the case.

"All of this is with a view to formulating a plan of rehabilitation, and carrying it into execution. For in the Wayward Minors' Part, the defendant is never brought to formal trial unless it is absolutely necessary. Rehabilitative plans are carried out *pending* the court consideration of the case, and if these are successful, the case is dismissed and the girl is never adjudicated a wayward minor."

For the boys, the court sought to spare them the stigma of a conviction; for the girls, to avoid an adjudication of any kind.

Girls' Term

Judge Peter M. Horn, now retired, was a person in many ways very much like Anna Kross. He was captivated by the idea of Home Term Court and was one of its early judges. When Judge Kross felt that a new court—an improvement on the Wayward Minors' Court—should be developed, she knew she could count on his help and did so.

It was to help girls in the 16–21 age group. The words "Guilty" and "Not guilty" were not to be used, though the offenses to be treated were the real thing: incorrigibles, runaways, delinquents, prostitutes, and the sexually promiscuous.

The girls were not under arrest. They were "respondents," not "defendants," and came to explain, rather than defend, their conduct. Physically the court had very much the same appearance as Home Term: judges without robes, no dais, no "trappings," no jury box.

As Home Term had come into being through the approval and authority of the then Chief Magistrate, Edgar Bromberger, Girls' Term had the blessing of former Chief Magistrate Abraham M. Block, another pioneer in the social courts. Block was another of the "sensitive" judges who had developed an instinct for determining "the deep hidden causes of adolescent misbehavior."

"We are able to ignore the black-and-white areas of the criminal law and explore the gray areas of emotional disturbance."

The objective: "To find out what really causes each girl to go wrong and then by court order to plan a cure, so that the victim returns to society as a useful citizen with no criminal stigma upon her." This was Judge Horn's definition.

The most important authority to be granted to the judges was this: "We are permitted to deprive a girl of her liberty for fifteen days after her preliminary hearing. During this interval, girls were not subject to release by habeas corpus. No one could force us to give her up."

Judge Horn was so impressed with the early results of the Adolescent Court for Girls, impressed with the social-work study that was made of each girl, that he sought legislation to extend the same protections that girls over sixteen but under 21 weren't getting. Beyond sixteen, girls were judged as common criminals.

After three years of study, Judge Horn wrote the Girls' Term Act. In the Albany Assembly it had strong support from Senator MacNeil Mitchell. It was studied by Governor Thomas B. Dewey and vetoed. Two years later it was again offered, and again vetoed. Judge Horn was about to withdraw his advocacy and his hopes but Senator Mitchell urged him to give it one more go, and this time it won the approval of the Governor. Judge Horn did not know that Dewey had a secret "rule"; even if he disapproved of a new law, he would not veto it a third time. He figured it must have merit his penetrating eyes had not uncovered.

But what can you do in only fifteen days' custody for a girl with a flaming record? The answer is that you can do quite a lot.

First, the treatment of the girl herself: the girls weren't moved about in prison vans. They were taxied unobtrusively in an unmarked station-wagon under the escort of a woman attendant who was not in uniform. No fingerprinting. No prison garb.

Where did the girls spend these fifteen days? Some were taken to the Euphrasian Residence in Manhattan. It was operated for the court by the Sisters of the Good Shepherd, an order of Catholic nuns, worldwide in their range of activity. It took in, and does now, unfortunate adolescent girls irrespective of race or religion. Barrett House was another non-sectarian facility, operated by the Florence Crittenden League. Here there was no dorm but a private room and bath for each girl, and a huge wardrobe where a girl could pick out her own clothes. There was a Jewish Youth Service. There was a home for 48 pre-delinquents, run by the

Salvation Army, and the Wayside Home and School in Valley Stream, Long Island.

Half of the girls who reached this court changed so remarkably in those fifteen days, they were paroled to their homes or to sympathetic relatives.

Prior to this, there had been nowhere to send such girls except to the Women's House of Detention.

During her "residence," a dentist might cap a broken tooth, a mole might be removed for cosmetic reasons. School instruction continued. Surrounded by others like herself, with no one getting "tough," her fears melted away. She felt that all those working with her were on her side.

An example of what Judge Horn would say to a girl before him:

"I don't think you're a bad girl, Dorothy. . . . You may have done some bad things, but I think you're really running away from a bad home. So I'm going to take you away from your mother for a few weeks."

What had Dorothy done and why had she done it? This:

She had run away. She had complained that her stepfather operated a still in her bedroom; that she couldn't study or sleep. One night her stepfather's brother forced himself on her in her own home. She complained to her mother about this, to which her mother replied: "Oh, men are like that. You might as well learn to put up with it."

But she didn't want to put up with it and presently a guidance counselor summoned police, who raided the home and indeed found the still.

Dorothy was sent to St. Helena's, adjacent to the Euphrasian Residence, an open, unfenced shelter for girls. Dorothy went to her own school from there and the second day was waylaid by the man who had seduced her. Judge Horn ordered this man to his court and told him he could not write to the girl, see her, or phone her. Nor send a message by a third party. The man promised to abide by this. He did not do so and intercepted Dorothy again. Judge Horn gave him thirty days for criminal contempt.

This power to give a jail sentence could be used against any person who, in the court's opinion, obstructed the court's program on behalf of the girls.

When a ward of this court was paroled, however, what continuing protection was there for her? Couldn't all those who wished to get their revenge? No, they couldn't. To avoid this very thing, judges summoned to court the parents, brothers, all the family, and acquaintances and associates, too, and gave written instructions to them all. Compliance with this could be ignored except for the power the judge had to jail anyone flouting this order. Do-it-or-else.

In all of the Girls' Term history (eleven years), no one was ever jailed for breaking the court's order on this point.

What about the toughest girls, the real incorrigibles? They were sent to Villa Loretto at Peekskill, where they could be committed for an indeterminate period not to exceed three years. But they could also be graduated from high school from this facility, and many were.

In the view of many, it is unfortunate that this court, with its "modern" approach and creditable "cure rate," has ceased to be. It disappeared—as did Home Term Court—in the 1962 reorganization of all the courts. Today jurisdiction of girls sixteen to eighteen is controlled by the Family Court. Parents of girls who are eighteen, nineteen, and twenty still apply for assistance under the Wayward Minors Act but most judges refuse to entertain the application, so these girls have to stand in Criminal Court, the very thing Judge Horn's act was circumventing. Many of the Probation people I got to know at 80 Lafayette Street are heartbroken that this umbrella plan, good on paper and in most of its other uses, is missing these central segments. Some girls, badly equipped and poorly used by the world, are still out in the rain.

Anna Kross as Commissioner of Correction

Not all the meetings that used to take place "under the clock at the Biltmore" were gay get-togethers of Yale and Vassar juniors.

On the afternoon of December 27, 1953, Anna Kross kept a three o'clock date with a tall, lean man, classically sinister. It is doubtful if their conversation, either for brevity or content, will soon be duplicated under the old Biltmore clock or any other.

"The Mayor wants you to be his Commissioner of Correction."

The man speaking was Carmine de Sapio, a typical American in

that he had risen from nothing but brains and an instinctive sense
of what was good for himself, to be head of Tammany.
"That's quite a job," she said. "When does the Mayor want to
know?"
"Two hours."
It was time enough. To Anna Moskowitz things have always
happened suddenly. In the spring of 1917 she married Isadore
Kross, a brilliant surgeon. The day after the marriage Dr. Kross
was shipped overseas to a base hospital with the Harvard Medical
unit. Surprise and vicissitude were a part of her life.

She believed then, and does now, that inmates should be rehabilitated, kept busy, taught commercial skills and paid for them,
returned to employable living by means of a planned program that
built their earning power; that this power should start the same
day a prisoner starts serving his time; that they should make
money; and have it when they leave. She believed this was a duty
implicit in the word "correction," and that it could be made to
happen. "Just give me the trained professionals."

Brave? Naïve? Unworkable?

Many thought she wanted too much. Others that she wanted it
too fast. None would go to bat for her to get the money. And it's
certain she wasn't easy to be around when not getting her own
way. Which was most of the time.

She had the body of a wren, the endurance of Paavo Nurmi and
the tact of Genghis Khan. She was the only Commissioner in the
whole history of New York City to be the target of three investigations at the same time. If she wasn't the most controversial figure
in city government, surely she was the most controversial woman
in American law.

The stamp of her thought and action has spread throughout the
state; her warnings, pleadings, innovations, failures, predictions;
her sass, energy, and dishevelled idealism; her hard pragmatic
insight, her empirical savvy, her quick compassion, her postponed
cynicism, her indestructible belief in a world of hard-core non-
believers—this odd-ball amalgam of ferocious honesty and Billy
Sunday crusading is today all present in the vast disarray and
whopping opportunity that is the condition of America's courts,
jails, prisons, shelters, and detention pens. All of them.

And today it would all be a bit different if Anna Kross, in the forty years she was booming and hollering and kicking shins, had had the truly effective support of New York's Mayors; or the recognition of her skills, as doer and prophet, by any articulate bloc of voters, editors, educators, or clergymen. She had a few of each—never more. Never enough. And never any money.

Probably, too, there has never been an American woman in such dreadful need of a P.R. man. Nor a woman so determined to misuse such if she had him.

On the same day that one important New York newspaper ran this headline: MAYOR DENIES HE PLANS TO PROMOTE KROSS, another New York newspaper had this view of it: MAYOR DENIES HE PLANS TO FIRE KROSS. She didn't see the papers that day. She was receiving an honorary degree from New York University. The citation reads, in part:

Brought to New York as an infant, by parents escaping persecution in Russia, the only one of three children to survive the steerage passage, she gained her public schooling by classes in the daytime, and factory labor at night; went on to the study of law with this University; was graduated two years too young for admission to the Bar. . . .

This had been a familiar contradiction throughout her life—not unlike John Vliet Lindsay's: public attack in the presence of proven accomplishment and unmatched courage.

These attacks, during her twelve years as Commissioner of Correction, disturbed her, sometimes hurt her to the quick. But they did not change her. Anyone in public life who is at once imaginative and determined is certain to get hurt. She knew this.

She also knew that some of her worst problems were not of the city's doing but of her own. Her bluntness was rivaled only by La Guardia's, a sorry and wasteful mulishness that finally set them apart and left them only half reconciled at the time of La Guardia's death. (Anna stuck up for gamblers, Fiorello's loathing was epileptic.) Ironical, too, of course, for their energies, methods, and objectives were identical, their practical good to the city beyond calculation.

How did she get into so much trouble? In New York it's easy, no matter what you do. If your purposes are pure, getting in trouble is inevitable.

During her reign as Commissioner, I visited all of the city's jails and prisons in her company, Raymond Street Jail among them. This was one of the oldest and rottenest in the East.

"This is a horrid place," she said. "I'm going to close it." It took some doing, but she was a doer and she did it.

How did Anna Kross get into such trouble? Here's an example, and it happened in that same jail:

In a corridor so narrow two people had to bump each other to pass, Anna Kross spied a little man with a large basket over his arm.

"Who's he?" she asked.

"He's Commissary," said her escort.

"What's Commissary?"

That simple question changed the lady Commissioner's life from that day on. It led to an investigation—her own investigation of her own department—that brought out the two main ingredients of her personality: her fanatical insistence on improving things; and her near-genius for being misunderstood in their doing.

She almost always won but she always got a terrible mauling.

She went to Commissary to see the man in charge, James Princhinelli, a fine man whom I met many times.

"Do you keep books?" she asked. He showed them. They were in good shape. They showed a gross business of nearly half a million dollars, and a good profit.

"What do you do with the net?"

"Pay salaries of the clerks in Commissary who buy the articles, make the sandwiches, and carry the stuff to the inmates."

"What do you do with what's left over?"

"It's used for the welfare of the inmates."

"In what way?"

He showed her: dentures, glasses, artificial limbs, for inmates who had no money. And most had none, none at all.

Princhinelli had the list of every item bought, its date, and amount of purchase. He was an impeccable bookkeeper.

"Are you people on Social Security?"

"No."

Anna Kross felt they should be. She also thought better use could be made of the profits. She told Mayor Wagner about the "department store" she was running. Then she went over to see the Commissioner of Investigations, Peter Campbell Brown, and asked him to look into the Commissary situation. She also consulted Joseph Schechter, Personnel Chief.

Both agreed the Commissary structure should be examined but both warned that putting Commissary on civil service would take the money out of her hands.

"That's exactly what I want," she said. "I don't *want* control of Commissary money. The Controller should control it." Her logic was unassailable. "And the Purchasing Department should do the purchasing," she added.

Today all Commissary activity is on civil service, the Controller controls the money, books are audited every thirty days.

But the word "scandal" got into the papers. And this is the classic irony that has pursued Anna Kross her whole life: there never *was* any scandal. She was and is as grandly unreachable as Seabury himself. Yet two years later a New York County Grand Jury investigated Anna Kross all over again and the word "scandal" once more appeared in the headlines.

Time after time, upon this most ferociously moral of all women, this word "scandal" tried to fasten itself.

Why Anna Kross should be so susceptible, so vulnerable, to the big and little digs and gouges of metropolitan spite and municipal attrition is a mystery to all those who have known her and worked with her through the years. But there are theories. One is that perpetual exoneration can get monotonous. Another: that she doesn't *look* like a Commissioner of Correction; that anyone so tiny, so passerine (she weighs just a hundred) can't really belong to the world of shivs and sirens, of tear-gas, clubs and manacles; to the clank of security gear and the clang of iron doors. She looks like she's on the way to the A&P for broccoli.

There is a third theory: that whenever she speaks, which is a large portion of any average day, she speaks as one embattled; in the areas of her scorn, defenses go up. The beleaguered are ready with rebuttal, the churlish with back-biting, the lashed with revenge. Being totally seized by a sense of right, and totally bent upon its achievement, she has been throughout most of her career almost totally self-righteous. Another thing: because she goes on talking long after she's made her point, reporters always leave with an earful. Often they leave with a string of loyal and loving staff members chasing after, to tell the press Anna didn't mean it *quite* the way it sounded just now; a kind of corridor editing that is always too late.

This has been with her since the very beginning, and a single brief though illuminating sidetrack will make it clear to the reader right here:

As Assistant Corporation Counsel, Anna Kross began hitting the front pages. In 1924 she was fighting for the passage of a Minimum Wage Law for Women. Many times she appeared before the New York State Assembly, describing the bill she wanted, pleading for it, answering questions. On the day of the Assembly's closing session, she made one final appeal. But the bill failed. Most legislators were bored or preoccupied. They were packing bags for summer recess, and many of them, as she faced them, were conspicuously drunk.

The next day, at a dinner at the Women's Democratic Committee, reporting the bill's failure, she told what she'd seen, including the drinking. How did she put it? "A large number of legislators we have elected to get these very things done for us were drunk." And she named the drunks—at least all those she knew and spotted.

It was then that Tammany's Chief Murphy, by then her personal idol, took her to one side and tried to tell her something:

"There are times in politics, Anna, when it is wise to say *nothing*. True or untrue, yesterday was one of those times."

But she never learned.

She was constitutionally unable to sit still or keep still when anything shabby was showing. And much that was shabby had surrounded her offices during all her years as judge or Commissioner.

Through her whole professional life many ugly insinuations have hung about in the air when what she was trying to state was a hard if complex truth. She'd never been one to waste time on modifiers. The truth banged its way to the stage, ready or not, and there declared itself.

"Prostitutes don't belong in prisons. They're social accidents."

She never allowed the physical fact of her being in politics to abridge her right to say what she thought. What she thought *as of that moment*. And say it to whomever. Nor to abridge her right to suspect. In her make-up it was not a refusal to observe caution. She saw what she thought should be done and went after it. And got it done. And got hurt.

Drugs and Scandal

The day Anna Kross saw the little man with the basket in the Raymond Street Jail, it occurred to her that the system could be used to bring into her jails not only sandwiches but drugs, too. She soon found out it was going on.

With the help of Peter Terranova, Deputy Commissioner of Narcotics (another unusual public servant I knew), two detectives posing as inmates were planted in the Tombs. Ten days later testimony recorded in her office revealed that inmates who were drug users *could* get drugs at least three times a week in the Tombs. It was being smuggled into the prison in laundry bags. From where, and to whom, could not then be found out. Anna Kross requested the Commissioner of Investigations to continue looking into her department. He did this.

One day her phone rang. There was another investigation going on, one she knew nothing about. It was the District Attorney's office: "We have enough evidence to arrest eight of your guards," he said.

"Great. I'm glad it's being cleared up."

Anna Kross would have appreciated being told the D.A.'s office was making a parallel and simultaneous investigation of the Tombs. She never received this confidence, and though her objectives were identical to those of the D.A., and though her own investigations of her own jails had never stopped, headlines this time did her real harm:

PRISON SCANDAL TO BLAST ANNA KROSS FROM JOB

It was almost as if the mess uncovered at the Tombs was of her own doing.

The scandal in the Tombs involved very few men. But the racket was real and smooth-working. Favors could be bought by well-heeled inmates and for fixed rates: Scotch at $35 a fifth, delivered in eight-ounce medicine bottles; a choice cell could be had for $40; a visit to another cell, $1. For the passing of ready cash, from friends outside to inmates inside, the arrested guards were skimming thirty per cent. Two guards threw a drinking party for six inmates in the prison's sixth-floor blanket room. To hide the evidence (and the noise), the empties were wrapped in towels, smashed against the wall, and dumped down an incinerator hopper.

Three of the guards were found to have police records. One of those three had been appointed during Anna Kross's tenure. She was astounded that a prison guard with a police record could *be* certified by the civil service. Background checks of prospective employees through civil service were never available to her. She had no say in the matter. "We take what they send us. We have to."

The D.A.'s investigation continued. So did her own. It went through the whole system, all personnel, all detention houses, all prisons, cell by cell.

The vast majority of her total staff of 2,000 were men and women of unblemished record and provable loyalty. Overall, it was an experienced and effective custodial staff. Weak areas were corrected by transfer or reassignment. There were very few dismissals. But there was a rash of complaining, especially among the transferred men, who brought a grievance list to Mayor Wagner. He listened to the delegation, then to Anna Kross, whom he had appointed. Again the headlines, fogging the picture as they had before:

MRS. KROSS FACING REVOLT OF GUARDS

ANNA KROSS CLIPPED, TO BE FIGUREHEAD ONLY

KROSS SAYS SHE'LL FIGHT ON FOR CHANGES

KROSS TO GO

Kross stayed.

In answer to a primary charge (from the New York County Grand Jury) that she was a "bad administrator," she told her wardens: "I can be administrator just by closing my door on all of you."

Every man there knew what that meant: it was a direct reference to the Commissioner immediately preceding her. His door was notoriously shut to all, and for the full seven years he was in office. And no captain, no warden, or deputy summoned to that

Commissioner's presence had ever been offered the courtesy of a chair.

It is a wonder she never developed Blanda's toe, kicking at the pricks of patronage, custom, and desuetude. Her horror at ever being unavailable—as her feckless predecessor had been—took a reverse turn. She would listen to anyone, see anyone, read anything. She was criticized for being *too* available. At times this may have been true.

True or not, the theories and practices she set in motion are still moving. The dreams for reform—from overcrowding, understaffing, underpaying—wherever they are being revived now, are her monument to practical compassion. Where they have been ignored, the back-loads of unheard cases, medieval jail conditions, all our Atticas, Raifords, and San Quentins; the national breakdown of the dignity and effectiveness of the American court system, all of this wears the benchmark of her powers of prophecy.

Almost everything about New York's courts and prisons was bad and she said so and named it.

Overcrowding is not new. It's just surfacing where all may now see.

As Commissioner of Correction she found the overcrowding at Rikers Island so primitive that in 1956 inmates were sleeping on the floor. Why? No money. Blame? You? Me?

"If there was one judge in five hundred with enough interest really to inspect a city jail, jails wouldn't look like this. But judges never visit jails," Anna said. (Today at least token appearances are beginning.)

This was true enough to shame the judges who'd never inspected a single facility; and win the fury of the few who had.

At Rikers Island she had the prisoner overload transferred to Hart Island. In all of New York's prisons, jails, and detention centers, she separated the men from the boys wherever physically feasible. At the Women's House of Detention she fought to separate sentenced inmates from pre-trial inmates. Because of the congestion there, it was a common thing for a young mother, held for shoplifting on a first arrest, to be shoved into the same cell with an assaultive dope addict, a homosexual, an aging recidivist. The building, recently vacated (May, 1971), had 401 cells. The daily census was often over 650. "A lot of the young girls here are the helpless captives of eager lesbians. And not a few are held so long, they get accustomed to it, then to like it. The same for teenage boys thrown in with older men."

Though a lawyer since 1912 and a judge since 1933, the cant of legalism has never mucked up her own speech nor blurred her vision. "I'm concerned about inmates. No one else seems to be."

About everything she ever said had a sting to it, often an implied rebuke. "Dope addicts don't belong in jail." "We talk about crime prevention. But nowhere in the state is there a move to *do* something about it!" "There's nothing new about sex. If it's cut off naturally, it will be sought unnaturally." "The time to prevent juvenile delinquency is before the baby is born." "Most judges have never seen the inside of a prison, and never will."

These attitudes, convictions, and furies had been hers when Anna Kross was appointed Commissioner of Correction in 1954. She inherited a fetid, palustrine mess. The appalling inadequacy of plant, personnel, and funding—still grotesque—were Dickensian when she took over the job. She knew it would be bad. And she knew how bad. But she took it anyway and began banging away at committees, the press, the Mayor, the Board of Estimate, the city fathers, and any foundation that would let her in.

She had to do a lot of begging.

It is very doubtful if Anna Kross would have been of such dramatic value to the bench, or to New York's prison system, if she had had a different background herself. She was a woman whose education in wretchedness had been thorough. Unlike most, this had not killed her spirit. But it had altered it. It had left her hard; hard but pitying. It had left her unerring in her observations about people and the systems that controlled them (or failed to), but quick in her response to these; to both the mechanism and its human content.

She was always for or against everything.

She had been brought up in a ghetto. Christie Street isn't much different today from 1905, if you want to go down and look at it. As with many ghetto products, or any other phenomenon of survival, she could talk to the hurt and the outraged. With the eyes of a croupier, unblinking, all-seeing, beyond surprise, she could spot any faker. With the eyes of mercy, she could sense any misery. She knew misery. She'd lived it. And at a time when its penalties were heaviest—when she was a young girl. Though physically almost minute, she could create a row anywhere, whether sidewalk, Tammany Hall, or the Albany legislature.

Unlike almost any other political product in New York history, she was a loner. A joiner but a loner. You can be both, and she was. She never had a gang. She wouldn't have known how to use one. She never paid any attention to herself, nor to what was said or printed about her. She got where she did because strong men recognized her strength; the civic-minded recognized the purity and the pragmatism of her drive. Two-faced politicians liked to promote her because it put them, for the time, on the side of angels. Hard-headed executives saw in her the strange, infrequent power to get the job done no matter what; saw a certain mystical competence hidden in her character somewhere; a pure strain of some sort. What they saw was an Old Testament Jewish refusal ever to surrender, equivocate, betray, lie, or compromise.

Obsessive industry was there, too. With Anna Kross, you knew that she'd not only be on the job but be all over it.

If anyone had ever offered Anna Kross a bribe—and she was a Tammany graduate where venality was not only expected but traditional—he would have been publicly beheaded by her umbrella. Or flogged to powder with her purse. She was, and is right now at eighty, mettlesome, tense, contentious, positive, steamed up, and fully programmed. And she is unendingly compassionate. In fact, much of her character could be summed up this way: her apartment right now is always aswarm with people who don't know each other and who have come for lunch. Half of these people are world-famous. The other half are hungry. She doesn't care which is which.

She's instantly recognized on the street by former inmates (I saw it happen twice), who are always delighted and who always stop and speak: "I'm one of your boys, Commissioner." "Hart Island, Rikers, or the Tombs?" she will ask. She doesn't know them but they always know her. And very often the job they got after release was her doing. They remember. She doesn't. Her concerns were vital, basic, physical: job, shelter, clothes, food. In the prisons: shower-headings, toilet paper, ventilation, exercise, classes, bedding, vermin control.

She had no use for theory. If a suggestion weren't susceptible of immediate use on a hard physical basis, out it went. Her roof was leaking and it didn't need committees. It just needed tar-paper and a pail. That's how she viewed her work.

Thus, from the beginning, her concerns went way beyond the sanitary findings of most sociologists, their paper charts, their ceaseless self-flattering memos, nifty vocabularies, and university offices. She knew she could take a few sociologists into cells and detention pens where they'd just faint. Or might not come out alive. She had as little use for most of the "book" sociologists as she did for judges who sent men and women to prison every day but who had themselves never visited a prison, anywhere, even once. And who never would. They've all earned her savage scorn. And they still have it.

As Commissioner, Anna Kross would walk in unexpectedly at dinner time or breakfast time and eat a prison meal, use the prison toilet; or come by at night and sleep in a remand shelter. Nobody could tell *her* what it was like. Through the grapevine prisoners knew about this at once, and approved. Even the most chitinous inmate agreed there had never been a Commissioner who showed such interest. If they didn't feel represented, at least they felt recognized. They knew that *somebody* knew they were alive.

Often she went from one prison to another by subway. It saved time. She had a chauffeur-driven Cadillac at her disposal—as all Commissioners did—and her driver ran a thousand office errands for her every month. She didn't make much use of the limousine herself; didn't feel or look at home in it. Didn't like it really, being too small to see out. But for her driver she had only one order: don't use the siren. I had a hundred rides in this Cadillac and never heard it but once: to hold the Welfare Island ferry.

As a social creature, everything about the woman was self-effacing. As a civic force, everything about her was explosive. She was an original, odd mix of Orphan Annie and Queen Elizabeth— at one moment pathetically invisible, whipped, and tear-stained, at the next, imperious. In rages she could be quite terrifying.

"I went over the Queens Jail. I found a youngster fifteen years old in that jail. Fifteen! 'How long have you been here?' Eleven months,' he said. I was so outraged, I wanted to pull down New York. It was my first visit. I saw the yard. I said: 'What do we do here? How do inmates get into this yard?' 'They don't get into the yard.' In twenty years nobody had ever gone into that yard! Not enough staff. No money. The Tombs is even worse. Do you realize that one officer has to take care of 240 inmates in this monstrous new prison? How can he even *see* what goes on in the cell-blocks?" (1954)

"In New York City we have a Correction Department. But it doesn't do any correcting." (1956)

"When you talk to inmates, and I do it every day; when you see what they go through, you know we make more and better criminals." (1954)*

"Today we have a frightful problem of narcotics. Over 33 per cent of our jail population is involved. What do we do? We spend a million and a half to take care of a hundred. At any one time, never more than a hundred. Of course they get right out, and of course they come right back. This is insane. We do this at North Brothers Island. But most times, when I go over there, there are about fifty youngsters. But in our jails, I find narcotics addicts in the thousands. What do we do for them? Nothing. Nothing at all. When we looked for medical facilities, they were almost non-existent." (1954)

"Do you know any lawyers who know anything about correction law? They don't even know that such a thing exists! Do you know any judges who know anything about it?"

"I am as tough as nails. But it is not toughness that is compelling me to drive as I am driving. It is recognition of the danger to our way of life that exists within the prisons, throughout our whole country."

When a challenge like the above is delivered, impromptu, to the New York Bar Association, is it likely to go the Dale Carnegie

---

* In the New York *Times*, Nov 4, 1971, this quote from District Attorney Eugene Gold: "When will jails be a place where men are not made into better criminals but into better men? How many more prison deaths must we have, how many more suicides . . . before we give meaning to human dignity?"

route? No, it is not. Yet Anna Kross had so much platform magnetism, so many tough facts, such spiritual energy, and such horrifying predictions that sooner or later she reached everybody in front of her. She knocked off a carnation or two from Harvard Law lapels, but they knew she was not kidding. They knew that she knew more law than they did; that what she sought was not for herself. They knew she'd done things they wouldn't have had the nerve, the energy, or civic unselfishness to try. They knew, too, that no matter who else might be present, she was the most courageous person in the room.

They never met anyone like Anna Kross.

"Look at this!" she would shout. "I have one male psychiatrist and one female psychiatrist, one day a week. For 8,000 prisoners! How does the Parole Commission expect us to make a report?"

"In the new Tombs, the air system has failed. Does anyone think men down there might suffocate?"

"We know the problem. We don't need any more conferences."

"In 1953 there was an examination for custodial officers in the Department of Correction. Would you believe that the Civil Service Commission advertised, "No educational requirements?" Can you believe we are expected to do a job on this crime problem with such a standard?"

She had the problem then that every city is screaming about today: no money. Never enough to attract and retain the quality of personnel without which no practical plan could be kept in motion. And we are going to bump along for many decades, unwilling to face the tax bite that will have to be levied if we're serious about healing the nation's criminals. The plain truth is this: we don't care enough. And the melancholy probable: we never will.

Kross as Commissioner — Improvements in Correction

When Commissioner Kross resigned her office in 1965, the improvements she was able to effect in twelve years of trying were impressive. All were achieved in a climate she refers to as "progress through crisis in a constantly volcanic situation."

Specifically, what improvements have taken place? And where? Prior to the Kross era, female prisoners incarcerated in the Women's House of Detention spent 95 per cent of their time in unproductive lock-in.

It was earlier mentioned that when she took the job, the new Commissioner had a lot of begging to do, since the Board of Estimate's budget was too stingy to accomplish anything. It was volunteers that she found who equipped the beauty salon and the school. When Anna Kross first entered the Women's House of Detention, she saw a room with the promising sign: BEAUTY PARLOR. She went in. It was empty. But she got it going: a teacher, professional equipment, and a change in the state law (also secured for her by volunteers) that made it possible for persons with a prison record to obtain cosmetology licenses, join the union, and work as licensed beauty operators.

In the course of the years, a daily schedule was set up. The tremendous importance of pride in personal appearance, of neat dress and becoming hair-do, of well-kept hands and "style"—as a psychological part of the whole process of rehabilitation—has been known for a long time. And, in a few places, practiced for a long time. (The beauty parlor in St. Elizabeth's Hospital for the Mentally Ill, in Washington, has known and most successfully used this universal "secret" for many years. Even the mentally and emotionally ravaged like to look nice, and with the knowledge that they do look nice, many of them can meet the world again with less fear and hostility; with more acceptance of reality.)

So also with women prisoners. Each inmate in the Women's House of Detention was permitted a periodic morale-building beauty treatment.

In 1959 this meager little plant was licensed by the state as the Number Ten Greenwich Avenue Beauty School. Many of the inmates of this dismal holding facility have passed the state-prescribed courses right there in jail, have there received their state certificates, and have gone on, following release, to good jobs as beauticians and hair-stylists. No girl with such a certificate has ever been rearrested. It's good-paying work. Ask any woman. (Or any married man.)

Education? Many of the sentenced women were illiterate. They were taught to read and write. Spanish-speaking women, if they wished to learn English, were encouraged to do so.

At a level somewhat above this, an average of 25 girls a year were awarded high school equivalency diplomas.

This wasn't much, to be sure. And Anna Kross herself called it negligible. But better than nothing at all.

Girls could take courses in dressmaking. They could make dresses, skirts, and blouses for themselves to take home upon release; and they were allowed to make clothes for their families. Materials? From volunteers.

There was a sewing factory with new modern machines where inmates could learn to handle the tools of the needle trades.

There were cooking classes and classes in table-waiting. The teachers, once again, were volunteers.

Volunteers came in to teach commercial subjects: typing, filing, mimeographing, office procedure, library cataloguing. (The waiting-list here was huge.) Volunteers, dragooned by the energetic Commissioner, made all this possible.

There was an active sports program on the screened-in roof of the building. There was a record library.

But the Commissioner had to beg for everything.

Volunteers donated money to indigent prisoners, money for carfare for relatives who couldn't afford a visit otherwise; temporary lodgings for needy discharged prisoners, aid in finding jobs. Prior to 1954, women were discharged with "a dime and a bologna sandwich." (Men from the Tombs or Rikers also got the bologna sandwich but the pay scale was higher—25¢.)

It was Anna Kross who said, after studying what was wrong with the Magistrates' Court system: "Abolish it." And of the Raymond Street Jail: "Close it." About the Women's House of Detention she was also explicit: "Replace this vertical monstrosity." Replace it with what? "With a horizontal layout that has a full rehabilitation program."

She never swears, yet one senses even today (and she's over 80) a rich lode of profanity under every quaver of her italics.

A project, started in 1961 and subsidized in 1962 by the National Institute of Mental Health, involved the New York University Graduate School of Social Work in correctional social service work on Rikers Island. This was a very head-on program, right at the mines where the ore is. A master's degree in social work, after two years of classroom lectures (on the university campus), plus field work conducted among prisoners on Rikers, was granted. A number of members of the Department of Correction staff completed this course, the emphasis, of course, being on the effectiveness of casework in depth.

The same year that brought support from the National Institute of Mental Health also initiated a professional training affiliation with the New York School of Psychiatry. This school participates in the psychiatric residency training of doctors assigned to state mental hospitals. Under Anna Kross, and for the first time in the history of the Department of Correction, psychiatric residents were utilized to shore up the mental health resources of her department. Reciprocally, doctors employed by state hospitals were receiving training in correction. New York's jails and prisons were being used as a lab post-doctoral study of correctional psychiatry. Under this program, seventeen psychiatrists-in-training were providing treatment services to the inmate population two years after the experiment started.

In 1963, the New York School of Psychiatry expanded its correctional training program to include training in the clinical and administrative aspects of the prison psychiatrist's role. Reality and immediacy were brought to this program through lectures, from selected correctional personnel, by wardens, deputy wardens, captains, correction officers (both male and female), and members of the department's psychiatric staff.

In 1964 a new training course for psychiatrists, made possible by funding from the National Institute of Mental Health, was started. It dealt directly with the rehabilitation of individuals who had committed criminal or delinquent acts.

The same year saw the birth of a new and immensely practical project designed to develop employable skills among sentenced adolescent prisoners on Rikers Island; skills that would mean jobs the day they got out: tailoring, shoe repair, baking, salad-making, auto repair, printing, surveying, greenhouse work, and roofing. A school paper, put out by the "students" and titled *The Open Mind* first appeared that year.

With the help of her Educational Advisory Committee, and its liaison with the Board of Education, Commissioner Kross saw the beginnings of Public School 616 on Rikers Island ("600" schools refer primarily to high schools located in prisons with a student body made up of sentenced prisoners from sixteen to twenty). This is called the Adolescent Division. The Adult School, with much the same opportunity and curriculum, is for prisoners older than twenty.

In addition to the learning of specific trades and mechanical skills, they could earn high school equivalency diplomas the same as the girls did in the Greenwich Avenue facility. About fifty men a year on Rikers Island have "gone through high school" this way. And ninety per cent of those qualified to sit for final exams have passed. But in her final report, Commissioner Kross noted: "We are still very far from our goal of educating every prisoner up to his potential."

Excellent ventures, worth support from every point of view, often must be abandoned. It's always for one or two reasons: the money ran out, the personnel vanished. I hear this report from wardens everywhere. Commissioner Kross was very high on a television series, for example, designed for illiterates (there are more of them than you would like to think) called Operation Alphabet. It was offered in nine separate Correction facilities, and it was a whopping success everywhere. But it had to be pulled— no money to pay the crew. A big crew? No. A crew of three.

Another fine project that had a three-year go was set up in the Adolescent Division on Rikers in 1961. It was a sort of "cram-course" in pre-release guidance; two months of intensive preparation for young fellows about to rejoin the mainstream of life, and even though it was brief the follow-up survey showed a dramatic reduction in the rate of recidivism. It was hooked into the R.Y.T. (Restoration of Youth through Training) program and financed by Federal money. But when the money stopped, so did the program.

"These have been laborious years of struggle," she has written, "to overcome the centuries of antiquated philosophy and of apathy with which today's public is still saturated."

It is still so saturated.

Despite new construction, during her regime, of detention facilities in Brooklyn, Queens, and the Bronx, every single facility holding anybody at all was holding a lot too many.

What to do about overcrowding? "Change the laws that now send persons to prison who are not criminals. Remove right now from all our prisons all persons whose main fault is senility, narcotics addiction, alcoholism, mental illness, vagrancy, or poverty. They're Welfare cases and hospital cases."

In the course of a long-continued and comparative bail studies project, interesting findings came out at once: a third of those held in New York City jails and prisons are there for about thirty days; a quarter as long as a year. They've no money to pay bail. Anna Kross endeavored to prove it was safer *not* to hold such persons. If they can't go their own bail, let them out. Don't keep them. Take a chance. Hope they'll show up when their case is called. Anna Kross believed it would work.

It was a daring idea. What happened? Of those arrested persons who were experimentally permitted to remain in the community while awaiting trial, a much smaller percentage failed to appear than in the case of those who had paid their bail and who then forfeited it by not appearing.

Today it is a common thing—as a direct result of this innovation—for an arrested person, adjudged reliable upon investigation, to be released on his own recognizance. It's called ROR. If this procedure were applied as widely as it should be, the reduction in overcrowding would be "striking," to use the Commissioner's word. She has called overcrowding "cruel," "stupid," "idiotic," "medieval," "totally unnecessary," "intolerable," and she banged away at it every day for all the twelve years she had the job.

It is still everything she said of it; and for the same reasons.

Why did the Women's House of Detention get so much publicity? Because it was the worst thing of its kind in the country? Not at all. Because lesbianism was so widespread? Again, no. It got knocked around (and a good thing it did, too) because it sat right out in the front yard of New York City where everybody could *see* it. And *hear* it. It was right smack in the middle of where a lot of what is typically New York not only makes its living but makes its home. In all five of its boroughs you can't name a facility that was seen daily and nightly by more people. It was a true part of the neighborhood. For 36 years the El roared right past it. You could wave at the girls. Millions did. And they waved back. Right up to May 1971, you could holler from the sidewalk and get a show of heads, a shower of giggles, or a curse.

Any jail is sordid, clanky, combustible, and sinister. And all of them are ready at any moment of the day or night to turn on their own battery of polygot expletives so robust they'd back Al Capone off the curb.

Many of our "best citizens" (by the way, who are they?) lived only a block away, on lower Fifth Avenue, and naturally did a lot of tsk-tsking when they read about all the poor girls and all the carryings-on. Or *heard* the commotion, perhaps, on their way back from dinner at Charles.

The stories were so repetitious, a form of public hysteria began to grip that part of Manhattan. We can have a riot in the Tombs, and television very quickly brings it right home to us. But there is this difference: ask any New Yorker where the Tombs is and he won't have any more idea of its location than he will have as to why it's called the Tombs. But the same New Yorker knows exactly where the Women's House of Detention is. He could direct you there by bus or subway, and has himself passed it a thousand times.

The overcrowding and the lesbianism got so many New Yorkers so steamed up that Commissioner Kross was directed to eliminate all doubling-up of female prisoners.

And here began an exercise in pure municipal idiocy. How *do* you eliminate all the doubling-up? Easy. You move the overflow somewhere else. Where do you move it? These girls—the overflow—were transferred to the Adolescent Remand Shelter in the Brooklyn House of Detention for *Men*. This was already the most overcrowded institution in Brooklyn. But once the girls were out of the Greenwich Avenue pen, public interest evaporated. There was one girl to a cell in the Women's House of Detention and we could now all have nice Christian thoughts about it. Which is to say, forget it.

Not so the Commissioner. She had to go on paying attention to the *problem*. The adolescent boys had to be removed from the Adolescent Remand Shelter to make room for the girls. But where did they put the boys? In the already overcrowded Bronx and Queens House of Detention for Men.

How was this accomplished? Doubling up everybody, men and boys. Here it created the exact situation, for men, that had been thought so degrading for women. In 1957 Anna Kross had put a stop to the demoralizing practice of putting young boys within reachable distance of older criminals. But this culture medium, the most virulent known, could now flourish in two prisons instead of one!

This is what happens when the yapping of pious amateurs gets enough newspaper headroom to push aside authority; the same pandemonium that occurs when hysterical passengers take over the bridge while the ship is traversing an ice field.

I spent hundreds of hours in these jails and prisons, meeting with and getting to know most of the Commissioner's aides, captains, and wardens. Milton Luger one day told me: "When Commissioner Kross took over the big job, she inherited a bad press." I was a reading man and knew it anyhow but it says a tremendous lot. Inheriting a bad press is like trying to fight your way back to a good credit rating after bankruptcy. There is nothing dramatic about goodness, and the goodness this Commissioner was able to effect did not wait to be interred with her bones. It got shovelled out of sight while she, its initiator and administrator, was very much in motion.

She started the night school on Rikers. In one month there was more activity than there had been in any full year under her predecessor. Recreational activity picked up proportionately, some of it in areas where only the most unusual woman could be expected to bring results: baseball. Rikers soon developed a "varsity" ball club, playing all of New York City's service teams—Police, Fire, and Sanitation—as well as ball clubs from Mitchell Field, Fort Wadsworth, Kings Point, Governor's Island. Only fifteen games the first year, but in three years it was up to seventy games, with two games on weekends. The night school on Rikers had a course in umpiring. It was conducted by a former semi-pro ball umpire who was doing time on a bum-check rap.

There were courses in painting and drawing. Subway posters began to come from the Rikers print shop. Courses in blueprint reading were offered; courses in music theory. There was a glee club. Trees for the Parks Department were grown on the acres of the Rikers "nursery"—110,000 trees. And the bakery baked the bread (sold at no profit) for the Board of Education and the Welfare Department. A peach orchard appeared, planted from pits thrown in with city garbage. The poultry farm produced fifteen cases of eggs a day. Industries included motor repair, plumbing, carpentry, electrical repair, shoe-making, and a mattress factory.

It sounds like more than it really was. And Anna Kross never blew it up to make it sound or read impressively. But it was a start.

If she had to name the principal villain of correction anywhere in the world, perhaps it would be idleness. I heard the same when visiting Attica. No prison has the patent—you hear it everywhere. Stupidity would be close behind:

"In eight years (1962) we haven't overcome these monstrosities: prisoners hanging around in long alleyways. No tables, no chairs, no benches. Nothing to sit on, even when doing nothing. I ask the question and this is the answer I get about chairs: "They'll hit each other with chairs." So I tell these city dignitaries: "I'm a judge. So do husbands and wives hit each other with chairs. I know a lot more about who's hitting who than most people in this town." But she did, finally, get some sort of solution to this one: chairs and benches that fold back against the wall. Immovable. "You can sit on them but you can't throw them."

With her own staffs, she was looked at differently from day to day, and for such reasons as these:

She got wardens' pay raised from $7,600 to $11,400.

But she also made the Department of Correction band mad at her. It was a good band, composed of the best brass and wood players from all her thirteen institutions. They played only two or three times a year, however. And they kept their own instruments in their homes. Anna Kross pointed out that the instruments belonged to the city. She made the players turn them in, in order to start an inmate training session. Then she thought a stronger incentive to apply themselves would be afforded if the band itself periodically performed for the inmates. She was soon told: "The officers' band objects to playing for the inmates." "Oh, they object? Well, they can object, but they're playing." They played.

About programs: "There must be a *minimum* time in which inmates have nothing to do. The goal should be for *no idleness* at all. And for the industries we have: better compensation for the prisoner work that is done. More money, for them, for what they make. They should be allowed, be enabled, to buy the things they want or need from money they make on prison jobs."

Rikers was like other prisons: over half the inmates had no money; none at all. And most couldn't make any, this in contrast to state prisons, where the pay, though wretched, often permits a prisoner to buy his own tobacco. Most at Rikers could not afford even that. Better pay for prison work was a fight she never won.

About promotion she was tough but fair: a physical and a psychiatric exam both, then these results to be fed into a full evaluation by including the candidate's past record. "If he's had trouble as a Correction Officer, he'll have trouble as a captain." This kind of exam was new. And no candidate could be advanced if he flunked any part of it.

"I am trying to elevate civil service standards. It's outrageous that we can seek recruits by advertising "No educational requirements necessary." We can get recruits that way. And they'll all be idiots. I want to upgrade the quality of every guard in every prison. You are more important in this picture than I am. Commissioners like me come and go. Just look in the papers. But career services remain. You are permanently here. I am only briefly here. I will fight for you. I will fight for better salaries for you, in and out of office."

They knew she meant it because she had done it.

"If you think you have worked hard, you know I have not worked less. I am called a bad administrator. The *Journal American* called me that yesterday. Yes, I am a bad administrator. In this job, you have to see people. In this job you have only this choice: to be a bad administrator or to be a non-administrator. I am accused of being too accessible to my department heads. I shall continue to be. By being accessible to them, I am a bad administrator. By being inaccessible to them, I would be a non-administrator. I am never going to be any better than I am now. So get used to it."

If promotion was difficult, it was the more respected. Anna Kross added a fine psychological fillip to the promotion ceremony: she got Mayor Robert Wagner personally to swear in all Correction staff members who were promoted. This had never been done before. It brought dignity and importance to the job, a feeling that the city cared, though in truth it did not much care and does not now.

"For your own personal and professional protection," she one day advised a large group of her staff, "keep records. Keep careful records. Keep a desk diary. Keep an accurate notation of the people you call. Such things as 'I tried to get so-and-so for this job but he wouldn't work for the money offered.' Be specific. You are all in very sensitive and vulnerable jobs. You often have temptations. Some of them can be quite awful. If you know the temptations, you know that I also know them. You also know the penalties. A lot of the men you are guarding and protecting knew the temptations and the penalties. And made the wrong choices. That's why they are here as prisoners. Some of this is a matter of intelligence. Don't be stupid. You've got good jobs. So keep them clean. You know we had an escaped-prisoner alarm last month. And I went along on this one to see how such things are handled. Many guards and officers said "No" to the idea of a search. And you know why. We didn't find the escaped prisoner but we did find fifteen hams!"

Frustration plagued her. It plagues every public servant. People in jobs have certain ways of looking at them, and of doing them. "There are always those who like the status quo," Anna Kross has said. "Just jiggle this a little and they feel you've imperiled their whole security. Change means worry. Worry means fear. Fear means inefficiency." But right here she had trouble, and it has and will persist in any holding facility that is trying to improve things: improvement *has* to mean change.

The crew involved solely in rehabilitation work (they were called "Rehabs" and still are in many places) felt that they and their work were looked down on by Parole people. *Was* Parole hostile to Rehab? Real efforts were made—limited, of course, because the money, as always, was limited—to change prisoner attitudes. And some progress was made, mostly because Anna Kross herself had a different attitude about what a prisoner was and what could be done to change him; to reconstruct him so that upon release he would very much *want* to stay out of trouble.

"We must teach inmates that the law is not against *them*. Of course inmates are resentful. Resistant and cynical, too. But I tell them: 'There is no difference between a man on this side and a man on the other side of these bars. Both are equally human. It is not like the Army where differences are not only recognized but insisted on. I cannot get these new programs working without your help.' "

But too often, upon release, when a warden could point to a good recovery record of a prisoner—a record earned through the programs of recreation and rehabilitation that had been set up in city jails and prisons—nothing was done for them by the Parole Commission, and usually on the grounds of "Bad background." "Sure, his background is bad!" Anna Kross would blaze. "That's why he wound up in jail! But he's been improved by these services and this has to be taken into account by the Parole Commission."

The Rehabs say it is hard to implement their programs; hard to integrate them through the labyrinth of Custody; hard because Custody does not really know what rehabilitation is. It has not been taught.

It is a pioneering idea with Anna Kross that social and spiritual deterioration starts when incarceration starts, "And not in the first ten years. It starts in the first ten minutes."

It is a matter of prisoner-handling attitude, it is all wrong, and it is nationwide.

"Every year about 3,000,000 men and women go through our police system. 'Give him a taste of jail' is a common attitude. This is cynical and wrong. It is destructive. It is cynical by presupposing jail as purely punitive and never corrective. It is wrong because it carries none of the basic meaning of the value of a person or of society's obligation to protect him in *any* setting, even a jail setting. But with too many jails and wardens; with too many correction officers—this idea that a prisoner has a right to be protected, a right to an opportunity to be improved—this disappears at once. It disappears at the exact instant the man is jailed. The whole idea of rehabilitation, the whole purpose and plan of it, the whole philosophy of it—all this is unheard of by most of America's custodial personnel. So most prisoners come to prison with keepers indifferent to the conditions of the inmates. Most of them either don't give a damn, or else think they *ought* to be tough.

"This is one of the things I am spending these years of my life trying to change. It is damn hard."

It is also "damn hard" to be under investigation for most of the time you are in office. The ironies of much of it were scalding. She had asked Mayor Wagner, as soon as she accepted this toughest of all jobs, to investigate the whole complex of the prisons; and had made the same offer to the D.A.'s office. Two other investigations were going on, one of them running for two years.

Two of the reports—the Preusse Report and the Charles Tenney (Grand Jury) Report—blasted her administration for not doing the very things, for not accomplishing the changes and reforms she herself had immediately sought upon taking office: overcrowding, separation of men from boys, more programs, less lock-in, better pay. You name it, she wanted it. But no money.

Was she a "bad administrator"? If her boss, the Mayor, thought so, he could have and should have taken her out. But he supported her through the whole of his own terms, three of them, and Commissioner Kross served the full twelve years, always advocating the implementation of the same major recommendations; hitting the papers almost daily with her vivid descriptions of the conditions she had inherited, damning public apathy, making open proclamations of the true exigencies in this marvel of neglect; getting there first—months and months before issuance of the punishing "findings" of the reports.

Chairman Frederick Woodbridge, an architect and a good one, made this summarizing statement in the Tenney Report:

> We want it distinctly understood that her administration has been bad and still is bad, and we hope something will be done about it. We think an administrator who would be a good administrator would be a distinct improvement. We do not think Anna Kross is a good administrator.

I have met this gentleman, a truly superior man. His firm drew the plans for a dormitory at Hamilton, where I went to college. But the firm never drew plans for a prison. An acquaintance with prison architecture might have produced a keener sensitivity to prison management.

Serving with the architect was a producer of educational films and a salesman for a large publishing firm of secondary-school textbooks. This man, Morris Stokes, was and is well known to me. When I asked him how he had been selected to serve, he had no clues. When I asked him for his personal evaluation of Anna Kross herself, he had a yet more surprising reply: "I never met her." "Did you make an effort to see her or talk to her?" "No. We didn't work that way."

When you don't get the money, you can't do the work. And when your own drive is identical to the goals set forth in a report of non-feasance, you just have to ignore it and go on. But it hurts.

Yet her whole professional life, from 1912 to 1968, was beleaguered. Practical, brave, and giving but beleaguered nonetheless. She gave all her brains and strength and finally, these last few years, most of her eyesight (she can't read any more) to revolutionize a system that is thoroughly known, thoroughly wrong, thoroughly rotten.

Now, because of the public's refusal to act; because of the inability of local governments to respond to our most dreadful predictions or to accept its most prophetic vision, the revolution is proceeding anyhow—not by citizens, judges, or administrators, but by convicts. They are beginning to tear down the prisons and burn them up. It is not surprising. We've finally taught them how.

This part of the odyssey—my jail tours with Anna Kross and the stamp of sense and of dispatch that clung to all she saw and struggled with and deplored—comes to an end here. Mayor John Vliet Lindsay succeeded "Bob" Wagner in 1968 and Anna Kross retired from public life. Why did this little woman affect me so powerfully? It was not just me, it was the whole city of New York. Though she was past sixty when I met her first, she was still Tammany's Wampus Baby. As far back as 1938, Fiorello La Guardia, who hated Tammany as much as any New Yorker who ever lived, could and did reach out for Anna Kross the very morning he heard she was to seek election to the Supreme Court of New York State. And he said this: "To think of the possibility of electing a judge for the Supreme Court of our State who has not crawled and cringed and begged for nomination is so exciting as to make everyone in New York go out and work for the success of Anna Kross's election."

She was defeated. But she's never stopped.

The very first time I was ever in her office, one of her wardens called on the phone with a brand-new problem.

"There's a 12-year-old kid just got off the Hart Island ferry. Wants to bail out his father."

"What's his father in for?"

"Non-support. Sixty days."

"Has the boy got the money?"

"Well, I don't know, Commissioner. He's got his school bank book. It shows deposits of sixty-four dollars."

"I'll be over."

Perhaps that is why the New York *Times* has called her "something special." You've witnessed, in previous pages, why I feel the same. No woman ever did more.

It has come through to the reader, no doubt, that I loved her tenderness as much as I admired her toughness, a symbiosis rarely seen in such degree in the same person; a quality which, had she been in charge of Masada, though the stronghold could not have prevailed against the Romans, would have held off the siege through another winter. Alone and damning them all, she would have disregarded the dead behind her and the short, stabbing swords in front, and looked ahead only, to the social sanities that defeat can only interrupt but never bury.

Probation was one of her great interests, and is the subject to be looked at now in Part Two.

PART TWO

Family Court

PROBATION

THE PRIMARY PURPOSE of Probation is to try to keep family quarrels out of court by keeping the family together; to keep it together by adjusting the problem. Does this work?

About 55 per cent of the family fights that are handled by Probation are smoothed over and never come to court. It has been found, of course, where court action can't be avoided or where it seems positively indicated, that the trauma of a court appearance often increases polarization between contesting parties.

Who Does the Complaining?

The warring families come from all walks of life, all grades of education and income. But again, as is true the world over, most cases erupt in the lower economic groups. In any large city, however, there is always a small number of the affluent and their bitterness and rage is in no way assuaged by the material comfort they may enjoy at home. They can hack each other to pieces as primitively as the less favored.

A woman's attacks are mostly verbal; a man's response to it is physical. Some wives, of course, do commit physical assaults but the husband will seldom prefer charges in such a case, or even come to Probation for help or advice. He's supposed to be able to handle himself. When a woman goes after a man, her weapons are things around the house—spiked heels, nail files, lye, scissors, irons, bowls, or anything handy to throw—and a man won't make a complaint unless he's seriously hurt.

However, he will invariably make a complaint if his professional status is threatened; if he's embarrassed by his wife while at work; if a wife or mother or mother-in-law is a nuisance around the office; if she raises her voice in front of his patients (and we'll see such a case); or bawls him out in the presence of an office nurse.

Men hate scenes. Professional men won't stand for them. They're touchier than actors, and will turn in any woman who threatens to make him look ridiculous in the presence of his professional peers. But these are quarrels at the higher level. Most are low-level; poor people, hurt and fear-ridden. There is a frightening amount of raw living all about us, all the time, that we all suspect but never actually see. In Family Court you see it. You see it also in any Probation office. It is the family violence that takes place in America's kitchens, bedrooms, and living rooms.

An impression of its quality and range can be had from the samples that follow, verbatim notes I took down or later took from court stenographers. Some are sadly bizarre, and unexpected, as this:

OFFENSE: BEATEN ABOUT THE HEAD AND NECK
COURT: What were you beaten with, madam?
PETITIONER: Judge, he beat me with a live chicken. And he kept beating till he kill the chicken.

OFFENSE: HUSBAND CONSTANTLY DRUNK AND ABUSIVE
PETITIONER: "Sure, I'll give you a divorce," he tell me. "Right after I kill you."
COURT: Did your husband have a weapon?
PETITIONER: He had a rifle.
COURT: What happened?
PETITIONER: My daughter jumped on him. She took the gun off him. He chased her but he couldn't catch her. He tried to hit me. But I bit him. I bit him good. He threatened the other kids. He had a rope. I didn't know what to do. So I bit him again. Too much of this, Judge. We're so sick of it. So sick.

The case took three minutes and forty seconds. The husband got ninety days in the workhouse.

OFFENSE: ASSAULT
PETITIONER: I need an order of protection, Your Honor. I stood in the parlor. It was four in the morning.
COURT: Which morning?
PETITIONER: Yesterday. My husband was outside the picture window. He was trying to get in.

COURT: He has a right to get into his own house.

PETITIONER: Yes. Only I knew he only want to beat on us. He had a towel round his hand. He swing at the window and bust it and he come in after me and my baby.

COURT: Four in the morning? Were you dressed?

PETITIONER: In my nightgown. My boy was in his underwear. I ran and my boy ran.

COURT: Your husband broke in? And came in?

PETITIONER: Yes. We run to the vestibule. Then up the stairs. To the neighbors above. They let us in. We could look down and see what he do.

COURT: You could see it?

PETITIONER: We leaned out. Our apartment is only two rooms. He is smashing it all up.

COURT: Then you called the police?

PETITIONER: No. We had no phone. The neighbors either. I picked up my son and we run into the street.

COURT: In your nightgown?

PETITIONER: Yes. Nobody on the street. We run on to the highway. Cars wouldn't stop for us. Then one did. He picked us up even the way we were dressed. He drove to a place where there is a phone. But we had no money.

COURT: What happened?

PETITIONER: The man dialed the police for us. In no time the police come. We got into the police car. The police come right into the house with us. He is still smashing up things. He had kicked the television onto the floor. He was stomping on the lens. The hi-fi, too. All over the room.

COURT: Keep your voice up please, madam. We can't hear you.

Two minutes and 25 seconds for this one. Disposition: Order of Protection.

OFFENSE: ASSAULT

PETITIONER: (Young Puerto Rican woman, unusually pretty): "No, I am not going with you," I told him. "It is too late." Then he had this pistol and shoot at my head and I ran into a bar and the people come out, hearing four shots. And my husband run away, thinking he kill me. So they phone him I am not dead, and he so mad when he come home, he smack me.

One minute and fifteen seconds. A summons is issued to bring in the husband.

Hard-working mothers have bad times with hard-drinking daughters:

OFFENSE: ASSAULT

PETITIONER (Woman, white, 55, well spoken): I want my daughter out of my house. She's 32 and she's a drunk.

COURT: Has she been an alcohol problem very long?

PETITIONER: Somebody else can call her an alcohol problem. I'm old-fashioned and I call her a drunk. I had to call the police. She went to a hotel. She's always going to hotels. Always beats her bill there, too. Every time. So I get the bill. I work.

COURT: What do you, madam?

PETITIONER: Gift-wrap. Department store. My daughter wanted to get into my apartment. To get some coats, she told me. I left the door open so she could get in. I have nice neighbors. My daughter has known plenty of men but never married. Once she went to A.A. She thought they could teach her how to drink. You know, like a lady. Imagine! So she never went back. I mean, when they said she could never drink at all.

COURT: Is she there now? In your apartment?

PETITIONER: She's there now. And she's drunk. Tomorrow I'm having the painter in. My daughter left the dishes. Just stays in bed. I'm sure if she's there tomorrow when the painter comes, there'll be little painting that gets done. I want her out of my house.

COURT: But, madam, it's your home. All you have to do is close your door.

PETITIONER: But she's a luxury I can't afford. I want a TOP.*

COURT: You want protection? Against your own daughter?

PETITIONER: She came in at 4:30 this morning. Very drunk. Such a noise. And such language!

COURT: But does she threaten you?

PETITIONER: Threaten *me*? Lord, no. She threatens my *lease*.

Three minutes and 5 seconds. TOP granted.

Jurisdiction of a Probation Department

The power and authority in most Probation services is limited to assaults and to disorderly conduct: punching, cutting, hitting with a weapon other than a gun; and jurisdiction in cases involving married people, relatives, or common-law relationships.

* Temporary Order of Protection.

What is the procedure when a complaint is made? Normally the Probation Officer (referred to henceforth as the P.O.) makes a first contact with the Petitioner (or Plaintiff). He or she states the problem. The P.O. then sends a letter to the Respondent (Defendant), who is invited to appear at the Probation offices, with a date given.

This is not a summons. It is an appeal. Do Respondents respond? As a result of this first instrument, about seventy per cent do. If the situation looks or sounds dangerous (and most Probation workers develop a peculiar skill in making these guesses), they do have the discretionary power to take immediate action; if, for example, a man is waiting at home with a gun, a P.O. will alert a police officer.

Women seldom come to Probation seeking help after the first beating-up. It takes two or three or four. But when they do come, they want instant action.

At the first get-together in Probation offices (called the Intake Interview and usually attended by the husband and wife and a P.O.), a final determination is made by the Petitioner (usually the wife) as to whether to go to court or not. You've seen a few brief examples in the above pages where Probation recommended this. Here are a few typical cases which I attended and in which Probation had to make up its mind as to what to do next. These interviews took place in small cheerless offices that will seat five people. The location: 80 Lafayette Street, a most dismal part of New York City—cramped, airless, dirty.

HUSBAND: She gets out of bed just to avoid me sexually.

WIFE: I do not. He always grabs all the blankets. I get out of bed to warm myself.

P.O.: You have a heater you turn on?

WIFE: No heater. I light the oven and sit there. I put my feet in it. And he beats me.

P.O.: Your wife complains that you never take her out anywhere.

HUSBAND: That's right. We don't go out socially. We don't have the clothes for it.

WIFE: He smokes in bed and I don't like that.

HUSBAND: I don't think she ought to complain about that.

WIFE: A husband should take out his wife.

HUSBAND: I don't want her to work. A woman should stay home and take care of her man. She doesn't have a tough life compared to some. I do the work. She's a good wife. She's a good mother. She's a good housekeeper. Yes, I beat her once in awhile. A lot of other fellows got their eye on her. A husband can always tell.

(Notation on Probation sheet: Wife very coy here. She likes him to be jealous. Couple does not want to go to court.)

P.O. (After studying report): You were here a year ago.

HUSBAND: It's no better.

WIFE: It's worse. He tied my hands and threw me in a tub of hot water.

P.O.: Is this true?

HUSBAND: Yes, it's true. But not scalding water.

P.O.: Why did you do that?

HUSBAND: My wife goes to some crazy church and she can't drink or wear jewelry or go to the movies.

WIFE: We don't believe in it.

HUSBAND: Nightgowns! Jesus Christ, you ought to see what she goes to bed in!

WIFE: I'm a saint.

HUSBAND: She's a saint in a house too dirty for pigs. A pig would puke in my house.

P.O.: Besides throwing her in a tub of hot water, what other complaints would your wife make about you?

HUSBAND: Oh, she'd say I never stay home. That I have girl friends. That I don't trust her. She's quite right about all this. I'm most unhappy at home so I seldom go there.

P.O.: She says you beat her with a broom.

HUSBAND: Yes.

WIFE: When I was cleaning house. How can I . . . ?

HUSBAND: I beat her with a broom. But she was *not* cleaning house. She had the radio on and she was dancing with this broom.

WIFE: I was praying.

HUSBAND: Dancing and praying. With this broom. I never saw her clean—why, she wouldn't knock canary turd off a dinner plate. All the years she's never tried to better herself, even though I criticize her severely.

(Notation on Probation sheet: Petitioner showed signs of bad beating. Fainted during interview.)

P.O.: This report shows that your wife fainted right here in these offices when you were in last year. You'd beaten her pretty severely then, too.

HUSBAND: Well, yes. But she puts on a good show, though.

P.O.: You mean it wasn't so much of a beating?

HUSBAND: No, I don't mean that. But she can arrange to faint when she wants to.

P.O.: How does she manage that?

HUSBAND: By not eating anything. And putting blotting-paper in her shoes. Pulls the blood out of her head.

P.O.: Do you want to live with this man? Do you love him?

WIFE: Once I did. If he was just nice to me. Some of the time.

P.O.: I don't think we have your address, ma'am.

WOMAN (An ancient black): Top floor.

P.O.: Top floor *where*, ma'am?

WOMAN: I don't know the number. Near the tracks. But I can go right to it. I could take you. Top floor. That's where I live. . . .

(Notation: White woman, 25, pretty, alert. First visit to Probation. Left arm in sling. Eyes and lips puffy.)

P.O.: You want an annulment.

WIFE: Yes, sir. If I can afford it.

P.O.: You've been married just two months.

WIFE: Yes. My husband has been working in the Poconos. He comes to the apartment weekends only. But he's been fired. Twice he thumbed rides to get to the apartment and I gave him money. And fed him. Then he punched me.

P.O.: What provoked that?

WIFE: I didn't have any money that time, I hadn't been paid. While I was at work, he stole the furniture.

P.O.: As your husband, legally he's allowed to use the apartment. Even sell the furniture. It belongs to you both.

WIFE: But I can't go back to the apartment now. There were two policemen there only this morning. I don't want an Order of Protection for next week. I want one for right now. He's a criminal. He could kill me.

P.O.: Do you have friends nearby? People you know and trust? Someone who could spend the night there?

WIFE: Oh, yes. May I ask a girl friend to spend the night?

P.O.: Of course.

WIFE: But what if he tries to get in again?

P.O.: He's your husband. He has a right. . . .

WIFE: *He* has a right! What about my rights? He has the right to steal the furniture and sell it? To steal my jewelry? My rings are missing. My wrist is broken. My lips are split. That's why I'm here. I put new locks on the door. He smashed them off. What's it to him? He doesn't have anything. What good is an Order of Protection if it doesn't do any protecting? What good is an OP next week if he's going to kill me tonight?

These are some of the dynamics in the human collisions and cruelties taking place every day all over this nation, not just in isolated spots like 80 Lafayette Street. They are happening right now, within a few yards of where you are sitting, wherever that may be. Or happening in the apartment just below. Probation cushions what it can; what it can handle. And of course it can't force itself or its services on anyone.

The Intake Interview, examples of which we've now seen, is a voluntary procedure. It can be by-passed. You can't interview people who object to it—or whose attorneys, if they have such, object to it. But the people who come do need help, as is obvious, and some desperately and immediately need it. Under what conditions will Probation recommend a court hearing?

In the Probation services I've explored, there are five or six conditions, with a few small variations from one service to another, but all basically the same, and about as follows:

a. If the fear of future assaults seems real
b. When the authority of the court is clearly needed (as with a drunk and bullying husband)
c. When elements of bizarre behavior are present (he sleeps with a knife under the pillow, or with a can of chloroform on the night table)
d. Where the assault could be minor but the risk large
e. Obvious neglect of children
f. Use of weapons or possession of such

Probation's *first* objective, in its Intake Interview, is to understand the situation; how tough it is right now, and its likelihood of worsening. Often for these hurt and raging (or terrified) people, it's the first time there has been any chance for calm talk. For example, a quarreling couple has decided to quit trying to live together. The husband is willing to clear out and has said so. There has even been an agreement about the kids and the money. But a squabble over a TV set or a pet dog can be very bitter, every bit as tough as a fight over a child.

Intake does have this important *second* objective: to provide information to the court. ("He came in with a basket of snakes and threw them at her." Or: "He took the kids and just vanished. He phones late at night: 'Don't you wish you knew where we were? he'll scream at me." This much tells any judge a tremendous lot.) Married people can harass each other inhumanly and can do so without doing anything illegal. Really vindictive couples learn all the cutting edges that hurt most and learn them early.

Probation officers are also valuable where there is no assault but where the marriage is in trouble; where there is no spelled-out jurisdiction but where there is a big problem. For example, parents have a seventeen-year-old son who is taking heroin and stealing. He's suspected of both but caught at neither. So they come to Probation for help.

The Working Atmosphere of Probation

For the people doing the work, what is it really like, day after day?

"We work in a pressure-cooker. All day, every day. Many of the P.O.'s don't want to have to work here. For some it is just too demoralizing, too sad. It's easy to understand that, for we all see far too much social and spiritual pathology. People who can't let go. Normal people who have just had too much. And it hurts just as much if they brought this on themselves, whether some of it or all of it. We see the people who can't stand living another minute. Something is going to snap. Something more than what has already snapped. So we try to slip in another elastic gusset before there is any more smash-up."

One of the Probation supervisors (for New York's Family Court) is Charles Lindner. We've spent many hours together, and the above are his words. His is hugely involved in the work he does, in every case he handles or deputizes. He is perpetually beset, rumpled, quick-minded, unendingly patient, diplomatic, bemused, and himself vulnerable in the presence of any really upsetting or derailing situation. Wonderful, spontaneous sentences, rich in their cadence and their special italics, tumble out of him. I carried a pocket tape-recorder, and this is part of what he said:

"The people who come in here are angry, worried, scared, socially put down, physically hurting, spiritually dishevelled. Here at
Probation, whether it's in the offices in the building—and it's got
to be the most disreputable building in the entire court structure—
or some ratty walk-up on 130th Street, we have to *seem* to give
support to both sides, both parties. We must absolutely avoid
mass-production methods. Everyone on the staff must suffer his
own way through every case that sits down at his desk. It's a most
fatiguing effort. Rewarding? Yes. Of course. Especially when you
realize that nearly three-quarters of the men we send a letter to do
show up here. *They* also want peace in the family. 'Well, yes,'
they'll agree, 'I did knock her around some, but I didn't really
mean to hurt her. Not much anyhow.'

"I have children of my own growing up. To me, the awfulest
part of this work—*not* New York, not just America either—it's all
over the world—is the cruelty to the children. And this is going to
have its effect on future generations. It is having its effect *now*.
Kids raised in homes, American homes, that are crammed with
hatred and discord. Pure desperation. Beatings. God, the beatings!
The youngsters will carry this over into their own families, just as
soon as they begin to raise their own families. What we are doing
is easy to say—what we're doing to our children, easy to say and
thoroughly terrifying to think about: in America we are perpetuat-
ing *monsters*. I can take you into a thousand homes and *show* you
the process. And we've been doing it right here, and clear across
the U.S., for three centuries."

Here Mr. Lindner glanced at a typed card, picked it up, and
recreated a case, current then (1971), a true horror story, but one
that is repeating itself hundreds of times a day, wherever Americans live. Here is the story, as he told it:

"Ninety-fourth Street. The kids come in with wet shoes. How
could they avoid getting wet? It's raining outside. They're punished. But how? They're forced to kneel on beer cans. In the
garage. The rims of the cans cut into the tissue of the kids' knees.
The father stands there to see the kids don't try to escape. Finally
the girl faints. Her brother loses his balance but the father lifts
him up and forces him back. The boy flings a beer can at the old
man and hits him. So now the father grabs the boy, shoves him
into the back seat of the Ford, and cranks up the window on the

boy's wrists, literally hanging him there. And he goes back into the house, leaving his son imprisoned there. In the most frightful agony. Two hours later he comes out to see how the boy is doing. He isn't doing so good. He's still in the same position, semi-conscious. And he has a severe shoulder dislocation.

"Now right here is what is so awful: this boy, having been through this ordeal, is going to be *just as cruel to his own kids*. If he ever has any. Beaten and tortured as children, they'll torture their own. Beat them. It's the only way they know how to respond to sudden bad news, sudden rebellion, or any sharp surprise or disappointment or challenge.

"Of course, since we have to make *immediate* evaluations, we make mistakes. You've spent a lot of time with us now, Mr. Wylie, and you've seen it a hundred times. Take this case: a wife complains about her husband. She says he's slapped her and is threatening her and the children. Obviously we don't rush right out and have him arrested. The problem: is there *immediate* danger? We have to take calculated risks. We do prevent tragedy by moving quickly.

"This same case: no real assault. Just a slap and a threat. No physical damage. But the husband is extremely drunk. He's been on a three-day bender and locked himself in the basement. He's announced to the family that he's going to drink himself to death but that before he does, he's going upstairs in the middle of the night and kill them all. We know that he's marked up this family before. Now, is something going to explode? Or is he going to pass out first? Who knows? In this work, you move by instinct. By experience.

"In this case we act. First we get the kids out of danger. And the wife. We know the man has three rifles. But that is not against the law. And he has a right to get plastered in his own cellar. We send the woman into court and get a warrant for the husband's arrest, even though the assault, as I say, was slight. Now, did we prevent a suicide? Or a homicide? We never know. Not unless it comes out as a tragedy and we read about it in the paper."

Here Mr. Lindner picked up another report.

"No two cases are ever exactly alike. And some are bizarre indeed. Take this case of some well-to-do, well-educated orientals. Just last week. Chinese. University backgrounds, both of them.

And wide teaching experience. A real international attitude about everything. Everything but one thing. The husband had a good post in Long Island U. They lived in a penthouse.

"When their case came up, I knew there had been some psychiatric problems in their background somewhere, but now the wife had brought an assault charge against her husband. I was assigned to investigate. The judge thought there was something important floating around just below the surface. Some of our judges develop uncanny insight, sometimes you could call it precognition. I agreed with him that we were missing the main component. You sense these things. I went out.

"All the windows in the penthouse except one going to the fire-escape were barred. Evil spirits had been flying in the windows, harming the family. Normal wear on their clothes? No. Evil spirits had eaten holes in their coats. The child hadn't been bitten by mosquitoes. It was evil spirits. They were getting to her during the night.

"The wife was quite terrified. She kept backing into corners, her eyes following invisible flying objects. Blankets had been strung over all the windows. You had to turn on lights in the middle of the day so you wouldn't trip over furniture.

"We arranged for an emergency psychiatric evaluation. The wife was taken to Bellevue for a full study. Non-violent. She later spent six months in a state hospital. We got day care for the kid. The husband was overwhelmed that his wife had to be taken to a nut-house. Later we got a temporary homemaker to come in. Then Welfare provided a 24-hour homemaker service for four of the six months the mother was away. Things seemed to stabilize.

"The wife was discharged at Christmastime. But once home, the fears came right back. Now she could *see* the spirits. The Christmas gift certificates had to be returned. Most pitiable. A bleak time for the child. Always so hard for them. The whole family, too, so very far from familiar things.

"It's hard for an American to really inhabit the fears and feelings of such; their trying to make a go of it in a city so noisy, so foreign, so terrifying. A culture so hysterical. A lot of us would crack up if our situations were reversed. If we found ourselves in Peking, trying to make our way professionally, shoved every which way by a wave of chattering Chinese.

"Often a case can be so poignant, it just tears you up. In child-abuse cases, our people in Probation can take only a limited load. And only certain of us can take even that. The emotional experience is absolutely shattering."

"Yes, I know. I've been there," I answered.

Other Probation Officers began to drift in, each with his own comment:

"Our physical set-up here is self-defeating. Here we are, at 80 Lafayette Street, with our work spread all over the five boroughs, and a heavy concentration on 23rd and Lex. *Half* of our investigating time is just portal-to-portal, really. We live in subways. The geographical arrangement is cockeyed."

"So is the pay-scale," chimed in another. "Startling inequities exist. For the same work we do, the Probation staff in the Supreme Court gets much better pay. The same work. Their salaries have crept up well beyond ours. Ours have plateaued. Probation in the Supreme Court draws about fifty per cent more than our maximum."*

Charles Lindner agreed:

"This creates another severe staff problem. Due to the salary structure, we can't hold our people. Tops is $10,000 a year. I'm a supervisor. I've been here fourteen years and I draw $11,000. An ordinary school teacher, after fourteen years, is making $14,900. We keep losing our people to the anti-poverty agencies, to social work agencies, to state parole, or to state narcotics programs. We can't strike. We can't cause any public inconvenience. Pension? Yes. But no matter how many years we've worked, we have to be 55 to apply. And at the end of twenty years of work, we don't get fifty per cent pension pay. We get 44 per cent. Whenever the public thinks of civil service, they think of power. The power of collective bargaining, for example. But we Probation people are only 750, all told. So when you sit down to bargain with New York City, the city already *knows* that you're weak. So some of our best people get away. They just move on."

"How many complaints do you listen to in one day?"

"About six. There's such a terrible overload, we only handle a

* Probation salaries have improved since this writing.

fraction. A very *small* fraction. And of that fraction, of course, we take the worst.

"The primary goal of Probation is conciliatory. If the problem can't be melted down right here in these offices, we visit the home itself. We investigate every aspect of the reported problem. We see for ourselves. After that, there is a fact-finding hearing. Then a P.O. will take as much as two weeks—more if needed—to study the family background; look at school records, talk to doctors, talk to precinct police. A written report is prepared. All the essential facts are given to the judge. If the judge's disposition returns a child to its home, for example, there is after-care supervision. To see if the problem is levelling off and stabilizing. But the services are inadequate in scope. And 95 per cent of the staff is involved in the screening operation. There just isn't enough follow-up. We aren't staffed for it."*

"Suppose a child has been arrested?" I asked. "Can an intake officer or a member of the staff right here dispose of the case without a hearing?"

"Oh, yes. Provided no one objects. The amicable settlement is the one preferred, of course. And the keeping of the child in the home setting, the family setting. If the case doesn't go to court, the child won't have a 'record,' even though he's been arrested. If a child denies what he's accused of, he has to go to court. But what is said at Intake can't be used in court till after a verdict. He can admit something downstairs, then deny it in court, at trial. There are three judges sitting, and the same court set-up for all five counties. A boy under sixteen can't be convicted of *any* crime, no matter how serious, even murder first. He can only be declared a juvenile delinquent. Often this refers to a crime, which if it were committed by an adult, would get him three years in a state

---

* Because of lack of money and no other reason, Probation services all through New York State are in dreadful shape. Peter Preiser, director of the state's Probation services: "The system is badly strained. We are not doing meaningful probation work now." John A. Wallace, director of New York City's Office of Probation: "We are going to limit the number of cases we handle." Recommended case-loads: optimum, 30; maximum, 60; now being carried, 86. "We are cutting it to sixty-two. Of the city's 15,000 probationers, with present staffs, the most that probationers can expect from their case-workers is 15 minutes a month." (New York *Times*, December 6, 1971)

prison. We get both felonies and misdemeanors: truancy, beyond control of parents, burglary, larceny, theft, mugging. About 8,000 boys a year and a thousand girls. As for PINS—it's about even for the boys and girls."

"How do most neglect cases come to your notice?"

"Through the SPCC. Here's a typical case: the allegation says the father hits the mother in front of the kids. That he also hits the kids. Always without provocation. He's a drunk. He's drunk every day. And out of him comes a constant flow of obscene language. He has no interest in his children, in the home, or in his wife. He's chased them all out with a kitchen knife. The older boy, twelve, is so concerned for his mother's safety that he went to the principal of his school to get permission to go home and see how she's doing. None of the children is physically well. An eleven-year-old has last been treated at Gouverneur Hospital for asthma, another for rickets, mother for nervous collapse, father for a lung condition and alcoholism. He's had six admissions for alcoholism. All at the same hospital. The mother says the father will deny everything, not remembering what he did while drinking. On the Intake referral sheet is this notation: 'Recommended that an outside agency be the petitioner here, the mother not wanting the children to know she took action against their father.'

"Women-in-crises are often severely protective of the very men they bring to court.

"Here's a girl of fifteen. Ninth grade. Won't stay home. Yet this girl had been number ten in a class of 275. Now she's flunking out. She's been seen by an M.D., a guidance counselor, and the C.S.S.* Because of repeated runaways, all advised a court involvement. She always fled to her aunt's. There's a clue here, of course. She'd lived with this same aunt from the time of her birth to age four. We saw the girl. Couldn't or wouldn't say why she runs away. She "doesn't like" her parents. Likes the aunt. Both the mother and the aunt work. Mother is a phone operator. We saw the parents. Good people, most industrious: and no quarrelling. The aunt has kids of her own, who are in frequent trouble. The mother's position is simple: if she can't have her own daughter, she wants the girl placed. The mother won't let her daughter go

* Community Service Society.

to parties unless she knows all the people. Extreme protectiveness. The mother seems to feel the daughter has rejected the mother's standards. The mother is unable to view the daughter in terms of the daughter's adolescence. The mother is 'concerned' but has no warmth. Polite but frigid, and of fixed mind. A cold though respectable marriage.

"Interesting item: the parents cut the girl's hair to suit themselves. They keep her hair short. They belong to a little-known religious sect. Daughter not allowed to conform to the fashion of her peers. She is a black who likes white people but parents won't let her associate with them. She's in severe conflict with both parents. Lonely. Isolated. Is rapidly withdrawing from all currents and patterns of life. Self-exiled. She is a PINS.*

"The parents' background: terrible poverty and emotional deprivation. They have extremely good working habits, and both are well employed. No drinking. Good work records over the years. No 'girl-chasing' by dad. The daughter feels 'manipulated'—that was her word, by the way—by her parents. She's bright and perceptive. Wants to 'belong' but isn't allowed to. No freedom. Has to be chaperoned or not go out. This embarrasses and outrages her. So she's gone on strike about her school work. 'I'll-show-them' attitude."

"How did you manage this one?"

"We advised the parents to allow the girl to return to the aunt, on a temporary basis of four to six months, and they agreed. And a P.O. scheduled appointments for every two weeks. There was good progress. The girl felt liberated. And she was proud of her school record. With much coaching from the P.O., the daughter has come to feel that her mother is not trying to 'turn me into a nun.' But she definitely does not love her mother, and much prefers the aunt. Sometimes, in Probation work, it's better to do nothing; nothing but wait and see. And here it paid off. We felt we could do little more than allow the girl to express her feelings. And soon she began to do this. Then a most unexpected break: the mother had earned a three-weeks' vacation. She took it. She went to the island of Jamaica and took the daughter with her. The daughter was delighted for a chance to 'see the world.' She was

* People in Need of Supervision.

fascinated with the island and with the quality of the school she visited there. The daughter stayed on, the mother came back. The daughter wrote us, thanking us. She is living in the home of the school's headmistress.

"But fortune seldom intervenes so neatly. Often, of course, boys get in trouble irrespective of the family setting. This boy is thirteen. His father is an American, his mother Japanese. But the father abandoned the mother. She remarried. Married a Buddhist. The boy seemed to have none of the regular problems: no sex, no pot, no stealing, no truancy. Just glue-sniffing. There's an item here I've never seen before: 'He blew up a rubber condom in class.'

"If the case of the boy who blew up the condom is uncommon, here's one of the commonest: a young wife goes to work for the first time, to help out with the family income problem. Of course she meets men. And soon they want to date her. And do. The husband hears about it, is jealous, and beats her up. 'But he never took me out,' she'll complain (and this complaint is almost as universal as any). 'Why didn't *he* take me out?' Yes, why didn't he? Her response to the other men was human. Innocent, too, at first. The husband thinks the problem is related *only* to his wife working. It took us a long time to make him see he was failing to meet most of her needs. A lot of men feel that once they've paid a woman the large compliment to marry her, they can forget about her, with a sort of 'I married you, didn't I? What more do you want?' attitude.

"How much use do judges make of your services?"

"They count on us. The basic relationship is very good. Some judges are more versatile than others, more seeking-and-finding. And they use our findings to modify or to fortify their own judgments. They know what we send in is objective. In these courts the judges sit for only a month. Then they move on. When their month is up, they're all emotionally drained, every one of them. Just as we are. Physically, too. The cases are run through with great speed. Most of us here at Probation have heard judges say, on their last day: 'I hope I never have to come back here.' And believe me, we know how they feel. I could sum it all up in a single sentence: work in Probation is the closest thing there is to being a rabbi."

Family Court Mental Health Services

The resources of Family Court have been effectively extended, in addition to the work of the Probation wing, by its Mental Health Services. This court has much the same hope and responsibility that Home Term did when it first appeared in 1946: the strengthening of family life in the community. Dr. Henry Makeover has described it well:

"A study of the Family Court of New York City can provide only a glimpse into an institution which deals with so many of the frustrations, sorrows, acts of violence and tragedies of a large city's life. The court is viewed, by those who come before it, in many different ways—some with fear, others with contempt, hostility and defiance, many with hopelessness, and others with hope. Disturbed families, unable to control their own destinies, stand on the other side of the bench from the judges who are literally swamped by the sea of almost infinite trouble that washes into the court."

Where did this court come from, the present Family Court?

Magistrates' Court was established in 1895, Family Court in 1910. But it was part of the Magistrate system, and its basis of jurisdiction remained criminal. Much of its activity had to do with support cases. It was a crime to be found guilty of non-support.

It remained an appendix of Magistrate system until 1933. In that year Family Court and Children's Court were united, its jurisdiction changed to non-criminal, and its name changed to Domestic Relations Court. It had no real capability for social diagnosis, none for treatment. Such social intervention or assistance as existed was performed by a small Probation force that was limited to brief interviews with the disputants, with no official hearing before a judge.

The service was token only; spotty in its selections and never meeting a full need for any family. A survey that was run during 1945 revealed that of more than 10,000 summonses issued by the district courts, less than 300 families had been seen by the Probation bureau. Some felt the whole idea of any such collateral shoring-up was too "ivory-tower"; that this kind of social intercept would get in the court's way. All felt that if anything really good could emerge from the beginnings of this new consciousness, there should be an experimental court set up where a concentration of the effort and a true try at a complete "social" approach could be given an independent chance for its life; to see, in short, if such gentle-sounding altruism could survive in the stones of a gritty, uncaring metropolis. If it failed, no harm done. If it looked to have a viable future, then similar services could be developed in the other boroughs. These, it will be seen, were the same feelings that were in the air when the Kross court, Home Term, came to life.

Dr. Melvin I. Fishman, director of the Mental Health Services of the Family Offenses Term (the old Home Term) of the Family Court, had described Home Term and how its benefits were merged into Family Court when the 1962 reorganization of courts took place. Here is a part of what he told the New York Mental Health Convention about it in 1969:

"The emphasis is on the offender and his family rather than the offense. . . . Home Term recognized that the individual, rather than the delinquency, required greater study. . . . Its main objective was to effect lasting adjustments of family difficulties, with or without the aid of formal court hearings. . . . Unlike district courts, Home Term considered the offense in relation to the total personality and life situation of the individuals, as well as the physical, social, and medical needs of their families. . . .

"Imprisonment was resorted to when the family required immediate protection . . . although it was realized that commitment offered no solution to any of the family's underlying difficulties. . . .

"Home Term constituted a marked departure from legal formalism. . . . For a majority of cases it offered a flexible, informal, and socialized procedure. . . . In most cases Home Term attempted to render service on a pre-court level, for it was seen that court appearance, where persons were encouraged to voice their grievances in each other's presence, frequently tended to aggravate an already tense situation. . . .

"Helping people to resolve the *immediate issue* which brought them into court—thereby making court hearings unnecessary—was the initial aim of Intake activity. This was only the first step. It was followed by continued efforts to help the individual and family, by enlisting the support of all available community facilities.

"Many of the clients appearing at Home Term were malad-justed persons, emotionally disturbed, visibly in need of psychiatric help. In such case, the Intake interview referred the family to the court psychiatrist, who subsequently presented his findings to the judge. . . .

"The need for increased psychiatric facilities grew very quickly . . . and by 1954 a formal psychiatric clinic was actively functioning. . . .

"It's become apparent during the latter period of Home Term's existence that to be truly effective, the court clinic would have to render treatment services also. . . . At its inception, Home Term was unique, no similar court being in existence, so far as we know. Its experimental phase was passed through in the first two years—that is, by 1948—and in 1951 Home Term became a citywide court. With procedures that remained flexible, Home Term continued to grow, and to refine its techniques.

"However, its power and jurisdiction were limited. Families were still confronted with a bewildering assortment of courts. Each one of these had jurisdiction over at least one aspect of the family's problems. There was a pressing need for the relocation of those problems into a *single court*.

"On November 7, 1961, a major step was taken in this direction. The people of New York State approved the bill for reorganizing the court system, and one of the most important changes effected by this reorganization was the creation of the Family Court of the State of New York. For the first time, the state had a court which could deal with nearly all legal manifestations of problems arising from family relationships. . . .*

"The new Family Court is the result of a combination of three courts—Juvenile, Domestic Relations, and Home Term Courts.

"Home Term, with its Psychiatric Clinic and Probation Department, became the core for the citywide Family Offenses Term, a specialized court in the new Family Court system in New York City. With more power and wider jurisdiction than the old Home Term Court, Family Offenses Term started functioning in September 1962."

---

* Still missing: a court for girls, 16 to 20, that will spare them the stigma of criminals. See Girls' Term, pp. 56–59.

The Psychiatric Clinic, now part of the new court structure, is called "Mental Health Services Family Offenses Term." It is the major adult and family psychiatric service of the Family Courts in New York City.

Its director, Melvin I. Fishman, is a well-known psychologist and psychoanalyst, who, before assuming the directorship of this facility, was in private practice.

"There is very real illness, frightening illness, in many of the cases that come in here. Illnesses being suffered by people who had when judges had such frequent proof of the value not only of our pre-trial evaluations but the follow-up, they began to rely on us more and more. After the court reorganization in 1962, we realized here that all we were doing, however professional it might be, was clerical. That is to say, unless a treatment resource was created, our work here was mechanical only. It was like abandoning an operation right after you got the patient to sleep. It meant nothing. If the patient doesn't take the prescription to the drugstore and then take the medicine, he might as well not have come.

"Our treatment resource is a three-pronged attack: Probation, Clinic, Judiciary. We've cut through tons of red-tape. Centuries of it. All of us are deeply involved in what is being offered in court. Home Term Court, of course, had been the real breakthrough, even though the structure was loose. This very looseness was much to its advantage at the start. It had to keep flexible. It gave judges and social agencies a lot of room to maneuver. Something else too: for the first time anywhere in court history that we know of, the full range of pathology that is right under the skin of every city—this could be measured. Measured and dealt with.

"There is very real illness, frightening illness, in many of the cases that come in here. Illnesses being suffered by people who had never had any psychiatric treatment; people who didn't know they stood in terrible need of it.

"When the court reorganization occurred and both Magistrates' Court and Domestic Relations Court were eliminated, the efficiency of the criminal courts, now citywide, was noticeably increased. And the same for Family Court, which is now statewide. Home Term Court, the true creation of Anna Kross, was the only part of the old Magistrates' Court to survive. Though it's been absorbed in the larger structure, we've kept its best features, all of them. Plus the enormous sense that is its basic philosophy: a social-work orientation with a court setting. Which is to say, within an 'authority' setting.

"And we've brought the clinic along, too. No Family Court, in any American city, can make real sense unless it maintains a clinic. The real, exigent need to *humanize* has been known for many years. Now, here, with this showcase opportunity, we are demonstrating how it pays off. And why.

"Of course, many of the cases we see are the cases *least* accessible to therapeutic intervention. The reason for this is simple: we see the sickest. And we see them too late. It isn't just the underprivilged and the poor. Many who come here have the resources to get good outside help. But they won't take it. 'I lost my temper,' they'll say. Or, 'I'm all right. I don't need any help. Who says I'm sick?'

"Yet their need for help is often appalling. If they try to duck it, the court gives our clinic the opportunity to show the client that he indeed does have a problem. With the court involved, we can make a referral that will stick. In many ways, it is not a court process. But the fact that a court is present makes it effective.

"It's a fact of life that many people don't want to be interfered with, told what to do, touched or advised, even though you may be saving their life. Or their children. Or their marriage. Or even their sanity.

"Being able to avoid a court appearance entirely does have many advantages. On the part of outside agencies, there's a reluctance to help. Private agencies have a harsh view of such people as have been to court. They see them as criminals. Or at least tainted to some degree.

"Sending people to Bellevue Hospital on a non-voluntary basis —of course that's hard. But it has to be done. And very often. The evaulations there take from a week to a month and average about ten days. And if Bellevue thinks they're sick enough for a state hospital, they must of course be certified.

"And right here is another problem: a great many families dissemble and rationalize about the matter of mental illness. They put off doing anything about it till the situation becomes intolerable. Even then they won't assume responsibility. They equate mental illness with shame They wait till there's been an explo-sion, then bring the matter to court. (See Family Court, Case Two, p. 139.)·We, the court, send the unfortunate person to Bellevue. They, the family, duck the onus of it.

"Of course, when someone is sent to Bellevue, the family may be secretly relieved, in that they knew it was needed. An awful time at home has been eased, for now anyhow. Sometimes, too, the family will hurl abuse at us for being so heartless. We point out a few truths: that this is *not* punishment. That we're helping someone who is terribly ill. We remind them that if they had a fracture, they'd get a splint on it. They'd immobilize the limb so it could mend. We tell them that the psychiatric services of any large city hospital are doing exactly the same thing for the head and the heart that the same hospital does for a busted arm. We *talk* to them. They *see* we're involved.

"Of course when we do send a person to Bellevue, we don't know what the doctors there will find. Or what they'll recommend. If the case is tough and the patient has to go to Pilgrim or Central Islip or Rockland State, there must be two signatures on the certifi-more help. And we point this out to the family, as well. And then cate of admission. Two psychiatrists who think this patient needs we finally let them know, as discreetly as we can, that they them-selves are in serious fault for letting the home situation deteriorate so badly before making an intelligent move."

"What about those you send to Bellevue who are *not* certified?"

"They're returned to this court with a report. And we take it on again and go from there. One of the greatest time-savers—a tre-mendous economy for the court, the patient, and the clinic, is what we call 'short evaluation.' This is an emergency screening, a procedure we established here years ago. This is supplied to the court. It helps the judge make determinations about psychiatric hospitalization, separation, custody—and to do so *on the same day* the family is before him. This procedure alone has reduced the number of people previously hospitalized by the court—the cases we've been able to evaluate—by over eighty per cent."

"How do your staff problems compare with those in Probation?"

"The same. Money. Insufficient staff. Overwork. The service we offer is solid, and professional. Showcase really. But pitifully limited. And the pay is so bad that all those who work for the clinic have a private practice. They couldn't survive otherwise.

"No one works less than fifteen hours a week here, nor more than thirty-five. We're open from nine in the morning till nine at night, Monday through Friday. We should be open all the time. Weekends especially, since we have to by-pass so very many legitimate people who can't come any other time. They're at work, too."

"If the pay is so poor, why do they want to work here at all?"

"Everyone here has a personal feeling about what he's doing. It's a true dedication, and with these people that is not just a word. A labor of love, if you wish, the pay being so nominal. They know they're making a contribution to something they believe in. In terms of quality, the clinical staff right here in this ratty building represents a higher standard than any other clinic in the city. Or in the state. The morale is extremely high."

"How much staff turnover?"

"When I said they were dedicated, I meant it. We have *no* turnover."

Mental Health Services Staff Presentation

Each week the full staff of the Mental Health Services holds a meeting, each week exploring a family problem of unusual interest or complexity. I was invited to attend one of these and did so. I believe a report of it will interest you.

These meetings have three purposes:

a. to keep the full staff working and thinking as a team

b. to give them all a continuing chance to share and to sharpen each other's skills, and principally

c. to give a disintegrating family the practical benefit of the staff's full resources.

The case before the staff that morning was the family of Mr. and Mrs. Skone: Victor, 25, and Henrietta, his wife, 17.

Before the presentation of the Respondent (in this case it was Victor, the husband), each had been interviewed at length by two members of the staff, husband separate from wife. The charge: Henrietta had charged her husband with assault. Findings of preliminary interviews:

VICTOR

Admits he beats Henrietta
Claims she "walks the streets" every night
That she neglects her own baby
That she's now pregnant and if the baby isn't his, he'll "kill her"
Claims his wife is a nymphomaniac
Victor dependent on his mother for money
Once a bartender (for eight months), this period of work being the steadiest in a spotty work record
80 per cent of his life unemployed
Four hospitalizations for alcoholism
No sex problems, though an active "wolf"
Responsive and "open" in this private hearing; good at interchange; responsive. Very nervous nail-bitter
In closed interview, very emotional, wept often
Chronic alcoholic since age thirteen
Sado-masochistic
Goes with self-punitive women
Cruelly treated by rough father
Pronounced tic in right eye
Holds self unnaturally stiff
Voice often cracks; combination of "tough hood and obsequiousness"
All defenses transparent
Intelligence average
Blurred ideas about all time relationships, dates
Admits striking and hurting wife; says she's childish; calls her a "five-minute" mother (i.e., attentive to child, with love, food, playing, changing, bathing, etc., for five minutes, then finished with it for five hours or so. Child is mother's plaything; is instantly out of mother's thoughts when child is put down. Mother's basic duty has been performed is idea)
Says wife will jump into bed and pull covers over her head; tries to "hide," blot out the world
Victor impulse-ridden
Claims to have just contracted gonorrhea from wife

HENRIETTA

Admits Victor loves the baby, even though not his
Wants Order of Protection, afraid of being beaten again
Background: Parents divorced while she was still unborn
Now 17½ years old; most seductive
Jewish, but converted to Catholicism
Her mother remarried year after divorce
Stepfather "treats me like a dog"
Early put out for adoption—no takers
Raped at twelve (apartment-house roof)
Remembers "incinerator smell"; same odor now will bring on sudden sex block
Quit school and went steady with older boy, who disappeared
Four suicide tries
Slept with baby's father to "hook" him, but he abandoned her before baby's birth
Has had severe (physical) fights with half-brother.
Suffers with visual hallucinations, bronchial asthma, irregular menstruation
Total affect: bland.
Fingernails bitten to quick, one finger bleeding
Lies easily and quickly, mechanically
Evasive, but more responsive as interview went on
Lives in fantasy
Happy-spirited basically, but hurt, vulnerable
Physically strong; definite sex-appeal, dainty, well-molded body.

The Skones had been married the previous May, six months before the interviews. They married two weeks after meeting. Living apart now for the past six weeks. Only the one child (by previous out-of-wedlock marriage), now seven months old.

The full staff of eighteen is present. Large rectangular table, seating twelve. Others scattered about the room in chairs against the wall.

Victor enters, is offered chair beside the leader's chair at head of table. The large group does not visibly scare him. Suede jacket. Clean. No tie. Handsome. Hard-eyed. Cold smile, brief. His speech is good.

Q: When did you see Henrietta the last time, Victor?
A: Last Friday night.
Q: Does she go out nearly every night?
A: She goes out *every* night. Sleeps all day. She's no housekeeper. Does no cooking. I told her to get out. Pack your stuff and get out.
Q: Is she with her mother now?
A: Stepmother. Yes, I presume. (*Very cool so far. Not poised, but his pose is carrying him all right.*)
Q: What's your own situation, Victor?
A: Well, we had one reconciliation. Then I found I had clap. I went to the M.D. and got it cleared up right away.
Q: You mean you got this from your wife?
A: Yes. Then I found I got it again. Penicillin fixed me up again. Three or four days.
Q: Didn't you ask the M.D. to examine your wife, too?
A: No. We split. I told her to go.
Q: Do you know if she ever did go to the doctor about this?
A: I don't know.
Q: What are your plans about all this?
A: When I left her the last time, I said "You're not the girl I married."
Q: What are your hopes, Victor?
A: I want to stay married. I'd like her to be what she was when we first knew each other.
Q: For how long a time would you say you had a good life together?
A: Maybe three months.
Q: Then what happened?
A: Well, my mother told me that my wife had said, "If my husband doesn't like the way I clean, he can go to hell."
Q: What does your wife like to do?
A: Discotheques mostly. She likes to stay out all night.
Q: Drink?
A: She drinks. But she doesn't have a problem.
Q: And you, Victor?
A: I drink the same as I always did.
Q: When did you know you wanted to marry her?
A: Well, really it was a whim. She seemed like a good mother. I met her casually. Through a friend. I went to see her in the hospital. Before the baby came.
Q: Had the father of this baby abandoned Henrietta by this time?
A: I don't think he ever came to the hospital to see her. I thought I could provide a good home for the baby. And for her. But it

hasn't worked out. The baby cries all the time. Has to be held all the time. Or fussed with. And Henrietta's out most of the time. Every night. She has a lot of growing up to do. I know the streets she walks on. I know where she stops. It's my neighborhood, too.

Q: You grew up there?

A: Yes.

Q: Would you call it a rough neighborhood?

A: Yes, I would.

Q: Do you remember when you had your first drink, Victor?

A: Very early teens, I'd say.

Q: Victor, did you ever notice, when you're drinking, whether you. have a personality change or not?

A: Oh, sure. It depends. More on who's around me and how I feel than in how much I drink. I can be the life of the party. Or get very depressed. I get into fights. Anybody brought up where I was is bound to get into fights. I've been real bombed a few times. I've blacked out, too, once or twice.

Q: Have you ever had any psychiatric treatment?

A: Yes.

Q: When was that?

A: When she left.

Q: Why did you seek help?

A: To see whose fault it was.

Q: Did you find out?

A: I found out we were both very immature. Mostly due to my drinking. Little things bugged me. Things that shouldn't. And I was terribly depressed when she left.

Q: Have you ever been hospitalized for drinking?

A: No. (*The staff knows better, of course.*)

Q: Is it possible you infected your wife with clap, rather than the other way round?

A: (*Slight pause*) Yes, I guess it is. Not likely but possible. It's all over the neighborhood.

Q: When did you see her for the first time?

A: In the hospital.

Q: Just before the baby came?

A: Yes. Very appealing. That's when I fell in love with her.

Q: What did you see in her?

A: Companionship. Not like the local tavern girls. She was clean.

Q: Any feeling about her being pregnant?

A: Anybody can make a mistake.

Q: Did you want to accept the whole burden—mother and child?

A: Yes, I wasn't going to take the girl and throw away the baby.

Q: About a home—were you equipped to maintain a home for her?

A: Probably not as well as some. But I had a fairly good place.

Q: Did you know the father of your wife's child?

A: Well, I knew who he was. But I never met him. I've seen his picture.

Q: What's the longest time you've ever gone with one girl?

A: Never long with any. I was a Don Juan. Took what I wanted. In the Air Force it was real easy.

Q: How long were you in the Air Force?

A: Four years.

Q: The child's father—does your wife see him?

A: I'm not sure. He said he'd marry her when she was eighteen. Big deal. Doing her a big favor. She told me this.

Q: You think she's still seeing him?

A: Now that I'm gone?

Q: Yes.

A: I think so. I'm not sure. But she says she always hated him.

Q: Was she seeing him before you separated?

A: Yes.

Q: You didn't mind?

A: What can you do?

Q: Has she been associating with other men besides him?

A: Well, from May to September she wasn't playing around. Then she began. Or maybe she just started up again. She'd visit bars while I was working.

Q: Do you love the child?

A: Yes. Very much. And I don't really feel it's his.

Q: Because he doesn't seem to care it's alive?

A: Partly. But also because I was there when it was born.

Q: Is the child well taken care of?

A: As to feeding and changing and things like that, yes, he is. As to environment, no. My mother-in-law. Her brother. A stepsister. Six people. All living out of boxes. Everywhere, boxes. Boxes.

Q: How often do you see the baby?

A: Not often.

Q: How do you feel about us, Victor?

A: I feel you're educated people trying to help me. And her. I feel sorry for her. Hangs out with a crowd of rum-dums, pot-smokers, bums, hoods, creeps, junkies, pimps. What for? God, what for?

Q: But it's your crowd, too, isn't it?

A: Some of them, sure. But I'm a man. It doesn't do anything to me.
Q: She's complained about your hitting her.
A: (*Shrugs*)
Q: Do you hit her when you're boozed up?
A: Sometimes. Two cans of ale. . . . Is that drunk?
Q: Is she a fragile girl?
A: No. Very strong. Emotionally fragile. I mean—sort of—she's just not there. Not with it.
Q: What do you want now, Victor? What do you want most?
A: To get back together. To start over.
Q: Good. Do you need a job? Now?
A: Yes, very much.
Q: We're going to help you Victor. Today is Monday. Can you be right here this Thursday? Ten o'clock?
A: Yes. I can. And I'd like to thank you all very much.
Victor exits.
STAFF COMMENTS: (*informal and ad-libbed, right after Victor left*)
   "He needs a ready-made wife, child, and mother."
   "He needs a ready-made family."
   "Inadequate personality."
   "Environmental starvation."
   "Passive-aggressive."
   "No noticeable drinking disorder." "Yes but he wasn't drinking this morning."
   "Stormy personality."
   "A periodic near-psychotic."
   "Needs a job."
   "Needs treatment."
   "We must have his mother in right away."

As it was further explored, this sad story just got worse and worse. Both Henrietta and Victor did come back but it was obvious that they could not or would not keep coming. At least not long enough to effect a real second chance in a union so bizarre, in a family so problem-prone.

Henrietta presented to the staff a "mixed diagnostic picture," an "ambivalent attitude toward men," a "severe personality disorder," and "severe confusion as to her own sexual identity." Defeating factors, not uncovered in earlier interviews, came to light: pathological home environment (she'd moved into her stepmother's menage); overcrowding; hostile relations of Henrietta to her sixteen-year-old half-sister and her mentally defective brother. Stepmother "destructive."

Staff recommendation: "An attempt must be made to *gradually* [*sic*] enable Henrietta and baby to leave home."

Easy to say, hard to do. This multiple-problem family, unstable in all departments, was far too sick to maintain any ongoing contact with the clinic. The people just couldn't be scheduled. After a few calendar dates, they just stopped coming, though the court kept the case open, as did the clinic.

Victor had a high opinion of himself, but it was easy for the staff to penetrate his pose: he liked appearing as Henrietta's "rescuer." He was trying to gain self-esteem by being helpful to someone he felt to be less fortunate than himself. He was not interested in treatment for himself; nor in any of the suggestions of the Social Service Bureau, nor in a private agency to which the clinic referred these lost people.

They vanished, as do so many in these anonymous multitudes, born to nowhere on the outgoing tide of the unprepared, the infantile, the hurt, the broken, the lazy, and the poor.

Trained, compassionate, skillful people, giving their lives for others' lives, come to the end of the sidewalk here. They can conduct their charges no further. There is no follow-up. There is no money for it.

Alcohol Clinic

Mental Health Services maintain an Alcohol Clinic. Its director is Bernard Newman.

"We don't resolve the main problem," he concedes. "You can't jump people from one world into another, any more than you can do it with emerging African nations. Anyone going to Alcoholics Anonymous *knows* he has a problem. He knows it, he recognizes it. And he's dealing with it. Or trying to. But those aren't the drinking problems we see here. Or for that matter, for the alcohol referral situations in city courts anywhere in America."

"They all claim to be 'social' drinkers?"

"Exactly. The courts, and this clinic, never get the man or woman who says: 'I'm an alcoholic.' And that is the crucial difference. You can't force sobriety on anybody. It has to be sought. It has to be desired. Most alcohol clinics have a poor cure rate."

"What do you feel you *do* accomplish?"

"We smooth over the roughest cases. We just have too many. And too few to do the work. Everyone piles in here at 9:30. The day is a long jangle; women who've lived their whole married lives with sadistic husbands. We can't give them much attention. A little hope maybe. Most need money, of course. The drinkers—the hard-core drinkers that Dr. E. M. Jellinik called "Gamma alcoholics"—their problems are large and real. Immense and immediate. But you can't help people if they don't *recognize* their problem. And most who come here don't recognize drinking as being the source of their distresses. The awful confusion at home."

"Don't recognize it because of their lower social and economic level?"

"For the most part, yes. In the cultural middle class or upper class, men and women at that level when involved in a foundering marriage would seek help from a psychiatrist or a marriage counselor. Such people know it is paramount that they learn to get through to each other. To communicate. To be rationally communicative is important to them. It is a part of their value system. But these aren't the cases we get. We get the worst. And to such people, communication isn't important."

"What is?"

"When *these* folk come to this court, they come because they want this s.o.b. to stop smacking them."

"Why are the cases referred to you?"

"The judge wants an evaluation. Of course, if a man is really seeking help, seeking it for himself, then we can be effective. But most of them are hiding their problem. And they hide it well. Having just been to court, they're defensive. And most of them— to look at them—*seem* quite normal. But they aren't normal. Inside, they're in frightful shape. They've been dangerous. They've hurt people. But they'll drink again, so they'll hurt again. They have to."

America has six million alcoholics, but most of these sad and suffering people might do as well to save their busfare, stay home, and drink.

"Where there is no motivation, there is no patient."

New York is not handling its alcohol problem. No city is. There aren't enough facilities or enough understanding of the disease. And too many alcoholics. The clinic I visited and told you of in the pages just preceding is pitifully limited in depth, scope, and continuity. Its staff could be increased by 8,000% and it would still not be enough for New York. Not enough people; not enough money, and the alcohol problem raging all over the United States. The Department of Public Health confirms that we have in America today 9 million active alcoholics. We get another million every year.

What *is* an alcoholic?

You will get a different definition from all those you consult. Some years ago I had a long interview with Mrs. Marty Mann, the founder of the National Council on Alcoholism, a woman I consider to be the most valuable person in America today, if only in terms of the lives she has saved, the money, the jobs, careers, marriages, and families. She is an overwhelming experience, just to meet. I know you've heard of her.

Herself a recovered alcoholic, which is to say, an alcoholic who doesn't drink at all, she has, in addition to being a student of the disease of alcoholism since the year 1937, authored in my opinion the most authoritative book to appear thus far on this subject. Its title is simple enough: *New Primer on Alcoholism* (Holt, Rinehart & Winston, 1958),* and somewhere in that book is her definition of an alcoholic. This also is simple, as indeed all her prose is, blunt, clear, and on the line. Here is Mrs. Mann's definition: "You are an alcoholic if alcohol creates a continuing problem in any department of your life."

In a TV panel discussion, I heard Mrs. Mann make two slight adjustments to her own definition—not word changes, just changes of emphasis. "The two most important words in that definition," she told the audience, "are the words 'continuing' and 'any.' A *continuing* problem, in *any* department."

What could be clearer?

Yet most alcoholics—as the New York clinic finds many hundreds of times a week—don't *want* to find out that they are alco-

* Marty Mann has more recently published an extremely intelligent short book, a question-and-answer book, titled: *Marty Mann Answers Your Questions About Drinking and Alcoholism* (Holt, Rinehart & Winston, 1970).

holics. They don't want to believe it. They hate the word. Many just want to go on drinking. And they do. Of course, too, many who secretly or openly know they have a problem insist they have battled it and can't lick it. They insist that they are 'different'. They want to stop but they can't. They loath being branded with anything so socially searing. They can't stand the embarrassment in public, nor face their mirrors at home: men, late for the office but too drunk to shave; women too drunk to get a bra on (or off).

Perhaps "alcoholic" is an unfortunate word. Certainly there is no "perhaps" about its having been given a bad name. But the word, and public response to it, has such horrifying connotations as to keep millions of suffering Americans from seeking help that is nearby, and free. So they go on and on, smashing up their lives, their jobs, their families, and their cars—your car, too.

Alcoholics Anonymous is an organization that has now spread clear over the world (92 countries) and that has 10,342 groups in America, 1,815 in Canada, and 337 in Mexico. There are (1972) 783 hospital groups and 915 in American prisons.

Seven hundred and fifty thousand is a lot of ex-drunks, but it is about one-fifteenth of the casualty list for this country. The other 8¼ million are drinking. And they are in trouble. They have two choices: death or insanity.

In my foragings about this country while making television film in our insane asylums, I spent many hours in each facility—Columbus, Cincinnati, Kankakee, Cleveland, Chicago, many others —studying the case histories of our mental patients. In the etiology of all the precommitment records that I looked at (2,300 commitments), alcoholism was listed as a "presenting symptom" in 44 percent. I've done the same in most of the prisons I've visited. For prisoners the figure is higher still, and when combined with drugs, I have found that drugs and booze were involved in the antisocial behavior of 91 percent of our inmates. This relates to male prisoners, and in facilities where I had time and permission to study records. Though I've spoken to women prisoners in eleven facilities, I've had permission and time to explore records in only two: the "training center" at Albion (now closed) in the extreme northwestern part of New York State, and the Women's House of Detention (now on Rikers Island) in New York City. My figures for women may have no meaning, because of the scantiness of the survey and the time lag (about ten years) between my visits.

Indeed, not being a professional, I make no claim for the statistical significance of any of these "findings," if such they are, and I know that the variables and methodologies of one state, both for the mentally ill and for prisoners, may be quite different from those in the state next door. But the preponderance of evidence, its universality through the whole of America's contrasted climates and geographies, was to me quite overwhelming. It hit me right in the belly and is with me now. And sharply in my mind whenever I start down the dark halls that do little for any of those inside, beyond keeping the rain off.

"Alcoholism," Mrs. Mann has said, "may be the only disease from which the patient does not *want* to be cured."

From her, and from others I've met through her, other interesting items have emerged: many people who want help for their alcoholism are reluctant to approach Alcoholics Anonymous because they think it is a religious organization (which it is not); or that it is made up of Skid Row bums (Skid Row accounts for less than 5 percent of the problem drinking in the United States); or because it's a "confessional" of some sort (no one speaks unless he or she wishes to, though speaking is encouraged); or that it costs something. (It doesn't cost anything. Though AA groups are self-supporting through their own contribution, the average contribution, per member, is 32 cents per meeting.)

Why do they so often meet in churches? Three reasons: the space is available, usually convenient to members, and rents are cheap. Churches are glad to get the revenue, from $2 to $100 a month, depending on the size of the church and its rural or city setting.

For many years, from the time of its founding in 1935 (in Akron, Ohio), AA did not see a hereditary factor as being involved in individual drinking. But they are beginning to now. Medical research is beginning to prove it. The item is not of particular interest to AA bodies. What alcohol does to the man or woman who drinks it is their main interest, how to intercept it. But the inherited susceptibility to alcoholism is hugely interesting to an increasing number of medical installations all over this country.

For people who spurn or shy away from Alcoholics Anonymous (and many do, partly because they doubt the effectiveness of its anonymity claim; partly because they're afraid they're going to meet a lot of new people—which they most surely will), there are now many hundreds of facilities in this country that deal with this semi-invisible but crippling problem. Some of these facilities are good. Some are no good. Some are solidly professional but "wrong-headed." (No psychiatrist has ever cured an alcoholic.) Some few are notably, even dramatically, effective.

Of the latter, I'd like to mention only two: one in Seattle, Washington, the other in Fort Worth, Texas.

Similar to Mrs. Mann's definition, given earlier, for alcoholism, is the definition of the Schick Hospital in Fort Worth, Texas: "The problem drinker is anyone who drinks to the extent that it interferes with his life—his health, job, marriage, or other interpersonal relations."

This hospital is the "companion" facility known as the Shadel Hospital, Seattle, Washington, founded in 1940. These two hospitals were established by the Schick-Eversharp Company in conjunction with the directors of the Enzomedic Laboratories. The cure rate for each is about 66 percent. (AA's note: 50 percent never drink again after the first meeting, 25 percent quit in a few months or years, 25 percent never "get" the idea and die drunk.)

These institutions recognize that alcoholism is a drug addiction; that alcoholism is (often) inherited; that it is progressive and, if not treated, fatal. They also realize and publicize that alcoholism is rarely listed as a cause of death.

At these hospitals, before any treatment is started, patients are given a physical and neurological examination; a test that evaluates every body system; an examination for alcohol effects and for its toxic effect on every body organ.

The patient's mental status is explored and evaluated by a staff psychiatrist who studies each patient and directs a program of psychiatric treatment for the few who need it.

As the patient is withdrawn from alcohol (with many patients the experience almost as unnerving as heroin withdrawal), detoxification is carried out. The alcohol level in the blood is gradually reduced, and medications are given to prevent withdrawal effects, or at least to reduce them.

The Schick Hospital, among other procedures, employs the *conditioned reflex aversion technique*. What does that mean? It means the drinker is conditioned so that the sight, smell, and taste of alcohol become abhorrent to him, so that the physical compulsion to drink is destroyed.

This process takes place during alternate days of a ten-day treatment and is later reinforced by two follow-up treatments. On the "non-conditioning" days, the patient undergoes the pleasant experience of sleep therapy. He is completely relaxed. His anxiety problems drift away, and disturbed sleep patterns return to normal.

Patients are encouraged (as they are in AA) to "interrelate" with other patients and are directed toward this by a staff of counselors who are themselves all recovered alcoholics. Patients soon come to realize they don't *need* alcohol; that it *is* possible for the alcohol addict not to drink and not to *want* to drink. That he can walk away from it and not miss it.

The entire procedure is medically oriented. Registered nurses (they have no others) administer the light doses of sodium pentothal (for those who cannot sleep, a common concomitant to alcohol sufferers); all the doctors are M.D.'s, and the dietitian, psychologist, and psychiatrist are all certified.

There is nothing "religious" about any of it, and the only requirement for admission is a desire to get sober and stay sober. Limousine service is available at the airport for those who can't make it on their own (many arrive extremely intoxicated, having been drinking hard on the plane); and a fine motel is located near the hospital to accommodate friends or relatives who may have made the trip with the patient, whether spouse, son, friend, or business colleague.

The Schick Hospital is sun-lit, modern, attractive to look at and to be in. It is a 42-bed facility of both private and semiprivate rooms, all furnished with attractive decor. The food is excellent. In professional terms, it is unusually commodious: modern lab facilities, air-conditioning, and such other assists as closed circuit television for monitoring, through their "bad" hours, all patients in the intensive care area.

The cost? It is closely comparable to that of an equivalent stay in any first-class general hospital. Your identity remains unrevealed, except to staff members. Patients may enter at any time of the day or night. The entire staff is "shock-proof," something not often seen, even today, in many of America's finest hospitals. (They hate the alcohol problem and when they can duck it, they do.)

Not so at Schick nor at Shadel. While it is true that general hospitals throughout the United States are more and more nudging their slow way to an acceptance of alcoholic diagnosis, not many as yet have the sophistication or the desire to go to work on an alcohol problem as they instantly would, for example, with a case of ruptured appendix. But in most hospitals it's been very slow in coming and is shamefully scanty in most American cities right now. And will remain so for many years. A fine exception (to mention just one) is the alcohol floor in New York's Roosevelt Hospital. But Shadel in Seattle and Schick in Fort Worth are in no other business than getting drunks, of whatever age, sex, degree of illness, ethnic background or circumstance, out of the trap of alcohol.

The Schick Hospital (Dr. Robert B. Dunn, M.S. and M.D., director) is located at 4101 Frawley Drive, Fort Worth, Texas 76118, and the phone is 817–284–9217.

No psychiatrist can cure a drunk, and any psychiatrist who today is still telling patients "We'll take care of your problem as soon as we find out *why* you drink" should have his license suspended.*

Research conducted through the enterprise of Schick-Eversharp has uncovered many startling, unsettling, valuable, even eye-popping findings: that many children are alcoholics; that many who never drink a drop are alcoholics; that there is a powerful heredity factor in alcoholism, the inheritance usually coming through the father, or the mother's male relatives.

My father, a well-known Presbyterian minister, hated booze,

---

* "Some of the worst therapists in my experience have been highly trained psychiatrists who have done far more damage than good to the alcoholic and his family." Frederick Lemere, M.D., quoted here from the *Quarterly Journal of Studies on Alcoholism*, No. 24, pp. 705 et seq., 1963. And: "After all, modern psychiatry has had the opportunity and responsibility for treating the alcoholic for well over 40 years with such poor results that patients had to start treating each other." (Alcoholics Anonymous)

knew nothing whatever about it, and closed a number of saloons in Ohio when I was a child. His mother, a one-woman matriarchy and irreversible tyrant, came to visit us (in Ohio) once a year, was much given to dizziness, and many times each day sent me upstairs to fetch her tonic. She fell easily, stumbled over footstools, and needed her tonic—it was called Peruna—"to settle herself." I thought it was tonic, and she thought so, too.

Forty years later, when making store checks (for the shelf movement of Camel cigarettes, a large account in the agency in which I then worked), I was one day in an unheard-of tiny town in the mountains of eastern Tennessee. Here I saw a large display of Peruna. I immediately recognized it, picked up a bottle, and examined the label. At the time my grandmother was in such need of its benefits—it was 1910 or 1911—the law did not require a listing of the contents of such nerve-steadiers. Now (1948) it did. Peruna was 48 percent alcohol! My grandmother may not have been an alcoholic, but my grandmother was a dedicated drunk. Often she couldn't find her way around her own living room. Had she known she was drinking BOOZE, I'm quite certain she would have killed herself. And for the good reason the reader will appreciate at once: Grandmother Wylie was the *founder* of the Women's Christian Temperance Union in North Dakota!

Home Term Has Come a Long, Long Way

You can see, can you not, that people *do* care? Then why isn't it better than it is? Indeed why is it worse? You are beginning to absorb some of the answers yourself: money, inadequacy of personnel (you've just read what Charles Lindner and Dr. Melvin Fishman had to say, and will presently get quotes from two judges who couldn't take it any longer and who quit).

The concept and the structure of Family Court is nonetheless praiseworthy, and its work recruits and retains many of our best citizens. This is true of every city, the shabby showing of the end-result notwithstanding. Superior people are killing themselves trying to make the thing go.

The tempered, intelligent talk of the psychiatric backfield that is a part of Family Court; access to past records bearing on present dilemmas; the patience of overworked professionals; the overtime; the rotten pay; the intensity of a judge's preoccupation with the special sides these sad (occasionally comical) dramas always carry; the teamwork, the insights, the guesses, and the hopes—all these are laid on the table of the judge's mind and there fitted into the design that will be his recommendation when all the resources open to him have been tapped.

By recharting courses for the lost and confused, by patching small accidents before they are fatal—these courts and the personnel maintaining them are saving lives just as certainly as surgeons are saving lives.

Over the past thirty years, half a million cases much like the ones to follow would stand as an acceptable monument, I would think, to the architect who first conceived all this. In the presence of nothing but wreckage, Judge Anna Kross saw an entire new dimension in the accelerated use of courts: courts to be instantly answerable—not six months hence but right now, today—to people in trouble; courts expanded, quickened, simplified. You've seen a bit of it. You'll see more, for the "socialized" aspect of her invention is here to stay.

She lit up this jungle, took the terror out of it, put in roads and guard-rails, showed the way to the frightened, the mauled, and the defeated. The framework of Family Court has many of her fixtures, and the Family Offenses Term is a direct grafting.

In Family Court a large number of the cases are assault cases: wives wanting to see their husbands punished or humiliated or softened up; the same with husbands against wives, as you've seen. Some have reason, some don't. But in nearly all cases, the sudden, sad, degrading element, the blow, the aggravation, comes out: *why* he hit her, locked her out. Or she him.

The mordant anxieties and bickerings that build up over money problems are at the root of much marital distress, though some of the cases—about one in every twenty-two—are collisions between warring parents or marriage partners who are well heeled, but even among the solvent the bitterness can be fierce.

I've said I pity these judges. So would you. No observer can sit in any of these courts for many hours without developing a permanent respect and a quickening admiration for the deep well of pure patience that judges must draw upon day by day. Explosions, interruptions, bad temper, invective, sass, and unchecked counter-accusations spin through these rooms like a sudden fall of summer hail.

The creative vitality, the angry demands for simplification were carried on by others when Judge Kross left the bench in 1954 and became Commissioner of Correction, and a big thing happened that same year. A report of great urgency and influence made its appearance. It was assembled by The Special Committee of the Association of the Bar, a group appointed in 1952. It spent three years studying the cancerous spread of court-proliferation, a metastasizing wildness in the bloodstream that went through the whole of New York State, striking at and disabling the court structure organ by organ, joint by joint. And the cancer wasn't statewide, it was nationwide.

The goal was easy to state: "Simplify and unify the court system of the state." Substantial revision of the state's constitution was required to get this moving. Some of the legislation and some of the recommendations have come in. What is pertinent to this part of the book is the verified data the committee found and reported. It will (as it did me) knock you off your swivel-chair, and for the sake of economy I have compressed, to only fifteen particular trophies, the mass of material the committee had to comb through. This compression, though arbitrary on my part, is characteristic of the courts' disease, a disease long and malignantly incubating, but it will have immediate meaning to any lay reader, for these fifteen trophies are real beauties. It is hard to believe the courts' machinery could operate at all.

Where Did Today's Chaos in the Courts Come From?

The full story is complex. I would like to keep it clear and simple. And will.

The big muddle, as all know, is historical. It is a matter of accretion really; the hard, impermeable mound that we have now and that came, in fluid form, from England, from the fresh flow of English law three hundred years ago; a flow that has slowly dried up, then petrified by uncontrolled evaporation; the evaporation of what was good at the time it came here from England to what is inoperable now. All of these solidified pyramids have been dented, now and then, by state legislatures, but they've never been dissolved.

Dean Roscoe Pound was the first to describe the problem—the anachronism of old English courts in modern American cities—and did so in 1922, in only two paragraphs:

To understand the administration of criminal justice in American cities today, we must first perceive the problems of administration of justice in a *homogeneous, pioneer*, primarily *agricultural* community of the first half of the nineteenth century, and the difficulties involved in meeting those problems with the legal institutions, inherited by us, from seventeenth-century England.

We must next perceive the problems of administration of justice in a *modern, heterogenous, urban, industrial* community and the difficulties involved in meeting those problems with the legal and judicial machinery received from England and given fixed shape for pioneer, rural America.

That was 1922. Twenty-five years later (1947), Judge Kross, in a typical malediction regarding this same absurd and wasting evil, was more blunt than the Dean:

The end-product of a long series of reorganizations has produced a court progressively adapted to conditions of *seeming* efficiency, notwithstanding the rise of many new and difficult problems of which the tremendous increase of traffic cases is only one example.

In spite of their new name, they are just what they were in 1798: *police courts for preserving the peace.*

We are using the same old apparatus.

In 1798 there were *no* cases growing out of labor disputes. Now we have thousands. Men and women are arrested for picketing in a rent strike. The magistrate, sitting in a court organized to hear cases of disorderly conduct such as existed in 1798, must decide questions worthy of the Court of Appeals. Such as:

Is picketing by several persons disorderly? Is walking four abreast disorderly? Is carrying posters disorderly? How about Negroes? In an effort to force local stores in a Negro neighborhood to employ Negro help, is that legal?

Changing times have brought new problems to our courts, without provision to care for the new conditions.

Eighteen years ago (1954), the "Gelhorn Study," concurrently with the "Report of the Committee on Administration of Justice

Relating to the Family," brought up to date, and clarified, the unbelievable horror that court fragmentation and overlap had come to mean to us all. From it I have extracted what I referred to as my fifteen "trophies," and that is the way they jumped at me as I went through the material. Some of these will surprise, even anger you. And they can't be dismissed as "quaint" just because they've been around so long. Here we have hard evidence, meticulously compiled, of what has been choking us to death.

For example, in the matter of *Jurisdictional Unity*, see this:

If an expert lawyer were hired for the express purpose of devising a system that would defeat the ideal of jurisdictional unity, he would be hard put to make the present structure worse.

Or this, in the matter of *Administrative Unity*:

There is no administrative unity.

Or *Fiscal Unity*:

Fiscal chaos rivals administrative chaos. This Committee has never been able to determine how much our court system costs. This lack of unity is not a situation peculiar to New York State. It is a common problem across the nation.

In the matter of business basics (see section on "The Dilemma of Our Cities" for a statement of current conditions), this court structure, even to the lay reader, would appear in poor shape, and indeed it was. But it gets quickly worse:

From time to time attempts at major simplifications of the court system have been made. They have generally failed. The consequence has been complication without permanent solution.

And later:

All the courts have different jurisdictions. Courts bearing the same name differ in jurisdiction. Courts having identical jurisdiction bear different names. Jurisdictions overlap. Authority over a single situation may be so divided among a number of courts that no just result can be reached by any of them.

Still later:

Nowhere is this fragmentation of jurisdiction more damaging to the cause of real justice than in the field of problems relating to *children and families*, yet no problems touch so close to daily life.

Here now are the fifteen specifics, a punishing lay-down of the facts:

1. In many instances the court to which the case is first brought is the wrong court.

2. In many instances the right court can give only partial relief to a situation which originates in a common underlying cause that has many symptoms, each of which symptoms is now treated in a different court.

3. If a drunken husband beat his wife, she can bring him before a Magistrate and if the Magistrate sees fit, he may send the man to jail.

4. But the Magistrate cannot enter an Order of Protection.

5. If the wife also needs support, she cannot get it from the Magistrate.

6. She must go to Family Court, which can enter an Order of Protection in connection with an Order of Support.

7. To secure a permanent separation, she must go to the Supreme Court, where the usual requirement of counsel makes the proceeding, as a rule, unavailable to the poor.

8. The Family Court has jurisdiction only in support cases of a *married* couple.

9. For the support of a child born out of wedlock, the mother must go to the Court of Special Sessions.

10. Matters involving the custody of minor children may require disposition by either the Family Court, Children's Court, or the Supreme Court, depending on the nature of the case.

11. Delinquency involving children under sixteen is handled in the Children's Court.

12. But if a minor over the age of sixteen commits an identical offense, he may be tried in any number of different courts, depending on the nature of the charge, and on the county in which the crime was committed.

13. The records of one court, dealing with a family that is involved in other courts, may not be available to the other courts.

14. A couple may be found to be unmarried, and the child illegitimate, in the Court of Special Sessions.

15. The same couple may be found to be married, and the same child legitimate, in Domestic Relations Court.

"Proper disposition requires that the whole family fabric, with all its torn and tangled strands, be viewed as an integrated whole, and in one tribunal."

The thinking embodied in that last sentence, plus a ton of evidence similar to the above entries, had much to do with the reorganization of the courts that took place in 1962 (and that is still going on); that sought to end such cockeyed fragmentation, confusion, and overlap, three of the real villains of case overload.

In a single sentence, the main purpose here was to put a family problem before a single judge. This has been a great help in many ways, particularly to the bewildered mother, married or not. It has protected her from "being knocked around in the courts as if in a pinball machine"—to quote from the Committee's own summary.

Family Court, Case One

As the reader will now see, the Petitioner (the Plaintiff, a woman) is an egregiously spoiled and self-serving housewife. The Respondent (the Defendant, her husband), not without faults himself, is a plagued and long-suffering man and a neighborhood doctor. Almost any layman, were he to witness a typical flare-up in this family, would surely feel the husband had earned the right to belt his old lady. At least once. And that it was limited to only the one thwack seems a mark of commendable restraint.

This case interested me because it illustrates four things that keep appearing, if one spends a matter of months rather than days in attending these hearings:

1. The patience of the bench under severe provocation
2. The high cost of intemperate speech or manner
3. Sane solutions to insane situations
4. The sharpness of the judge in spotting something essential that is being understated or by-passed (it is usually the children) by the litigants.

Here is the verbatim exchange, the case already being underway:

COURT: (*To Respondent*) Do you sleep in the same bedroom?
RESP.: No, Your Honor.

PET.: We do sometimes, Your Honor, when he busts into *my* bedroom.

COURT: I'm questioning your husband, madam. Please don't interrupt.

PET.: Well, he comes in anyhow.

COURT: How much money are you giving your wife, under this arrangement?

RESP.: $125 a week.

PET.: Oh, boy. It's $75, Your Honor. Never more!

COURT: Madam, if you keep butting in, I'll have you taken out.

PET.: Well, I just don't want him to get away with a lie like that.

COURT: I expect we'll pretty well know who's lying before we finish. And something about provocation as well. We will go on. Now— this $125, is that for your wife alone?

RESP.: For her alone.

COURT: You have two daughters in boarding-school. Who pays those bills?

RESP.: I pay all their bills.

PET.: That's a lie. I just outfitted them. Last week.

COURT: I've warned you, madam. You're the Petitioner here. And you'll be heard. In full. (*To Respondent*) You heard your wife.

RESP.: Oh, yes. I heard her all right.

COURT: Well, what about the money?

RESP.: The $125?

COURT: Yes, the $125.

RESP.: I put it in her account. Every week. It's her money.

COURT: Who outfitted the girls?

PET.: I did.

COURT: (*To Respondent*) Is that true?

RESP.: Well, perhaps my wife thinks she outfitted the girls. But I think I did.

COURT: Explain that.

RESP.: My wife took our two daughters to Peck and Peck, De Pinna, Saks, and Arnold Constable, and outfitted them.

COURT: Well?

RESP.: And I just got the bills. It's $1,734.

COURT: (*To Petitioner*) Is that true?

PET.: Not exactly.

COURT: What exactly is true?

PET.: I'm paying out money to the girls all the time.

COURT: Have the bills for the department stores been paid yet?

PET.: I wouldn't know. It's his responsibility.

COURT: (*To Petitioner*) Madam, do you buy clothing for yourself and charge it and let your husband pay for it?

PET.: I would never do such a thing.

COURT: (*To Respondent*) Did you pay the store bills yet?

RESP.: I paid over $1,200 of it.

COURT: Not all? Is this on account?

RESP.: No. After they got the stuff home, the girls decided they didn't like some of it and sent it back. I've paid for the things they kept. Things they took back to school.

COURT: Sir, do you own your own home?

RESP.: Oh, yes, Your Honor. Sixteen years.

COURT: How many rooms do you have?

RESP.: We have fourteen.

COURT: Servants?

PET.: I do all the work. Mostly. Dishes, cleaning. He'd make me shovel snow.

RESP.: We have two servants, Your Honor. A live-in cook. And a cleaning woman twice a week. A twice-a-month gardner, and a contract window cleaner, once a month.

COURT: What does your wife do around the house?

RESP.: Well, she spends a lot of time fixing her hair.

COURT: Anything else?

RESP.: She markets. And listens in on my professional phone calls.

PET.: That's a lie. I hang up if it's not for me. There's an extension.

COURT: Madam, on the morning you claim your husband struck you and abused you, can you tell me what provoked this? Can you tell me just what happened?

PET.: Yes. The phone rang. I was downstairs. In the kitchen. Washing the dishes. He picked it up. In the bedroom. Then he shouted to me to take the receiver. It was somebody making an arrangement for us to meet a judge about our separation and my moving out of the house and I said I wasn't ready. It was too quick. I had to do my hair. This call came in very sudden. At that particular moment, I couldn't make it. Couldn't see anybody.

COURT: You and your husband were to go out immediately and meet a judge? Do you have an action in another court?

PET.: Oh, yes. Support Court. And Supreme Court. But that morning I couldn't go.

COURT: What was the reason?

PET.: Well, I just couldn't get ready in time.

COURT: How long does it take you to get ready?

PET.: It depends.

COURT: An hour?

PET.: Sometimes more. So I said I would be glad to meet with the judge but not that day and would he please make it some other time. And I hung up and went back into the kitchen and just as I was starting the dishes again, he was in the kitchen calling me the vilest names. . . .

COURT: What did he say?

PET.: He called me a ghoul, a bastard, a parasite, and he said he'd kill me.

COURT: Did he say he would kill you?

PET.: Yes. And I turned around to get away from him—from his anger—and went into the dining room. And he knocked me down there and beat me on the back with a stick and beat me on the head and my shoulders with his fists and he is a dentist and he has very strong hands. (*Petitioner loses control here.*)

COURT: Oh, come now. You're not on a stage. You're giving testimony. I want to know everything that happened from there. As best you can recall. And don't get hysterical. This court is here to help you. To help both you and your husband.

PET.: Well, he kept on beating me on the back and neck.

COURT: With what?

PET.: With his fists. And pushing me. And he pushed me right out through the front door.

COURT: Did you call the police?

PET.: No. I wasn't dressed for it.

COURT: How were you dressed?

PET.: I had on bedroom slippers. And my hair—curlers, you know. Wound up. And a house dress. So I couldn't.

COURT: What did you do?

PET.: Ran to Mrs. Miller's—a neighbor. I had tea. And a pill to quiet me.

COURT: Were you bleeding?

PET.: I was hurting.

COURT: Did you call a doctor?

PET.: No.

COURT: When you got to Mrs. Miller's, did you then call the police?

PET.: I never did call the police.

COURT: But the information here indicates you've called the police before.

PET.: Oh, yes.

COURT: Then why not this time?

PET.: Well, I had an Order of Protection once, so if he hurt me I could have him arrested. But it was only temporary. And I looked terrible. Just to look at me, I mean.

COURT: Where were your daughters?

PET.: Thank God, away at school. Mrs. Miller loaned me an electric pad. So later I came home but right away my husband climbed in through the window. The door was locked.

COURT: Did you lock him out?

PET.: No. He locked himself out.

COURT: You didn't lock the door on him?

PET.: I thought I ought to. To be safe. But it locked itself.

COURT: You got in. But he couldn't?

PET.: Yes. He came through a window.

COURT: Did he beat you any more?

PET.: Not that day.

COURT: Have you still been living in the same house with him?

PET.: Yes. Where can I go?

COURT: Did you at any time get or ask for a doctor?

PET.: No. I didn't want to hurt his business.

COURT: No one ever saw the marks and bruises?

PET.: I saw them. And God saw them.

COURT: That is all. Now, I'd like to ask your husband some questions.

PET.: He'll lie to you. From beginning to end.

COURT: I don't think so. He's under oath not to. And so are you. You might remember that, madam. You mentioned God just this minute. Sir—about the phone call—did you answer it?

RESP.: No, Your Honor. My wife did.

COURT: Did you hear her?

RESP.: Yes.

COURT: On the upstairs extension?

RESP.: No, when my wife's on the phone, anybody can hear. She's a loud woman.

COURT: Loud enough so you could hear her upstairs? Wasn't she in the kitchen?

RESP.: You could hear her to Yankee Stadium.

COURT: What happened that morning, after she hung up?

RESP.: I came down and told her it was an extreme discourtesy to a busy judge—he'd cleared a whole morning to adjudicate our case— to refuse to go just because she hadn't fixed her hair. I told her she was a slob. And she picked up her coat and I said, "Where are you going?" And she said she was going out and none of my business and I gave her a sharp crack over the buttocks with a croquet mallet.

COURT: With the head of the mallet?

RESP.: No, it had no head. It was a stick I used as a stake to mark vegetable rows. With string, you know. To keep a row straight. I have a garden.

COURT: You ever strike your wife before?

RESP.: I've felt like it.

COURT: That is not an answer.

RESP.: No, I never hit her before. Not really.

COURT: Shoved her around?

RESP.: Well, more like push her. I've pushed her.

COURT: So hard that she fell?

RESP.: I pushed her into a sofa once. But I never hit her. Only the one time.

COURT: That's all. Now, madam: do you want to live away from your husband?

PET.: More than anything.

COURT: Then why don't you?

PET.: Because we—my daughters and I—we haven't been given an apartment to live in.

COURT: Aren't you getting $125 a week?

PET.: Well, in a sense. And I am looking for an apartment. But the $125 is just for food and clothing. After you live in fourteen rooms and have servants—

COURT: You said you did all the work—Now, both of you, listen to me. Only one thing concerns me and it has little to do with either one of you. You are a pair of social pigs—you're both selfish and both disturbed. I think both of you have lied to me. You, madam, more than your husband. There is no allegation of any gross wounding, or damage. If he struck you across the buttocks with a croquet mallet, and if it inflicted pain, a previous court already granted you an Order of Protection. You never made use of it. You did not seek or need a doctor. You had recourse to the police, but never availed yourself of it. As a mother, you never once talked about your children—your two daughters who are in school. Your husband—at least he's paying their bills. And yours. You pretended to be the one doing all the work, all the housework. You are a liar. It's my guess you're also a lazy woman. Now, with a multitude of courts and none of them really getting to the heart of this problem, it doesn't seem that dragging your case through one more court is going to correct this situation. Of course, I could make a disposition of this case. My interest, and my intention, however, is not to see that you two are protected from each other.

My interest is seeing your daughters are protected against this absurd and juvenile friction that has been the climate of their upbringing for many years. In these courts we often ask people from the counseling services to help us. And I am going to do that now. Since there is enough money to afford counselor in both your other court actions, I suggest you get with counsel right now— I see you are both Catholics—that you both attend sessions with the Catholic Charities people—

PET.: He won't go.

COURT: Don't tell me he won't go, madam. And if you interrupt one more time—we have a stick we use in court. It's called contempt and it will hurt a lot more than the croquet mallet, I promise you. Now, sir, would you sit down with a counseling service that I am going to recommend to you?

RESP.: Yes, of course. I certainly will.

PET.: He never will. He never will! I know him! You've no idea what he's like. It's all lies!

COURT: Madam, I've warned you five times. And I'm sick of it. Now you're going to jail. You're going to the Women's House of Detention for ten days. It's a tough place. And I hate to send anyone there. Perhaps you'll learn a bit of restraint. And the rudiments of courtesy in court. The next time, it won't be ten days. It will be thirty days. Now, take her out.

Family Court, Case Two—Son Against Mother

The evanescence of psychosis, the unpredictability of its timing, its swing, its capricious flight-and-return, has been noted by many. In court it can sometimes be cunningly regulated, ingeniously concealed or disguised by the "patient," whether witness, plaintiff, or defendant. It can deceive every member of a full jury, and thousands of jury trials have gone the wrong way because the "insane" party so masterfully hid his insanity.

Juries, to some defendants, represent the "opposition" more sharply than does the prosecutor; a test to be met, an adversary to be brought into camp. The case itself can become quite secondary. And in this below-the-surface contest, a certified psychotic can summon a surprising display of logic, composure, sharp memory for detail, and a seemingly humane concern for others. (See section on Child Abuse, p. 150, vicious parents successfully posturing tenderness.)

If the disturbed person is a good enough actor, he (or she) can show up as the sanest one in court; as the most convincingly aggrieved. All judges of any experience have seen it happen many times. And will see it again.

Some judges have told me that the mere presence of a gallery (a jury) has something to do with this. The nature, depth, and quality of the psychosis has more. But the display factor, the powerful sense that something important, critical, significant, at once garishly public yet acutely private is being staged—all this is very often involved in any sustained, successful concealment of serious mental illness, even of imminent breakdown. It is as if the performer—with all the world watching—refuses to break down, at least right now. They have an act to put on. Many have done it very well.

Not so in the "social" courts that have no jury.

In the more natural surroundings of Family Court—as I've before noted—courts without any of the trappings or the ritual or pageantry of formal procedure, without robes, gavel, or formal risings, a very different climate is presented, and it is a climate that induces different responses.

What, specifically?

Everything here seems to be at room temperature. No one is seated above anyone else. Windows have curtains. It's a roomful of equals—no glare, no tension, no visible rules. And no August Presence.

There is not even an audience to "perform" against, no arena, no place to turn on a show. And a pitiful few to see it if anyone tried.

In such a setting, normal stimuli have a normal chance for free play. Things will be seen as they are. People seem familiar. So do voices. There is no theatricalism of any kind at all.

What's the advantage of all this?

Quite a large one. In a few moments after a hearing starts, all voices are low (at first) and parties informally close, even butting into each other's talk. No one is boxed off by himself in a witness stand. The quiet talk, the reviving of old provocations (or, more correctly, the newest or precipitating provocation), soon sets in motion the exact syndrome that last month or last night or this very morning brought in the police

The "re-enactment" isn't staged. It is spontaneous. And the whole thing can start, does start, with a question as calm as this: "Tell us what happened."

Thus, in the case you will see next, the mother, most pathetically, is just being herself; herself in the *real* posture, not the histrionic put-on, that has plagued her son so often. She comes on as a very poorly structured woman, beefy, defiant, intrusive. Her gush of talk, her rage, her monstrous self-pity, quickly establish her as fitting almost exactly the psychiatric evaluation already made of her by a member of Dr. Melvin Fishman's staff in the Mental Health Clinic, the service we looked into in the section on Probation.

Of course, the "mother-in-love-with-son-and-jealous-of-daughter-in-law" theme is older than the Bible. It has an almost Jurassic historicity. But these courts are the first courts to deal, in precisely this way, with this ancient, universal aggravation.

COURT OFFICER: Would you remain standing, Mrs. Burt? Sir, your name is Anthony Burt?

PETITIONER: Yes.

COURT OFFICER: Your name, madam, is Pauline Burt?

RESPONDENT: Yes.

COURT OFFICER: This is your son?

RESPONDENT: Yes.

COURT OFFICER: You reside at 3 Maiden Court, Plandome, Long Island?

PETITIONER: Yes.

COURT OFFICER: You, madam, reside at 215 West Twelfth Street, New York?

RESPONDENT: Yes.

COURT OFFICER: Your son charges you with disorderly conduct, in that on the 11th of November, 1971, at 4:30 P.M., at 44-61 Elmhurst Avenue in Queens you came to his office shouting and screaming, "You fucking bastard! Those damn Drums!" referring to the Petitioner's wife's family; that you also went into the private office when work was being done on patients in the presence of nurses and patients; that you cursed patients in the waiting-room, saying your son had no license; that you refused to leave when asked, necessitating the calling of the police to remove you from the premises.

Madam, on this charge you may be heard in this Court; you can ask for time to get a lawyer or bring witnesses.

EXAMINATION BY THE COURT

Q: Sir, your name is Anthony Burt?

A: Yes.

Q: And you say that this Respondent is your mother?

A: That's right.

Q: And on the 11th of November, 1971, at about 4:30 in the afternoon, you say that this Respondent came to your office on Elmhurst Avenue in Queens. Now you say certain things happened there?

A: Yes.

Q: Tell us what happened.

A: Well, she came—I am a doctor.

Q: Yes?

A: And she came into my office, as she has other times in the past and has created a scene—

Q: What did she do? Tell us.

A: Well, she comes in and sometimes she sits down, and then— starts to cry when nobody pays attention to her, and carries on; and then when nobody pays attention, she walks into the private offices where my nurses are, and sometimes there are patients present. And, finally, the last time I was forced to call the police because it was getting to—

Q: This was November 11th?

A: That's right.

Q: All right, what else? You called the police. Did they do anything?

A: They removed her; they asked her to leave.

Q: And they sent her out? They didn't arrest her at the time?

A: No.

Q: And you say in this petition that she was shouting and screaming and using profane language?

A: Yes.

RESPONDENT: Lies.

Q: Do you know whether she was under the influence of intoxicants?

A: I don't think so. I don't believe so.

Q: And you say that this was being done in the presence of nurses and patients?

A: That's right.

Q: And she refused to leave the office until the police came?

A: Yes.

THE COURT: All right.

EXAMINATION BY THE COURT:

Q: Now, madam, your name is Pauline Burt?

A: Yes, that's right. That's my son, and I put him through college. He wouldn't be where he is—

THE COURT: Now listen, we don't want a lot of talking here.

RESPONDENT: And I am very unwanted by his wife.

Q: On the 11th of November, 1971, at about 4:30—

A: No, it was not 4:30, sir.

Q: (*Continuing*)—did you go to his office?

A: It was 8:30 in the evening when he is usually through, sir.

Q: Did you go to his office on that day?

A: Yes, sir. I think I am entitled—

Q: Tell me what happened then.

A: And it was in the evening around 8:00 o'clock; and usually he is through around 8:00 or 8:30; and I went in and there wasn't a patient in the office sir. And he was in fact, in his reception room like fixing up the magazines and things, and like getting ready to go. So I said, "Oh, Tony." "What are you doing here?" he says to me. And I only went over for a kind word. I am so lonely without him. And my husband is gone, dead and gone, and this is because of his wife. My son's wife. This goes way back.

Q: All right. Did he ask you to leave?

A: But I'm his mother. I sat down for a minute, and I never said "boo." He says "screaming"—and what else? And making a lot— I never screamed or raised my voice.

Q: He said that you were using profane language.

A: I know he did. I never swore before in my life. But now it is his wife is the cause of this. My poor husband when he was alive used to say, "Who does she think she is? Why doesn't this boy call us up?" Because his wife has him brainwashed, is why. His wife is living the life of a queen in his home.

THE COURT: But, madam, that is his home. He has a right to have his home the way he wants it.

RESPONDENT: He shouldn't unwant his mother and father who are the best people in the world and handed him everything on a silver platter and never got a cent in return. And as soon as he gets married, she doesn't want us. I lost my husband. He was so aggravated because of her; and she was trying to kill me. A week after my husband was dead, she said, "It's a good thing he dies." Imagine that.

THE COURT: You see, madam, by everything you say—we have this unfortunate concept of mothers-in-law. You see the way you talk about them?

RESPONDENT: Yes, but I'm trying to say something—

THE COURT: But you shouldn't interfere in your son's marital affairs.

RESPONDENT: But I never interfered, sir.

THE COURT: But you were doing it. And you are now. You were talking about his wife. How can you expect her to like you?

RESPONDENT: She is the one that started. One week after they were married—

THE COURT: He asked you to stay away from his place.

RESPONDENT: I never want to see him again. What he's done to me since my poor husband is dead—the best guy in the world. He knows it, too. And the best mother in the world. His friends up in the house every night in the week before he was married.

THE COURT: All right, I make a finding in this case.

RESPONDENT: And this is what I get.

THE COURT: Have her sit down in the back.

COURT OFFICER: Have a seat back there, madam.

RESPONDENT: You give the child the most and you get the most trouble from them. Back of the hand, Believe me.

THE COURT (*To the reporter*): Will you take this down, please?

(*The parties took seats in the back of the courtroom.*)

DR. FISHMAN: Pauline Burt and Dr. Anthony Burt were examined by Clinic Psychiatrist Dr. S. K. Eastman on 2/21/71. As a result of this examination, Mrs. Pauline Burt was found to be actively psychotic, extremely depressed, agitated, and in need of immediate hospitalization. It was Dr. Eastman's recommendation that this woman be remanded to the Department of Hospitals immediately.

THE COURT: Did you talk to the son about this? Does he know what the recommendation is?

DR. FISHMAN: I don't know.

THE COURT: I mean: You didn't tell him?

DR. FISHMAN: No.

THE COURT: All right.

COURT OFFICER: Do you want them back, Your Honor?

THE COURT: Yes. Come up, please.

(*The parties came forward.*)

THE COURT: I have had a report from the Court Psychologist. What do you wish us to do, Doctor? How do you feel about this?

PETITIONER: I want what is best for my mother and my family at the same time. If she needs help, I would like her to have help.

THE COURT: It appears from the examination that the Respondent needs hospital care. Do you yourself feel that this is the best thing?

PETITIONER: I would think so, yes. If they feel it's necessary. I can only go by somebody else's opinion.

RESPONDENT: May I say something?

THE COURT: Yes, madam.

RESPONDENT: You're talking about hospital care. I have never been sick a day in my life. Thirty-one years married to my husband; never in a hospital; never; never been to a doctor, and neither my husband. Now all of a sudden I need hospital care? All I need is a kind word. That's all I need, believe me. I had a good job for six years. They said I was the best worker they ever had. I left myself. They said I could go back any time. I need hospital care? I think his wife is the one who needs the hospital, believe me. Another person would have collapsed long ago from what I've gone through. I know now how it feels. An innocent person going to an electric chair.

THE COURT: The calendar for the 3rd, is it still—

COURT OFFICER: The 3rd will be fine, Your Honor. It's an arbitrary date. She may return sooner, and it may be extended.

THE COURT: I mean: We are not overcrowded for that date?

COURT OFFICER: No.

THE COURT: I wonder if we need get any Probation inquiry in the meantime.

DR. FISHMAN: I doubt it.

THE COURT: No. All right, the Respondent is remanded to the Department of Hospitals for psychiatric examination to March 3, 1964.

RESPONDENT: Oh, my God. What are you—I need no more psychiatric care than a man in the moon. I need a kind word; I need a kind word.

Many Courts Are Just "Too Much" for Some Judges

Many, many times I have sat down to have lunch with a busy judge only to see the same thing: after the morning sessions, they were too drained and dragged out to eat. They'd worked four hours already—they'd worked all week—without loosening a visible chip from the backlog.

They were beat, baffled, and discouraged. Angry, too. Instead of eating, perhaps they'd finger a martini while the flounder just sat there, cooling; sometimes they'd leave the table without lunch at all, a single bite of pie and some tossed-off coffee, poor for their own nerves, poor for the families waiting.

In the featureless, airless waiting areas, the smell of cramped and nervous visitors, of fighting relatives and squalling kids can be worse than oppressive. It can be overpowering.

Nervous people give off an odor the calm do not. After ten in the morning, it becomes noticeable. By noon it is pervasive and sticky. It hangs in the dim atmosphere as something contaminating and touchable. It is still there when the cleaning crew comes in. But the crew can't dispel it either, for it has attached itself to the skin of the walls.

I remember this smell. I had encountered it before, when making tapes and documentaries in fourteen of America's mental hospitals, for both radio and television. It's a steerage smell, feculent, fecal, and there's death and despair in it.

But this is life for many judges.

Though there are no visitors save me, the pressure on the judges comes from the punishing ceaselessness of the daily procession. It has no end.

I soon grew to pity the judges and the grinding, mauling regimen of the papers that were choking them. The American illusion of the remote judge, dignified, unhurried, and rather splendid in his isolation and omnipotence, is an illusion only. A picture of most city courts is more like life in a motorcycle repair shop, judges jumping like grease-monkeys from valve to piston to sprung forks and blown rear tires, sweat everywhere, and court officers bobbing about as if with welding torches instead of the briefs, depositions, and probation reports of suffering people; people who will not be heard that day, people who will take the wrong bus going home.

Many of the courts are rickety-rackety midways and not courts at all. Funless charades unrelated to order, efficiency, or sense. This Grand March of the stationary and the waiting is a world of herded Neanderthals, of scared lemurs and garish mandrills, dressed for a circus that seems never to start or end, all tensed up for cues that no one gives. It is strangely dead yet strangely animate, like a huddle of slaves waiting to be whipped or hanged or shipped out.

Because of these melancholy back-ups, every city in America loses good judges every year. They can't stand the spiritual degradation of the climate they have to work in. They cannot any longer take the assault on their skills and training. They cannot, or in conscience will not, put up with such shabby handling of local justice.

They just close their briefcases and go home. And resign.

Stepping down after more than 22 years of service, first as Magistrate, then county judge, and finally Criminal Court judge, was Judge Simon Silver. Here is what he said:

"I am fed up with the congestion of the courts. I have had to spend more time on adjournments than in devoting my attention to listening, considering, and disposing."

Judge Simon faced a calendar of more than 150 cases a day.

"We need more judges, at least forty more. And more courtrooms. I find I can't dispose satisfactorily of more than fifteen cases a day. The rest are adjourned. It's just as bad in the Bronx and Brooklyn as it is in Manhattan."

To Judge Silver it was a loss of a $30,000-a-year job. New York's loss was much more, for Judge Silver had an influential name, a big one, in the spreading need for the rehabilitation of addicts. He believed in and worked for residence therapy for addicts, not lock-in. His crusade that "anything is preferable to jail terms" instantly recalled the hammerings of Anna Kross on the very same issue, years before. Judge Silver was one of the "tireless" judges, and was associate chairman of the Board of Directors of University Settlement, a body concerned with the welfare of the children of ethnic groups on the Lower East Side.

But last year Judge Silver quit.

This year Judge J. Howard Rossbach quit. He was from the same court. He had served sixteen years. His term was to run through 1975.

"My retirement is prompted by the feeling that in this court we are not treating human begins the way they should be treated. It is due to the horrible case-loads in some parts, and to the wretched facilities in which we have to work. The courthouse facilities are so shabby, I am ashamed to have anyone visit me there. By summer it will be worse: prisoners jammed into sweltering cells and

holding pens. Youths tried in sweltering courtrooms. For years we
and the Bronx Family Court have been promised a new courthouse. For years this project has been fiddled and faddled among
the city departments. We still have no courthouse worthy of the
name. In Manhattan I tried some cases in courtrooms measuring
ten feet by ten. Cubbyholes."

No money. Who cares?

There will be more of this. New York has no monopoly on
defecting judges.

Do People Ever Thank the Courts That Served Them?

In attending the closed trials of Family Court, or in reading
transcripts of the proceedings, certain phrases keep returning:

"To see what can be done to help him . . ."
"To straighten out your trouble . . ."
"To keep this family together . . ."
"To see the children have a proper home . . ."
"To stabilize . . ."
"To lift . . ."
"To remove these persisting frictions . . ."
"To help him keep his job . . ."
"To reason . . ."
"To try again . . ."
"To protect . . ."

The full thrust in the structure of these courts is affirmative,
constructive, and healing. Judges can be severe, and are severe,
when this is called for, but the overlay of practical, non-sentimen-
tal benevolence is present in every case. It fills the air. Quarrelling
couples, angry and hurt, come to these courts with heavy cargoes
of spleen, often to find the spleen dissolving in the climate of
sensibleness; or in hearing their situation reviewed by a fair,
searching man, or an attentive, searching woman. This, to them, is
new.

Petitioner and Respondent come in, embattled, and many times
leave disarmed, defused—leave with the feeling that they aren't
being tried so much as X-rayed. Resentments often evaporate or
begin to. Aggressions, once indulged, are regretted, or looked back
on with diminishing rancor.

Both sides have had a full chance to unburden. And once before a judge, though no one is rushed, the experience hasn't taken long. Workable solutions, calmly presented, are *seen* as workable. From the wisdom of the bench, emphases fall on the plusses, on acknowledged and statable values, on respect, on love of the children, on convenience of home, the blessings of familiar surroundings and a sense of belonging to a community, of being a living part of an operating microcosm which, though faulty, is basically sound, basically rewarding.

Their situation isn't quite so tough as they thought.

Very few leave any of these courtrooms with the same rage that brought them here. Most appreciate, in the true sense of that word, what has happened to them, and though they may not appreciate the judiciary evolution, the cost, the effort, or the apparatus through which they are being heard, they do sense its fairness. And they respect, without resenting, its authority. Most of them go away with quiet gratitude, their worst problem lifted.

Do they ever say thank you?

Hundreds do. And do so in words no fiction writer could make up.

To Court Clerk, Nathan Grossman,* 80 Lafayette Street:

I wish to thank the court, the clerks and all I met who were most kind and helpful when I was so helplessly hurt and confused.

> Thanking you . . . (signed by both
> husband and wife)

Att: Intake Desk: Sift Desk: Room 506

To whom it may concern:

On June 3rd of 1965, I, Mrs. Leona Marshal, filed a complaint against my husband, Martin, charging him with brutality. However it is no longer necessary for me to persue the matter any further. On July 10th of 1965 I learned that Martin had entered a hospital in Anniston, Alabama (his home), and will undergo a very serious operation that may well be the death of him.

Having already gotten my affairs in order, I am flying there tonight to be at his bedside.

---

* Nathan Grossman, now retired, was one of the finest, most dedicated and scholarly court clerks in New York's history. Respected by all judges, he would have made a great judge himself. He was a superior and gifted man.

In the event that he pulls through, we will be living there permi-nately. Thanking you for your kind understanding and concideration, I remain . . .

Mr. Nathan Grossman, Clerk of the Court
80 Lafayette Street
New York, 10013
Dear Sir:

I feel that our initial visit to Family Court made us more aware of our differences and caused us to review and see them in a new perspective. Therefore, the Court has been instrumental in helping to settle our problem and we thank you.

Dear Mr. Grossman:

Please express our deepest appreciation and extend our heartfelt thanks to your entire staff for the understanding and help they afforded my family in the trying months past.

We approached the Home Term Court as a last resort—having failed to cope with our problem ourselves. Every individual with whom we came in contact—receptionists, examiners, clerks, the probation officers, psychiatrists, and judges devoted their time and extended genuine sympathy and understanding to us. Each of these individuals made every effort to help with the ultimate solution of the problem on a personal, warm basis.

At this point, the problem is still not resolved; but thanks to your accumulative efforts is on its way to a possible satisfactory solution.

Please feel that your efforts are sincerely appreciated. We are sure that many others, like ourselves, are grateful for the help and effort which you continually extend.

Very truly yours,
(signed by husband)

Child Abuse

All over America parents are killing their children, burning them over open flames at kitchen ranges, burning them with ciga-rette lighters, electric toasters, radiators, hitting them with ham-mers and chairs, throwing them down stairs, scarifying their backs with paring knives, puncturing them with ice picks, blinding them, starving them, stuffing them in closets to suffocate, smothering them with plastic bags, whipping them with rug-beaters, throwing them out of windows, drowning them in laundry tubs.

In a vigorous effort some years ago to bring television cameras into Children's Court (so the public could see what the "children" had done and see the children who had done it), I met, among many other remarkable men, the then director—Alfred Cohen— of the Warwick Training School. Warwick is a facility for "incor- rigibles" in the Catskills. I am still haunted by one sentence that came out of him: "I've never had a boy at Warwick who hadn't been cruelly beaten at home."

This came sharply back to mind when I was talking with Charles Lindner, of New York's Probation Services, especially his remark about the kind of American home and the atmosphere of home life of the "problem" family being the breeding-ground of "mon- sters"; that the beaten child, if he survived, would torture his own if he had them.

Our prisoners come from these homes. Our murderers come from them. The abused child, early crippled, soon emerges as a chilling risk himself and is in trouble in his early teens. He's hurt, lawless, and vengeful. He has nothing but teenage strength, con- suming fear and hate, and no restraints at all. No hope, no regard, and nothing to keep him alive but feral self-preservativeness and a weapon.

But when this child was four years old, recovering from frac- tures of both arms, what did his parents say to the authorities?

"I had an epileptic seizure and fell down the stairs with him."

"She fell out of her crib and broke her leg."

"He was playing in the bathroom and fell in the tub."

In child-abuse cases all the parents lie. Hospitals make the repairs if the child is alive. Doctors do little "reporting."

Newspapers have gone after this, but most media, national magazines and television especially, won't touch the subject—too "offensive" to readers or viewers, too hideous to think about.

Over 700 cases were reported last year in Los Angeles County alone. If one was to prepare this statistic to be in proportion with every county across our nation, we would see where this involved thousands of children each year. I would hate to contemplate how many of these result in death.*

---

* From first paragraph of a letter by Mrs. Teri Ballas, ex-child abuser, and a member of Mothers Anonymous, Dec. 24, 1970, from the Appendix of the "Final Report of Mayor Lindsay's Task Force on Child Abuse and Neglect."

Some of these grisly horrors came to professional attention in 1962 when C. H. Kempe's article appeared in the *Journal of the American Medical Association* and the "battered child syndrome" was first discussed. Since that date many medical journals have carried articles on the same subject, and much legislation exists. In fact today all fifty states have child-abuse laws making it mandatory to report cases of child abuse, as proposed by the Children's Bureau. But the laws aren't working. There are four reasons:

1. The reluctance of physicians to report
2. Traditional yielding to parental authority by the courts
3. Overlapping of investigations
4. Interposition of numerous social service agencies

There also should be mentioned this additional reason: parents of these maimed or scalded infants and children take their small victims to one hospital after another. This way they avoid "pattern" detection. The very young, those under three, can't tell doctors what happened. Older children—four to ten—are fearful of more beatings if they reveal the true story.

Who does this beating and torturing?

"In evaluating our cases of child abuse at St. Vincent's Hospital and Medical Center, it appeared that the battered children were usually the victims of emotionally crippled parents, beginning with unfortunate circumstances surrounding the parents' own childhood. The "battering" parent reacts toward his own child as a result of past personal experience of loneliness, lack of love, lack of protection. Some of the mothers have been cared for by a variety of foster parents during their own childhood. Such mothers are unable to react normally to the needs of the infant and can't distinguish between their own childhood suffering and their vicious reaction toward their own children."*

A little more each day the situation for such sorry children is getting recognition; and, slowly, getting some help. But not enough, and not soon enough. From the same letter of Dr. Fontana, just cited, there are other and deeper obstacles:

* From a Letter to the Editor, by Vincent J. Fontana, M.D., appearing in the *N.Y. State Journal of Medicine*, Aug. 15, 1968. Copyright 1968 by the Medical Society of the State on New York.

It would seem at this time [1968] that a hopeless situation exists in assisting or rehabilitating the parents who are responsible. Not enough studies have been accumulated to give psychiatrists direction. . . . Hopeless also in that many of these parents not only do not seek out help but resist any type of psychologic or social assistance when it is offered.

Why do such parents refuse help?

E. Elmer, in "Hazards in Determining Child Abuse" (in *Child Welfare*, January, 1966) had this theory:

The array of emotional attitudes toward abuse, the sparseness of descriptive literature, the comparative absence of study, all lead to the hypothesis of a social taboo in this area. . . . We (average parents) resent the evidence that vindictive impulses exist in others and may, therefore, exist in ourselves. Hence the "cloak of silence" and the determined actions to eliminate the evidence, or to disregard it.

Our medical schools don't teach young doctors either the existence, extent, presenting evidence, or management techniques of the problem, any more than they do for alcoholism. Physicians are reluctant to report cases of child abuse for fear of law suits. Dr. Fontana advocates legislation that will make all doctors and hospital personnel immune to any possible civil or criminal action. In this area the traditional relationship of doctor-patient confidentiality must be broken up. It does not belong here. Murder is going on. Also to be discarded: the old concept, still very much alive in Family Courts: "Mother belongs to child and child belongs to Mother."

Why do parents get into insensate rages against tiny children? Partly, as has been said, because they had such a rotten time as children themselves. Liquor, joblessness, and immaturity load the risk. So do drugs. The physical condition of the child, at birth, is a factor:

"We noted that over 50 percent of these children who were abused or neglected were prematurely born and of low birth weight. These premature children were usually slower in development than the normal newborn. Parents of such infants are often unable to cope with the slow development of the expremature child. When the child is not able to perform, the parent may be "triggered" into a reaction, leading to inflicted abuse. . . . One can speculate that there might

be a conscious, or unconscious, rejection of the infant by this type
of parent."*

In March, 1969, the savage destruction of four-year-old Rox-
anne Felumero rocked this whole country; rocked it because it was
found out, not because it was new. The New York *Daily News* ran
an important campaign of pure outrage that many other papers
copied. The child was beaten by its mother and stepfather, its
sweater pockets were stuffed with rocks, then the child was thrown
into the East River. I am not going to get my oar into this, nor
name names. On two occasions I attended hearings in the court
where the judge, who returned this child to the people who killed
her, was presiding. She had received no reports the home was
dangerous. This judge seemed to me to be both compassionate
and perceptive, and I am convinced that blame for this frightful
misjudgment must be shared by many, for a prognosis of extreme
risk to this child was never given the judge. She suffered a breakdown and left the bench.

Offending parents can and do put up a convincing front of
innocence, of masqueraded love, and of caring. And they can, and
do, fool many social workers. Homes, attitudes, and the *seeming*
concern of parents in which the most unspeakable cruelties have
just taken place, can appear well ordered, even serene.

The three cases which follow illustrate this very point. These
cases were first published by the *New England Journal of Medicine* (Dec. 26, 1963). Aside from the shuddery aspects of what
was done to the children, you will note that experienced case-
workers who inspected the home situation found this to be all
right.

CASE 1

The patient was born prematurely after 6 months' gestation. At
the age of 1 year she was taken to a hospital emergency room with
a history of having fallen out of her crib. X-ray study revealed fractures of the right and left wrists. She was not admitted to the hospital at the time. Several weeks later the mother took her to another
hospital, where the mother stated that she had "tripped" with her
baby and noted swelling of the ankles. Fractured right and left

* "Further Reflections on Maltreatment of Children," by Vincent J.
Fontana, M.D., quoted from the *N.Y. State Journal of Medicine*, Aug.
15, 1968.

ankles were noted on X-ray examination. Two months later the patient was admitted to a 3d hospital with a fractured left arm and signs of malnutrition. X-ray study at the hospital revealed healed old fractures as well as the newly incurred fracture of the left humerus. The case was referred to social-service workers, who, after investigation, reported the parents' denial of having inflicted trauma and considered the home environment adequate. No further action was taken in view of the social-service report. At the age of 2 this patient was admitted to the hospital with multiple fractures and symptoms strongly suggesting rickets or scurvy. The case was again studied by the social-service section of the hospital, and again the home environment was found acceptable. The Society for the Prevention of Cruelty to Children investigated the family problem to rule out physical abuse of the child. At that time the mother stated that she was a victim of "epileptic seizures." The Society felt sure that the injuries sustained by the patient were due to trauma incurred during the mother's seizures and not any negligence or abuse on the part of the parents. Six months later the child was taken to the emergency room of a hospital, where she was pronounced dead on arrival. The mother stated that she had fallen down a flight of stairs with the child in her arms. At the time the mother brought the patient to the emergency room, there were no signs of trauma on any part of the mother's body.

On autopsy the following findings were noted: contusions of the scalp and face; subdural hemorrhages; cerebral edema; multiple abrasions of the face and extremities, with scab formation; old lacerations of the lips; multiple contusions of the body. A diagnosis of maltreatment was made by the medical examiner but no legal action was taken at the time.

CASE 2

Several months later the 1-month-old sibling of Case 1 was admitted to the hospital with a diagnosis of malnutrition, dehydration and possible vitamin deficiency. The patient responded well to supportive measures and was discharged in good condition. Two weeks later examination in the pediatric follow-up clinic revealed soft tissue swelling of the left wrist and left thigh. The patient was admitted to the hospital, and X-ray study showed fractures of the distal end of the left radius and ulna. The possibility of pathologic fractures was considered, but laboratory data were all within normal limits. Inflicted trauma was suspected, and data on the medical past history of the patient and siblings was obtained. The "accidental-death" report of the sibling in Case 1 prompted further investigations, which confirmed the diagnosis of maltreatment in Case 2. The parents persisted in their denials of inflicted trauma and abuse and expressed concern for the welfare of their children. The mother impressed both physicians and social-service workers with her affection and care of her 4 children. Her clinic visits gave further evidence of her "motherly" affection; the children appeared well dressed, and there was no obvious indication of neglect.

CASE 3

A 6-week-old infant was admitted to the hospital because of swelling of the right thigh of 4 days' duration. The mother stated to the examining physician that the child had fallen from the crib and struck its right leg on the floor. X-ray examination revealed complete fracture through the mid-shaft of the right femur with posterior displacement of the distal fragment. The patient was in Bryant's traction for 2 weeks and was discharged in good condition after application of a hip spica. A few weeks later the child was admitted to another hospital with multiple contusions and abrasions. Investigation by the social-service department indicated that the father had thrown the child on the floor, shattering the case and inflicting serious head trauma, resulting in bilateral subdural hematomas. The child was recently seen in the pediatric clinic, where multiple signs of intracranial damage were noted. The child was blind and mentally retarded.

Most active in the hidden battle to save the battered child is Dr. Vincent J. Fontana, Director of Pediatrics at St. Vincent's Hospital, and Medical Director of the New York Foundling Hospital. He prefers, and uses, the phrase "maltreatment syndrome" instead of "battered child syndrome" and for a good reason. He says: "A maltreated child often shows no obvious signs of being 'battered,' since this is the last phase of the spectrum." It is usually preceded by nutritional deprivation, dehydration, and emotional starvation.

The story the parents tell is usually quite different from the clinical and X-ray findings. The families themselves show evidence of being multi-problem families, severe problems existing at the time of marriage, with a multiplication of these right after. In his own writings, and in the preparation of the "Task Force Report," the contribution of alcohol is mentioned over and over again. So is the need for Family Courts to get off the dead stump of tradition, and for doctors to do the same: "The moral responsibility is to the maltreated child."

In courage and in public service, Dr. Fontana ranks with another great physician, Howard Rusk, who in a related field is patching up and bringing back to life and use many hundreds who would not have made it otherwise.

It is another example of Mayor Lindsay's awareness of who is doing what that he should have selected Dr. Fontana to construct the Task Force, some of whose principle recommendations will now be looked at.

The Mayor's Task Force in Child Abuse and Neglect

In 1964, the New York State Legislature enacted a child-abuse law. It contains the first registry of child-abuse cases in the eastern United States. In 1970 more than 1,700 cases of child abuse were reported to this Central Registry in New York City alone. It has its own phone—431-4680. It is in service all day, all night, all week, all seven days of it.

Its purpose: to be sure the 1964 mandate is working; that abused children are being reported. The Executive Director of the American Humane Society has stated that "no community in the U.S. has an adequate child protective program." The objective of the Task Force is to build one that is. Here is a summary:

1. The Central Registry to be a repository of information concerning *all* abuse and neglect cases. This will uncover all those cases, hitherto missed, where parents have used many hospitals to hide what they've done.
2. This information to be instantly available to the medical profession. It is now available only to the Bureau of Child Welfare.
3. The same information to be available to Family Court.
4. Inclusion of *neglect* (besides abuse) as part of the information, neglect often being more serious. ("All abused children are neglected, but not all neglected children are abused.")
5. Computerization of material, for instant retrieval.
6. *One* caseworker to be responsible for a reported case. (There were 7 in the Felumero tragedy.)
7. Use of separate divisions in protective and preventive services of the BCW should be abolished.
8. Since Probation admits great difficulty in following up court

recommendations in abuse and neglect findings, it is recommended that Probation phase out its responsibility here, letting it fall to the Department of Social Services and one caseworker only.

9. Since hospitals are viewed as "neutral" (non-punitive), and have the greater number of experts available, hospitals to be the locus for protective-prevention services.

10. Family Court judges, sitting in the child-abuse part, find it "emotionally draining." A child protective worker is even more deeply involved. The latter should have frequent rotation, comparable to that of the judge.

11. All cases of suspected abuse or neglect, when observed in schools, be reported through the principal's office to the BCW.

12. No case of abuse to be adjusted internally within the school, without the knowledge of the BCW.

13. Principals to be personally responsible.

14. Reporting to be kept confidential.

15. Homemaker and Day Care Services to be expanded.

16. 1,200 beds in child-caring and foster placements to be contracted for.

17. Increase of board rate to foster parents.

18. Those children "hardest to place" because they have the most needs or are from ethnic minorities: the city to provide new city-owned long-term facilities.

19. For "boarder babies," languishing in hospitals although they need no further care, some for over two years and most, on admission, only two years old: hospitals holding such children to be given a "Finder's Fee" for each temporary care facility (home) the hospital will recommend and the Department of Social Services will accept.

20. Since there is no psychiatric service for abusing parents, create one, on a pilot basis at first, to evaluate its impact. "If there's no motivation, there's no patient."

21. Group therapy for parents with the child-abuse problem.

22. Family House therapy: the whole family sitting as a single troubled unit, a multi-problem family with child-abuse as only one of many other problems.

23. Lay (surrogate-mother) therapy: introducing a parent-aide into the family structure while child is in placement.

24. A "homemaker" for persons in need of home assistance: to cook, clean, shop, and mind the child or children.
25. "Abusing and Neglectful Parents Anonymous"—rehabilitated former child-abusing mothers, called Mothers Anonymous— based directly on the Alcoholics Anonymous idea: that persons who have suffered a severe maladjustment problem, once recovered, can be of great help to those with a similar problem.
26. Hospital and doctor education must include: recognition or suspicion of abuse or neglect, plus immediate reporting of it to Department of Social Services or to BCW.

This new program was launched in March 1971. Anyone may phone in—teacher, private citizen, or neighbors (a frequent source of information—they hear the screaming).

Already very much in being is the facility called Family House. This is a projection of the Family Institute, a remarkable creation of the late Dr. Nathan Ackerman. Here troubled families—all members of it—sit down with a psychiatrist (Dr. Ackerman was one of the best) and "have it out." Each member, after the first few moments of self-conscious holding-back, begins to unload his or her beef. How the furies fly! Sass, profanity, weeping, counter-accusations, unbelievable caustic revelations tumble about the room. Incest, stealing, drug use, hidden resentments, fierce jealousy, pitiable loneliness, the deliquescent wasting of poverty, the lost aspirations and private defeats, the garish fantasies—from this spontaneous eruption, the psychiatrist presently fixes on the true source, in provocation; and fixes on the real persecutor and his (or her) actual victim.

I saw much of this action in 1969 and 1970, and wrote the story for the *Ladies' Home Journal* (March 1971).

Dr. Fontana used the word "hopeless," but that was in 1968. Now he heads up one of the sanest, most practical, most perceiving teams ever created for managing a human (inhuman) problem so common, yet so ugly, so barbaric, that most people can't bear to look at it or think about it. Today Dr. Fontana has hope, and said to me in his office quite recently: "Child abuse is a disease and it is preventable."

PART THREE

Where We Are Now

THE DILEMMA OF AMERICA'S CITIES

The Mayors

IN THE INTERMINABLE BACK-AND-FORTH about the crises in our cities, there is a conspicous omission. No one has pointed out that, in a very real sense, our cities have no status. Townships and counties do. Even election districts can claim a little. But our cities are municipal anomalies.

They are constitutional orphans with no known parentage but growth, greed, and enthusiasm. They are freaks of commerce, sports of nature, accidents of river courses, fortuitous spill-overs where the shipping could push no further because of the falls.

They grew up when no one was looking. Now, friendless and adrift, they don't know which way to turn. But large or small, they all have this in common: they're flat broke.

New York's Mayor Lindsay is not the first American Mayor to try to shake lettuce out of his state capital. All have tried. All have had to. But who owes what, and to whom, and on what basis is a real jumbo for which our best-lighted computer can't spit out an answer. Sometimes you get the money, sometimes no.

Conferences of Mayors bring out this one leavening or inhibiting (or stultifying) point of agreement: our cities have no inherent sovereign powers. Which is another way of saying they haven't much weight to throw around. No clout.

So Mayor Lindsay's beamish rides to Albany* and to Washington, his bruising confrontations there, and his melancholy returns are, to his colleagues in all our other cities, sadly familiar. They've done the same.

* "When I prepare for a journey to Albany, I think of Henry Hudson, who began his own journey as captain of the stately *Half Moon* and ended in a rowboat somewhere off the coast of Canada."—John V. Lindsay, from his book, *The City*.

163

Our cities are teeming Nobodies, located in geographical No-
wheres. It must hurt to work as hard as a Mayor only to find out
you are a Nobody; that important people don't have to recognize
you; that though they know your address, they don't need to answer your mail—and don't answer it. The Federals are as not-at-
home as the big houses in state capitals.

Cities are beggars without licenses.

Cities create most of the nation's wealth and most of its tax
base. Cities provide most of the jobs. And through Welfare, they
take care of most of the people who can't take care of themselves.
Whenever Mayors get together, their cry is the same. It is unre-
hearsed and terrifying: it is the cry of absolute desperation.

The dilemma was neatly expressed, in three tight sentences, in a
New York *Times* editorial in March 1971:

The central government siphons away the bulk of tax revenues. The
local governments confront the bulk of domestic problems. The
existing fiscal mismatch makes no sense.

The various conferences of American Mayors, and the more
recent exploitation of them in semi-spontaneous "road shows" has
changed forever the public impression of two things: what Mayors
are and what they do. And the Mayors have come out very well
indeed, for dedication to duty, for high-grade, practical intelligence, and, with a few North Jersey exceptions, for honesty. They
work day and night and get nothing for it but the public's elbow
forever in their eye. They exactly know what their cities need.
They just don't know how to get it.

Trying to ease immediate distress is not the principal job. The
principal job is trying to check the drift to complete disaster. The
case which the Mayors make for immediate Federal revenue-sharing would seem to be invincible, unanswerable. The race between
oncoming, visible collapse and last-minute Douglas Fairbanks rescue will be a photo-finish that we are all going to witness within
five years.

In April 1971, Mayor Lindsay and New York City (and Brooklyn's Brownsville) were hosts to a group of American Mayors
from all over the U.S.: Atlanta, Boston, New Orleans, Wilmington, Philadelphia, Detroit, Seattle, Baltimore, Pittsburgh, Newark,
Milwaukee. Others later joined the party.

Neither the abandoned wreckage nor the glassless window-frames of Brownsville nor its solid blocks of rubble surprised or shocked any of these fellows. It reminded them of home.

"It's just a difference of degree. We've got the same problems," said Moon Landrieu of New Orleans. "We're going down the drain."

James H. J. Tate of Philadelphia: "It's the same everyplace. That's what we're trying to tell Congress. Let me start by saying that we will lock up 26 playgrounds this summer. We don't have the money to run them."

Kevin White of Boston: "Boston is a tinder-box. It's worse. It's an armed camp. It means something that Louise Day Hicks got 49 per cent of the vote against me. Everyone—black and white—knew what she stood for. One black district voted against her 650 to 2. Look—we raise seventy per cent of our money with the property tax, but half the property in Boston is untaxable. One out of every five people is on welfare, and twenty per cent of our people are bankrupt. Could you run a business that way?"

Roman S. Gribbs of Detroit: "Unemployment is at the doorstep of the Mayors. In the inner city we have 25 per cent unemployed. Among young people it's 48 per cent. I have a "disaster plan" budget: cutting out city employees if we don't get more money. I'm going into every city service. I'll close fifteen to 31 recreation centers and six firehouses. And if you see services cut back, you'll see blowups."

Wesley C. Uhlman of Seattle: "We have 100,000 trained and educated people out of work—engineers and technicians in aerospace. It's a whole new class and no one knows how to deal with it. I love seeing these other Mayors—misery loves company!"

Harry G. Haskell of Wilmington: "We can't seem to get any help. We're dealing with alien legislatures, suburban and rural legislatures. . . . There's going to be a city that goes bankrupt because it can't sell its bonds. And that's going to happen soon."

Peter F. Flaherty of Pittsburgh: "I don't go to the state legislature to attack. I go in self-defense. I say: "Will you please stop giving new pension rights to every small group of city employees? I have to pay them and they're killing me! They don't cost you a dime!' What will I do if we get revenue sharing? I'll use it to stop

tax increases. I'll use it to keep people from jumping into the
suburbs."

Henry W. Maier of Milwaukee: "How bad is it? We have a
higher tax load than New York City and the most segregated
suburbs in the country. . . . The cities are financing social over-
head. The Federal income tax should be financing it."

Thomas J. D'Alesandro of Baltimore: "The population of Baltimore is 905,000. Of that figure, 305,000 pay the state income
tax. Of those 187,000 pay on an income *below* $3,000 a year. So
that leaves 118,000 substantial taxpayers as my base. The more I
hit them with increased real-estate taxes, the more they move out.
And the more Baltimore becomes a repository for the poor."

Moon Landrieu of New Orleans: "Our population is 593,000,
but we provide the transportation facilities, every major park, the
zoo, cultural facilities, and the airport for a metropolitan area of
over a million people. And we get nothing back from the suburbs.
They contribute nothing. We don't even get the sales tax because
of shopping centers in the suburbs. All we get is the poor. And an
eroding tax base. The trend is frightening. We tax anything that
moves."

Sam Massell Jr. of Atlanta: "Everything's coming to a head.
We need a second airport—$2 billion. That need didn't build up
overnight. The Federal government comes down and says we have
to have new water-pollution controls, but the Chattahoochie River
didn't get that way yesterday. We had to increase the police force
by 33 per cent but crime didn't become a crisis today. Now the
fire inspectors tell me City Hall should be condemned. Doesn't
meet safety standards. If we don't get help, I'm going to disap-
pear."

Kenneth A. Gibson of Newark: "We're as close to the bottom
as any American city—everything has been racial in Newark since
1967. Remember, we're sixty per cent black, ten per cent Puerto
Rican, and thirty per cent a minority group. If things aren't done
for the Newarks of this country, they will hit bottom. Then the
country will hit bottom."

The thrust of their remarks all sped toward the same target:
cities had reached the end of their taxing powers. If congressional
passage of a revenue-sharing law or if Federal takeover of all

welfare costs didn't come in time, national collapse was upon us. Doubtful of its ability to act, Mayor Uhlman of Seattle was alarmed by the make-up of Congress: who the men really were, where they had come from; their emotional remoteness from the raw horror that is now here.

"I'm just appalled about the rural and small-town types who run Congress. Maybe it would help if they were to see Brownsville."

Mayor Haskell of Wilmington obviously shared this view, at least as to the non-urban aspect of legislatures, calling them "alien." "Alien" meant rural or suburban.

Many of these Mayors had been in Washington, D.C., the month before their get-together in New York. They had come to get money, a "Marshall Plan for the cities," as Mayor Lindsay put it, with a 10-billion minimum.

Said the Mayor of San Francisco, Joseph Alioto: "The sky's falling in on us in the cities. It really is. We've had six cops killed in San Francisco since I took office. We need jobs. We need money for the poor and haven't money for either. Our people are trying to put Maginot Lines around the suburbs and zoning them. We can't go on like this. The way we're going, the capitalistic system can't survive."

"Wherever the cities are going, Newark is going to get there first," said Kenneth Gibson. "We have the worst infant morality rate and the worst maternity mortality rate of any city in the U.S. We have the worst crime rate. If we had a bubonic plague, everybody would rush to help. But we have a worse plague. And nobody notices."

Peter Flaherty of Pittsburgh: "No one can understand how lonely a Mayor feels with his problems. The people in our suburbs use all our facilities but won't pay for any of them. When I ask the county commissioners for help, they look out the window."

Roman Gribbs of Detroit: "We have to have $43 million right now, just to stay where we are. Last year we got $5 million from the state. But Michigan is now $100 million in the red. Revenue-sharing with the Federal government is our only hope."

Carl Stokes, black Mayor of Cleveland: "We're operating on $25 million less than we had a year ago. We're spending sixty per cent of our budget on police and fire. We've had to lay off 1,500 people. All our community relations activities have been wiped out."

James Reston, head of the New York *Times* Washington bureau, was as gloomy as the Mayors: "All are for revenue-sharing. But there is not enough revenue to share. Even if the President's revenue-sharing bill were passed, New York's share would add only two per cent to Mayor Lindsay's budget, which is not enough to sweep the streets."

I go back a long time and have a good memory. I remember a front-page story the summer of 1921, when Villepigue's Inn was raided for selling liquor during Prohibition. Villepigue's was a rightfully famous shore-dinner restaurant that catered to a truly colorful and sporty New York crowd: a procession of celebrities, libertines, stage beauties, gorillas, charlatans, gluttons, fighters, priests, and politicians that began coming in 1903, the year Big Jim Villepigue (who weighed 405 when he died in 1934) invented the American shore dinner and opened his vast firetrap that miraculously never had a fire. On any Saturday or Sunday in the summer, every table would have as many as five sittings. The place seated six hundred.

The location, at Ocean and Voorhies Avenues, was only five minutes from Coney Island and no more than that from the once-popular Sheepshead Bay Speedway (closed in 1915), where the first aeroplane-vs.-auto race occurred, and where Gaston Chevrolet was killed in a race which he won—he blew a tire and turned over, crossing the finish line.

Everybody who came to Villepigue's was Somebody. The night of the raid the head table had a dozen patrons, including New York's Mayor Hylan, and Police Commissioner Enright. Their statement to the press, after the raid, left an impression on me I still wear:

"Everybody knows you can't get a drink at Villepigue's. It's just as much against the law there as it is everywhere else." And that was all there was to that.

It impressed me, though—I was seventeen years old—because I had carried the drinks to their table. I was working there. I suffered what you might call an Acute Recognition of Power, or, the Mayor-as-God.

I have now lived to see a full 180-degree turnabout. It's a sad thing indeed that the gallantry, the hard bravery and sinewy resilience of today's Mayors is relegated to padding up the long, long sidewalks of state houses and the White House, each Mayor clutching a city-father hat in his hand.

This is undignified. It is also a good way for the United States to commit suicide.

In the jungle that is the overgrowth of the courts in New York City and New York State, five very different men—all of them strong, experienced, and extremely serious about the work they do, and all determined to find a way out—have started hacking at the horror that has grown up all about.

These five—a governor, a judge, a state senator, a Mayor and a district attorney—have chopped out enough of a clearing so that some sort of plan for survival can go up.

The plans are original with, and peculiar to, their respective authors, and they are very much worth a good look. Each man sees the same jungle, but each from his own bough.

Any one of these plans, if implemented, would bring immediate relief to many of the public areas that hurt most: the burned-out areas, the rained-out, the worn-out, the starved, the strangled, the smothered, and the squeezed.

Specific elements in most would serve at once to free courts of their awful congestion. Similarly, each would put a stop to the imbecilic, bird-brained, 300-year-old syndrome of prison congestion. There is sound and vigrous sense in all these plans and they therefore, because we are a race of squawkers, began getting hit on the head as soon as they were made public. Which, to some, may be "the American way" but which, if not stopped, will take us all the way down, and all the way under.

That may be where we deserve to go, deserving it as penalty for our abuse of privilege, our happy propensity to learn-nothing-from-nobody, our egregious, unconquerable, materialistic puberty, and will-the-president-of-Stauffer-Chemicals-kindly-admit-his-sulphuric-acids-have-contributed-to-the-stench-that-hangs-over-Houston? No, he will not. How can he? He's the president—he's paid to "explain" it.

I can't find anything really new to relieve the cities' agonies that is being urged on the public now that wasn't being urged on the public forty years ago by Anna Kross. Except for oil-spills, it was all here then. It is all here now. It's just worse now. We keep pushing the same big mess around while still managing to keep it in the same big room.

In the air, however, there *is* something new besides particulate matter—it is fury. That is good. Forty years ago the public might experience surprise, occasional embarrassment, even disgust. But no fury. Today America is getting a great big bellyful of *itself*; of its own massive, self-made mistakes. It has shame and that, too, is good. America is going through a cosmic kind of purification ceremony.

It has found a new Jesus in Ralph Nader, for example, a young man reared in the Jesus tradition, a man of the same geographical background, the same bold challenge. (No irreverence is to be read into this.) Nader has tipped over a lot of the statuary that has decorated the front lawn of American commerce for so long that some of our tycoons are now reading their speeches before making them.

We're beginning to know how we're being fleeced. We're wising up. Someday we may find a vitamin showing up in a Cheerio. We know who's been gypping us. We're sick of paying out so much and getting back so little. We're sick of seeing so many of our business leaders showing up as naïve, churlish, or incompetent; or major businesses run by lawyers who are champions of slack fill or public apologists for the watered hot-dog.

We are not yet at the moment of truth. But we are positively at the moment of accounting. "Consumerism" is not a mere word, as "rehabilitation" is a mere word. Consumerism means going up to the manager of a chain store and asking him what the hell he means by this tapioca.

There is a contagion of direct confrontation. It is going to stay in the American atmosphere a long time. There is a new climate of truth, a fierce challenge of half-truth. And there is a desperation about it: a sudden willingness to throw old beliefs in the ashcan. If it doesn't work, junk it.

You've seen some of the complaints, some of the angry bewilderments, of more than a dozen American Mayors. Your own Mayor could add surprises to those listed. It's an extraordinarily vocal era through which we are passing and some of our most articulate men now have the mike. They mean what they say and many of them occupy positions of such influence, they are going to see, in their lifetime, some healthy beheadings, and the conversion of plans into visible and coherent projects.

THE FIVE PROPOSALS

In the pages which now follow, there are five separate plans for change, big change, immediate change; recommendations by experts and battlers who know what's wrong and how to fix it.

The first is Mayor Lindsay's proposal: clear up the courts.

John Vliet Lindsay rang the full carillon when he went after New York's court system. He opened up, for all the public to see and consider, a long-smouldering feud between his own city administration and the judicial administration. Of course there was clamorous rebuttal. But everything has been spread out now, for everyone to look at. As usual he was quite direct, his language simple.

On Saturday, October 10, 1970, before the Administrative Board of the Judical Conference, he recommended the following:

1. The Lindsay Proposal

a. The courts should go into emergency session on nights and weekends until the backlog is cleared

b. The state narcotics program should fulfill its pledge to treat the thousands of criminal addicts now in city jails. If they were in state treatment facilities, the jails would no longer be overcrowded

c. Bail policies to be drastically overhauled. . . . But beyond cash alternative and bail reduction, the most important reform: a time limit on detention

d. This administrative board should take direct responsibility for the daily operation and efficiency of the judicial system. . . . Only the board can stop the flagrant abuse of adjournments by court officials and the private bar

e. The New York City Criminal Court should be abolished

f. Limit the criminal courts to serious crimes

Rebuttal, of course, was not long in coming, and from an appropriate source. State Supreme Court Justice Edward R. Dudley, administrative judge of the city's Criminal Courts, said the Mayor had "misplaced the emphasis"; that "he should have examined more closely the entire criminal justice system, not just the courts."

Justice Dudley then maintained New York had one of the most liberal bail systems in the U.S., and that of 80,000 cases pending in the city's Criminal Courts there were only 3,500 defendants in jail. He said, regarding bail, that judges every ten days reviewed cases of those unable to raise bail. (See the opinion of District Attorney Frank Hogan regarding bail, p. 173n.) He agreed to Mayor Lindsay's recommendation of a state takeover of the Criminal Courts, but claimed that judges handled 250,000 cases a year and had the highest disposition rate of any judges in the nation.

"We are all dissatisfied," Justice Dudley concluded, "but the Mayor is wrong in trying to put blame on the courts. You're going to have to look closer at the entire system—Probation, the Correction Department, Legal Aid, the district attorneys."

The Mayor *had* looked at all these, and for the full time he had been in office—about four years at that time. And he had severe counters, as he does whenever challenged.

"The prison riots we've just had are due partly to a clogged Criminal Court calendar. The riots themselves are the result of grievances so intense that desperate men were driven to violence despite the presence of overwhelming force against them. The crisis is very real. Whenever we deal with a problem in criminal justice, we inevitably end up facing the problem of court delay. As a result of these delays, the police become cynical and wonder what good the next arrest is going to do. The city prison becomes a human storage-house, and society pays the ultimate price." How so? "Felons bargain their serious crimes down to misdemeanors and the robber walks away laughing at the law."

The felon can go out laughing at the law. But you can't. He's really laughing at you. He's laughing at me. This is what is beginning to get through, finally, to the average man. If you wish a fine example of how felony charges (here the felon is a killer, not a mere robber) can be reduced to a point where any right-thinking, red-blooded, white-livered, true-blue felon would bust out laughing, here it is:

Nicholas Bianco, a reputed member of the Mafia, was indicted with fifteen other men for conspiracy to murder 22 men in the so-called Gallo War in Brooklyn. This was ten years ago, 1962. Twelve were killed. The executioners were members of the "family" of the late Joseph Profaci. The gunmen were not the best, for although they hit all 22, ten of them were merely winged, and they survived.

Conspiracy to murder carries a maximum sentence of fifteen years. The indicted men—Mr. Bianco and his fifteen colleagues—pleaded guilty, but guilty to a lesser offense. For himself, Mr. Bianco pleaded guilty to "conspiracy to commit assault," which is a misdemeanor.

He was sentenced to three months.*

Justice Dudley had mentioned Probation, Correction, Legal Aid, and district attorneys. Mayor Lindsay had immediate responses: that the city's adult detention facilities were, as of that moment, at 183 per cent of capacity (nearly double), and that sixty per cent of the inmates "are suspected narcotics-addicts who, by law, should be in a state treatment facility."

Other facts: 54 new judges were added to the Supreme and Criminal Courts during the previous year (1969); Probation money had tripled since 1967; the Correction Department budget had doubled.

After the riots, some hideous causes came into sharper focus. The records of the full prison population for the year 1968 were studied to see how long they'd had to wait for trial, this delay being their principal grievance.

Forty-three per cent had been in detention for over a year.

---

* Plea bargaining, which started in the Middle Ages as a way of tempering justice with mercy, has some positive humane use today, despite its abuses. One assistant district attorney put it this way: "If you get an eighteen-year-old for possession of an ounce of marijuana, you don't want to see him get a felony record and ruin his life, so you offer him a chance to plead to misdemeanor."

Further, serious overload of cases in New York makes plea bargaining a necessary evil. In the words of D.A. Frank Hogan: "It can readily be appreciated that if half of the 7,000 defendants accused of crimes in Supreme Court had demanded trials, the situation would have become completely unmanageable. Plea bargaining thus becomes a necessity because prosecutors, judges, courtrooms, and defense counsel are too few to staff the number of possible trials."

Put another way: not enough money to do the job.

Of the same population, half of those detained through trial were found not guilty, or, if convicted, were sentenced to time already served. Only 2.6 per cent finally received sentences of more than a year.

When the catch is so skimpy, why bother to arrest?

"These figures pinpoint our delay problems," the Mayor pleaded. "They reveal that too many defendants are subjected to the tragedy of lengthy detention before guilt or innocence has been decided. Above all else, we must fulfill the mandate of a speedy trial. A defendant should be held only a set time before trial. A sixty-day limit on detention would reduce the current detention population by 46 per cent. . . .

"In February 1969, the Administrative Judge of the city's Criminal Court stated that the judges' work schedules were lax. He criticized their failure to put in a full day's work. He said the courts were improperly run. Why build expensive new court facilities when the public sees existing courtrooms in session only a few hours each day?"

That is a real good question. The Mayor had some others: "Can anyone tell us the nature and numbers of the Criminal Court case backlog? No. Costly analyses have produced only frustration with the incredible state of court records. Researchers have derived, from the same data, backlog figures ranging from 90,000 to 345,000 cases! How can you make plans with figures like these?

"In summer months, calendar listings are scandalously low in number. Even in the courtrooms that are open, activity is often limited to two or three hours. How should we characterize a system of discipline that permits this to continue, while detained prisoners lie crowded in the scorching heat of a prison?

"Long calendar calls by judges produce adjournment rates in Criminal Court of between forty and fifty per cent. This situation goes on and on and on. Some defense attorneys procure adjournments as a lever to collect their fees. Do countless unproductive calendar calls represent good management?

"In State Supreme Court, a prisoner may wait five to six weeks before a grand jury indictment is returned. Why?

"In State Supreme Court, many convicted prisoners must wait sixty days or more for sentencing. Why?

"As of June 1970, of State Supreme Court defendants in deten-

tion, only 43 per cent were awaiting trial. Fifty-seven per cent
were awaiting indictment, or awaiting sentence after conviction.
Why?

"These facts cry out for change. If drastic reforms are not
forthcoming, I am prepared to request a delegation of management authority for courts within the city, from the state's judiciary
to the city's executive branch. New York City spends almost fifteen per cent of the total criminal justice funds expended by all
state and local governments in the entire U.S. That's a heavy load
for a city with just four per cent of the national population. Since
New York City is paying most of the judicial bill, the courts must
be publicly accountable to the city's taxpayers. Citizens have as
much right to expect performance from the courts as from the
police or hospitals."

His full report and accompanying comments are too long to
reproduce, but aside from the half-used courtrooms and summer
layoffs, an amazing waste of time and money relates to the city's
effort to control gambling. Figures the Mayor produced showed
that the city spent forty times as much in one month, enforcing
anti-gambling laws, as it received in fines! "No one was sent to
jail," said the Mayor, "and in one borough, a month of fruitless
anti-gambling action cost the city $230,000."

2. A State Senator's Proposal

State Senator John H. Hughes of Syracuse, chairman of the
Joint Legislative Committee on Crime and one of the finest public
servants this body has ever had, brought some insurance runs to the
Lindsay team. His was a completely independent appeal for over-
haul of the justice system, before the "system ended in total
breakdown." His speech in the Albany Assembly came at about
the same time as did the Mayor's in New York. Like the Mayor,
he stressed "professionalism of management." His principal warning: "The past pattern of increasing penalties which are not imposed; legislating new crimes which are not enforced; creating new
rehabilitative agencies which do not rehabilitate is an exercise in
futility." He'd seen the same attrition, as an upstate legislator, that
Lindsay was—is—living with in Manhattan, and adjacent boroughs. (The situation is so bad, it recalls Allen Ginsberg's neatly

pejorative description of the general condition of America today: "Apocalyptic drivelhood.")

The proposals of Senator Hughes:

a. Administrative responsibilities of the court system should be turned over to professional managers employing modern business methods to relieve judges of non-judicial duties

b. Para-judicial personnel should be added to all criminal courts to relieve judges of the time-consuming pre-trial hearings

c. Legislation should be enacted to create a single state agency to supervise the custody and rehabilitation of all persons held prisoner, including those awaiting criminal charges

d. A program of career service for assistant district attorneys should be developed to provide continuing professional staffs for elected district attorneys (on this point, see District Attorney Frank Hogan's proposal)

e. A constitutional amendment which would create a state department of justice

f. New legislation to strengthen the grand jury system

g. A new board to review all sentences passed by judges in criminal cases.

h. State financing of all courts having felony jurisdiction

i. A review of the Family Court and its procedures

j. Consolidation of small police departments in the state into larger, more effective units

If you think the last item is of little importance, you are wrong. Overlapping or blurred and disputed police authorities is a gigantic waste of the public's money; and it is nationwide. In a very limited section of Rockland County, N.Y., for example, the treasurers of seven towns pooled enough municipal money to pay for some professional help, and secured the services of one of New York City's "grand old men"—now retired—of the police department—former Inspector August Flath—to study the problem.

He did so, and found 23 separate and independent police jurisdictions within an area of sixteen miles. Much of this duplicating and overlapping (and costly) police sprawl was in and around towns within sight of the Hudson River and Tappan Zee Bridge, the short stretch along the west shore from Piermont to Upper Nyack, and inland as far as Orangeburg and Blauvelt. Inspector Flath and a police colleague unified the services, and saved these communities many thousands of dollars a year in salaries and equipment maintenance.

Such fragmentation is not uncommon. It is general. Ramsey Clark, in his book, *Crime in America,* reports that the U.S. "has a crazy-quilt pattern of 40,000 police jurisdictions. Major urban counties have scores of police jurisdictions within their borders. . . . St. Louis County has more than a hundred."

The attrition of effective police management of local areas gets worse, not better, as populations grow. A startling figure emerged when Milton Levine, supervisor of the town of Fallsburgh, told a New York State commission, on June 21, 1971, in White Plains, that the state was crippled by trying to operate under *3,485 types of local government.*

It is the local governments, of course, who are the fathers of each of these 40,000 police jurisdictions. One can easily see how the "children" of such ancestry, sired by fortuity, local custom, and regional prejudice, can range in discernment and natural aptitude for police work, from the very good to the altogether grotesque and satanic.

What does such sprawl and splatter mean to an offender? It means, for example, that if you are one of America's twenty million users of marijuana and if you are arrested you can be sentenced from six months to *life.*

It depends on *where* you were arrested.

This is the kind of nonsense Senator Hughes is trying to correct (the last item in the decalogue just seen.) *

3. Governor Rockefeller's Plan to Improve State Courts

Less than a week after New York's Mayor Lindsay placed most of the blame for court congestion on the judges, Nelson Rockefeller offered a nine-point program. He made no reference to the anger the Mayor's remarks had flung into the air but he did note, in a brief prefatory statement, that "recommendations for improvement of our judicial system which are limited to the courts

* The same fragmentation has infected courts. What does Senator Hughes mean, in the first item, by "non-judicial duties?" In an interview after his formal talk, he supplied a clue: "One judge I know has had to spend most of his time recently arranging for the painting of his courthouse."

alone are by themselves inadequate." He characterized his own proposals as both "judicial" and "executive." Here they are:

1. Increase state aid for the construction of additional court facilities
2. Establish a special narcotics court
3. Remove additional non-criminal cases from the courts
4. Reoffer an amendment to allow felony defendants to waive indictment by a grand jury
5. Create additional judgeships for New York City
6. Emphasize court reform projects financed through the State Crime Control Planning Board
7. Remove automobile-accident cases from the courts
8. Develop an effective statistical reporting system for courts to improve accountability and administration
9. Support the efforts of the Temporary State Commission to find ways of making major court improvements

It was to this Commission that he addressed the above recommendations. "I will give my full cooperation and support to such efforts to develop sound programs to meet the pressing problems we face. The most destructive, devastating fear enveloping our families today is the fear of crime."

4. Judge Fuld's Plan for Court Improvements

Chief Judge Stanley H. Fuld is chairman of the Administrative Board of the Judicial Conference, the group before which Mayor Lindsay had leveled his attack, virtually accusing judges of being responsible for the stop-motion, dishevelled conditions obtaining in New York courts, including the pile-up of unheard cases and the prison riots in New York City. Justice Edward Dudley's response to the Mayor's charges, which we have seen, was mild indeed compared to the sense of professional, even personal, outrage the Mayor's remarks provoked in Judge Fuld.

I believe both of these meetings took place in the mausoleum austerity of the Century Club. It's a good thing they didn't occur in a saloon. It was quite a row, and the fur is still falling. Judge Fuld's eight-point proposal dealt mostly with ways to improve existing procedures, and followed by one day what we've just seen of Governor Rockefeller's plan. But in a 2,000-word statement that preceded the laydown of his recommendations, he threw a couple of punches himself.

"It serves no constructive purpose," he said, "to charge that the courts and judges are principally to blame for the conditions in the jails in New York City, or for the disorders that have occurred there. . . . Jails and inmates are the responsibility of the city. The fact that the municipality has so ordered its priorities that it assertedly lacks the funds for this important function does not lessen its obligation in this regard, nor operate to shift it to the judicial system. . . . [Accusatory] statements like the Mayor's not only do incalculable harm to those who have long struggled with ever-increasing caseloads, but also render a disservice to the public, since such utterances lend agreement to those who seek to destroy the rule of law. . . . This is neither the time nor the occasion for recriminations or reproach. Such a tactic serves only to obscure the basic problem."

Then Judge Fuld announced that Harold A. Stevens and Marcus G. Christ, presiding justices of the appellate divisions in the First and Second Departments, which encompass the five boroughs, would take the following steps:

1. Transfer judges from civil to criminal courts, which will be increased in number. If this is not sufficient to reduce the case backlog, a long court session will be held, including weekend sessions
2. Transfer Supreme Court Justices from the Third and Fourth Departments (upstate judges) to hear cases in New York City
3. Seek additional space for trials
4. Schedule more meetings between administrative judges of various courts and lawyers, for a review of untried cases, with reports being sent to Justices Stevens and Christ
5. Arrange meetings on a regular basis with judges, district attorneys, Legal Aid Society lawyers, Correction and Probation Department officials to make recommendations for the improvement of the criminal justice system, including bail, delays, congestion, and conditions in the detention facilities, with reports going to Justices Stevens and Christ
6. Continue bail review procedures
7. Take immediate and positive steps for the enforcement of Rule

20.1, relating to the hours during which the courts are to be in session

8. With respect to the calendaring of criminal cases, take such steps as may be necessary to expedite the processing of such cases

Rule 20.1 (item 7 in the above) of the Administrative Board mandated that courts remain in session for at least six hours a day. This does not mean judges actually to sit on the bench for six hours a day. It means they are supposed to spend that much time on judicial work in the courthouse. That's the mandate. But the practice is somewhat different. The practice is that most judges set their own schedules. (Of course this charge outraged all judges whose schedules were inhumanly over-pressing.)

Mayor Lindsay's recommendation that the courts go at once into emergency night and weekend sessions to reduce the backlog of criminal cases was opposed by Judge Fuld, who said such extra sessions would involve new funds and new planning; that the adoption of the idea "is not feasible at this time."

In their respective statements the two men were in accord in the matter of removing several types of offenses from the Criminal Court, a proposal that has enthusiastic support from the legal profession.

"Matters such as alcoholism, prostitution, housing violations, to name but a few," wrote Judge Fuld, "do not belong in the Criminal Court system. They should be transferred to social agencies."

In the opinion of many judges, gambling has often been included as another of the "victimless crimes" that should not clutter the nation's Criminal Courts.

But this has been recommended for forty years. And that is the whole core of the backlog problem.

In 1917, when she'd been a lawyer for only five years, you will recall from the first chapter in this book that Anna Kross was banging around New York, irritating a lot of people by insisting that prostitutes weren't criminals and didn't belong in jail. Later on, when she achieved power and position, and was probably the most undeceived, disenchanted, persistent hell-raiser New York ever had, certainly among its women, she was the best friend that ladies-of-the-evening were going to meet in their lifetime, however short or ill-spent.

And the same for alcoholics, peddlers, and two-bit gamblers.

Criminals are people who commit *crimes*, she argued. And the identical argument is before us all once more. It has always made moral and social and sociological sense. But what do you do with them? You put them away and repair them. But the "crimes" of poverty, senility, insanity, alcohol insensibility, the roamings of whores, dykes, and daffodils—these are *not* crimes. They're hospital cases. They're psychiatric casualties, specimens of social deformity, end-results of biological aging, rejects from blighted community services; the innumerable marginals that live and die without name; that die with numbers only.

Such do not belong in courts and no iron door should ever be slammed on such wrecks and wretches. They aren't crooks—they're cripples.

Who keeps slamming it? Why do we tolerate it? What keeps it going? Municipal stupidity? Pervasive hypocrisy? Community ignorance? The dragging grind of custom? Or just the clerical inconvenience of making changes?

Through these foolish decades this wasting parade is kept in motion by the prods and pokings of all this. And, I think, one more: too many public servants of the recent past, never anticipating the shrill and scream of today's emergencies, felt they had made their Contribution when they had made the Great Statement. Or smashed the bottle over the bow at the launching, without knowing the credentials, without even knowing the identity of who was in the wheelhouse. Majestically, the ship sailed out, beautifully fitted from keel to main-truck, and was never again seen.

There was no one aboard.

Anna Kross gave this aspect of the big problem a full half-century of her best effort and she couldn't bring it off. It was on this clear, clean, flinty issue that she broke her pick. ("We don't need any more conferences.")

And here we are, once more at the brink of something sane and saving and decent, something of extraordinary sense, of simple yet glittering practicality, being urged on the public and the courts by some of the most vigorous thinkers and doers our cities have produced in this generation. Will they be able to tip it over? To bring it in? To bring it off?

Besides the atmosphere of fury, we are riven with fear and riddled with disgust, impatience, and delay. All these forces have finally built up into a powerful compression, of which the once-in-every-two-hours-in-America-a-bomb-goes-off is one expression of released pressure; of which the recommendations just seen, and the one to follow, is another.

About the perennial problem of alcoholism, for example—our number-three killer—we could end forever this self-perpetuating nonsense by building treatment centers, not cells, for alcoholics. And something equally plain for the gaudy nuisance of prostitution: by admitting it and licensing it and regulating it; by giving it community sanction through law; by providing community health protection through regular medical inspection of the girls.

With powers like Judge Stanley Fuld, the get-up-and-get-on-it energy of Mayor Lindsay, and the long-ranging wisdom of Frank Hogan; with senators and governors all fighting for the same thing, can't this be *made* to happen?

We'd be well on our way to hard-eyed social accountability. We'd be forever out of the Augean troughs of 300 years of judicial emptyings and stalings.

5. *Proposals for Reducing Delays in Criminal Justice in New York City*

The following is the statement of Frank Hogan, district attorney of New York County. It's the most candid and convincing review of the situation that has appeared. It is methodical, relentless, impersonal, fair, restrained. In fact, its very restraint, in detailing some of the real marvels of administrative weakness, achieve a special eloquence because of this low-key reporting.

The full statement is broken down into eleven parts: Here, in abbreviated form, are the main points:

Part I—POLICE DEPARTMENT

Arrests:

Courtrooms have been jammed with unprosecutable cases arising from poor arrests. Police officers should be judged by the quality, not the quantity, of arrests. There should be no quota system. . . . Bad arrests lead to bad law. . . .

Mass arrests of suspected addicts and prostitutes must stop. . . . Most of these cases eventually are dismissed in court. Many innocent persons are ensnared in the dragnet. Bail bondsmen and attorneys are enriched by quick fees.

Unexecuted Bail-jumping Warrants:

Thousands of defendants who are released on bail or parole . . . fail to return to court. There were 300 bail-jumpers in the Supreme Court in Manhattan in 1969, charged with felonies. In the Criminal Court . . . it is reported that 177,000 bench warrants for the arrest of Criminal Court bail-jumpers are outstanding. These warrants pile up in the office of the Warrant Squad of the police department; few are executed. Pending charges are left unresolved; non-appearance is itself a crime. . . . Recently Justice Miles F. McDonald, the administrative judge of the Second Judicial District Supreme Court, justly concluded:

"This situation approaches the area of a public scandal and a complete breakdown of law enforcement."

There is no centralized control over court warrants, no adequate record of what warrants have been issued and are still outstanding. The police department's Bureau of Criminal Identification is not notified that a warrant has been issued for failure to appear. Frequently, therefore, a bail-jumper is rearrested on new charges, but the authorities are unaware that he is wanted on a previous charge. Such defendants are often paroled again or released on low bail.

It is estimated that 63,000 warrants will be issued by the Criminal Court in New York in 1971. With a staff of only 42 (proposed as the enforcement branch of a new Warrant Squad), each officer would therefore be responsible for executing some 1,500 warrants—or six bail-jumpers each working day. A staff of 42 is inadequate.

In an attempt to encourage police officers to make a greater effort to execute outstanding felony warrants, our office has recommended to the police department that apprehensions of bail-jumpers be recorded as new arrests. Prior to October 14, 1970, when a detective apprehended a person wanted for failure to appear, he simply deposited the person in an appropriate detention center without arresting him on the new charge of bail-jumping. This meant that detectives expended many hours of work without any recognition.

A survey made in October [1970] showed that only ten of the 75 felony warrants issued by the Supreme Court in New York County were executed.

Criminal Records:

The failure of the Bureau of Criminal Identification of the police department to record the results of previous prosecutions seriously handicaps the courts and the district attorney in determining appropriate bail conditions when a defendant is arraigned. . . . In many cases the defendant's criminal record will show several prior arrests, but no dispositions; either the results are not recorded, or the defendant jumped bail and the case was never closed, which is also not recorded. . . . A squad of officers, assigned several years ago to gather this information from the courts, has wasted away. . . .

Laboratory Reports:

Narcotics cases are constantly adjourned in court and before the grand jury because the laboratory report of the police department (as to the content of a suspected narcotic substance) is absent. Many defendants are incarcerated for extra weeks because such reports are not filed earlier. The present laboratory facilities . . . should be enlarged promptly.

Appearance of Police Officers:

Too many cases are adjourned or dismissed because police officers do not appear in court. . . . No court should be forced to dismiss a case simply due to the non-appearance of the arresting officer. If a case is dismissed, the officer should be held responsible.

Listing of Witnesses:

Many trials are delayed because of the time needed for locating witnesses. Many witnesses cannot be located because their names and addresses were not made available by the police officer to the prosecutor. This is a simple matter which should be corrected by the police department and which would help immeasurably in speeding up the disposition of cases.

Part II—VERA INSTITUTE OF JUSTICE

Two of the projects of the Vera Institute of Justice, conducted on a limited basis, should be expanded by the administration of the Criminal Court. These projects have assisted in the reduction of delays in the disposition of cases:

a. A recent experiment, confined to the 14th Police Precinct in Manhattan: the police officer issuing a summons in lieu of an arrest, in certain minor criminal cases, swore to the complaint in the station house. This project of stationhouse verification in these "Vera Summons" cases should be expanded to the entire borough. Removing the verification procedure from the courtroom not only cuts down the cost of police officers for time spent waiting in court but increases the efficiency of the court.

b. The Appearance Control (Court Alert) Project is now operating in Part I, B I (misdemeanor hearings for bailed defendants). The project . . . excuses prosecution witnesses until they are absolutely needed. When it is necessary for a police officer to testify, he is notified by telephone to appear within the hour.

Part III—COURTS

Through no fault of trial judges, the time required for the trial of criminal cases has increased tremendously during the last ten years. Few murder cases can be tried to verdict in less than four weeks. Pre-trial hearings—unheard of ten years ago—as to the admissibility of physical evidence, confessions, and eye-witness identification, and as to the mental competency of the defendant to stand trial, have added to the time for trial. Expanding post-conviction *coram nobis* proceedings brought by prisoners also eat into valuable judicial time. Nevertheless, the time spent on a criminal case can be shortened.

Judicial Assignments:

From 1962, when our courts were reorganized, a major cause of calendar congestion and delays in disposing of criminal cases has been the assignment of judges with civil, rather than criminal, experience to work in the criminal parts. This has been particularly true in the Supreme Court, where justices with no criminal experience have been assigned to

preside over serious felony cases. Some civil judges dread
these assignments . . . one civil judge disposed of only
six criminal cases during the entire month of July 1970.

Another important cause of inefficiency in the Supreme
Court: rotation of justices between the criminal and civil
parts and between counties. Relatively short assignments of
judges to the criminal parts render them valueless during
the last week of their terms because of their reluctance to
start a case for fear it will carry over and disrupt their next
month's assignment. . . . Moreover, the rotating justices
are required to play a game of judicial musical chairs, moving
from county to county in one day, so that they can sentence
prisoners who were convicted before them previously in another county. Thanks to Presiding Justice Stevens, of the
appellate division, First Department, assignments of justices
to criminal parts of Supreme Court will be longer. Hopefully,
judges will be sitting in the criminal parts in the same county
for a year.

In the New York City Criminal Court, judges should be
assigned to felony arraignment and felony hearing parts for
at least one month at a time.

Court Records:

A more efficient method of managing and producing court
records must be devised. . . . In the last six months in the
arraignment part of Supreme Court, Part 30, files for the
cases on the Calendar were not produced in ten per cent
of the cases—in 65 cases in October alone. These cases must
be adjourned until the missing file is produced, causing intolerable delays.

Handling of Court Business:

Calendars in heavily loaded parts should be split into two
separate calendars, for morning and afternoon sessions. In
this way, witnesses, police officers, and attorneys would not
have to spend their whole day in court. Production of prisoners by the Correction Department would also be facilitated.

Sentencing of Supreme Court defendants is often adjourned
over the summer, leaving the defendant in custody unne-
cessarily, and contributing to the crowding of detention
facilities. This practice should not be repeated next summer.

Court business is periodically suspended during normal court hours for judicial conferences, meetings, and personal business. For instance, in the third week of June 1970, many justices of the Supreme Court in New York City attended a seminar session for trial judges at Crotonville, New York, sponsored by the judicial conference. Not only were these needed judges away from court during this period, but for several days before the conference and for the rest of June many of them declined to start new trials. Too much valuable court time is lost because such functions are held during court hours.

Trial and Pre-trial Procedures:

One concrete proposal endorsed by this office to shorten criminal trials is that the trial judge conduct the *voire dire* examination of prospective jurors in Supreme Court felony cases, as is now done in the Criminal Court in misdemeanor cases. Such a system is followed in the Federal Court, and was recently initiated in New Jersey. Presiding Justice Stevens has approved this proposal. . . .

The filing of defense motions on the eve of trial is a cause of delay in many cases. The law does not provide a deadline for the filing of pre-trial motions. This should be remedied by a prescribed omnibus checklist with deadlines for pre-trial defense motions.

Many defendants who clamor for trials suddenly change their minds just as their cases are moved for trial. These defendants then discharge their lawyers . . . and judges grant them adjournments. The ease with which defendants discharge lawyers at the last moment . . . is staggering. The judiciary must tighten control on all adjournments, particularly when the defendant gets rid of his lawyer to avoid a trial.

While practically no efforts are being made to apprehend bail-jumpers, the amount of bail set is diminishing continuously in recent years. Nevertheless, there can be no objection to periodic review of bail in the New York City Criminal Court and the Supreme Court. In the Supreme Court, moreover, all pending cases in which the defendants are incarcer

ated are on the calendar, and this constitutes an available
bail review each time the case appears.

Part IV—DISTRICT ATTORNEY

Administrative Needs:

A major cause of delay between arrest and trial is the increasing difficulty of getting witnesses to appear in the Criminal Court or before the grand jury. Too frequently we must
seek postponements because witnesses are absent. This is
often the fault of our own staff of process-servers. This group
is underpaid, overworked, and non-motivated. The average
salary of a process-server in this office is $5,200, far below
adequate compensation for an employee who frequently
must go into high-crime areas to serve subpoenas. Although
we are authorized to hire 35 process-servers, including the
supervisor, there are eleven vacancies. These cannot be
filled with competent persons under existing salary scales.

Court administrators should consider a system of computerized service of court subpoenas by mail, as is now
accomplished in Los Angeles County.

We take responsibility for these delays: holding a case
in the Criminal Court for action by the grand jury; and the
filing of an indictment after grand jury presentation.

One cause of this delay . . . is the desperate shortage of
clerical personnel who can type. The pay scale is not com-
petitive with the scale in private industry. Yet in order to
file an indictment . . . considerable typing is required. In
recent months some of our young associates have been bringing material home, typing it themselves, and then filing it
in court. Wives of junior assistants have joined in this home-
work.

We also acknowledge that the interval between indictment
and trial is frequently too long. Shortage of grand jury reporters is one cause of delay, since a copy of the grand
jury minutes is required for trial and for disposition of certain pre-trial motions. Presently there are five grand juries
in daily session, plus fifteen holdover grand juries, but we
have only four permanent grand jury reporters, whose salary
of $7,650 is not comparable with the $10,000 earned by

Criminal Court reporters or the $12,000 to $13,000 earned by Supreme Court reporters for similar work. . . .

Another absolute necessity is modernization and computerization of our own files, in a manner compatible with computerized court calendars and court records.

Part V—LEGAL AID

In a typical session in the New York City Criminal Court, soon after the judge begins to call the calendar, he is forced to order a recess to allow Legal Aid attorneys to consult with their clients. . . . Thus, a visitor to the Criminal Court may observe crowded courtrooms with no proceedings in progress. . . .

Legal Aid lawyers should interview clients and witnesses in advance of court appearances. . . .

Other agencies must increase their cooperation with the Legal Aid Society in order to make defendants available for consultation with their attorneys.

Stipulations:

Legal Aid attorneys refused to enter into routine stipulations that would save considerable time, and would not prejudice clients, such as a stipulation with respect to ownership of a stolen car.

Part VI—PRIVATE DEFENSE BAR

Appearance of Counsel:

Too often defense counsel are late in arriving in court for calendar calls and for trial. This tardiness delays proceedings and contributes to the congestion in the Criminal Courts. Shockingly, private defense attorneys often, without excuses, fail to appear at all when they have cases on the calendar. . . . Counsel who inexcusably fail to appear in court on time, or who are absent without giving good reason and timely notice to the court, should be disciplined by the court. Their unprofessional conduct should be brought to the attention of the Grievance Committee of the Association of the Bar.

Unfortunately, our judges are excessively charitable in their treatment of private counsel who are tardy or absent without excuse. Such conduct is not tolerated in the Federal courts and should not be permitted in state courts.

Availability for Trial:

"A lawyer should not accept more employment than he can discharge within the spirit of the constitutional mandate for speedy trial and the limits of his capacity to give each client effective representation." (From the American Bar Association Project on Standards for Criminal Justice)

The courts should enforce this standard.

Part VII—CORRECTION DEPARTMENT

Detention Facilities—Production of Prisoners:

Even with greater efficiency, intolerable conditions in our obsolete detention centers, will continue until more space is provided.

Release of more defendants, while desirable in the abstract, is not an acceptable solution of the problem. Judges have been setting bail at rock-bottom figures in thousands of cases, with the result that 177,000 bench warrants for defendants who have jumped bail are reportedly outstanding in New York City. Most of these defendants have remained in New York City, many committing additional crimes. Defendants cannot be let out indiscriminately merely to keep down the prison population. After every possible improvement has been made in our parole and bail procedure, there will remain a jail population much larger than, currently, can be accommodated.

We must construct a facility to supplement the Manhattan House of Detention for Men (the Tombs).

There is presently available immediately north of the Manhattan House of Detention for Men an entire square block ready for condemnation. A detention center constructed there could be connected with the Tombs by a bridge over, or tunnel under, White Street. Commissioner McGrath, supported by this office in a letter to the Mayor on November 24, 1969, has recommended use of this site for additional detention facility. . . .

We join the Correction Department in recommending split calendars—morning and afternoon calendars—to alleviate the problem of producing defendants.

Record-keeping:

Correction Department records must be computerized.

Part VIII—PROBATION

Bail Evaluation:

It is the obligation of Probation to furnish the arraignment judge with a report by the probation officer as to the defendant's ties to the community. A favorable report will often result in the release of the defendant in his own recognizance, and so this document is called the R.O.R. report.

A report which contains facts of employment, family life, or other background material of the defendant is of great assistance to a judge in considering bail. All too often the R.O.R. reports are not verified because of the lack of time or personnel. The R.O.R. staff should be increased. . . . There is currently no follow-up on investigations which are incomplete at the time of arraignment.

Youthful Offender Reports and Pre-sentence Reports:

In the Supreme Court when a defendant is eligible for youthful offender treatment, the Probation Department supplies the court with a comprehensive background study of the defendant. The Probation Department also supplies sentencing judges in the Supreme Court with pre-sentence reports. . . . These reports take from four to six weeks to prepare. The case is in limbo during this period. A jailed defendant just lingers in detention awaiting completion of his report. During summer months the delay is as long as eight weeks. We urge judges to be more selective in ordering probation reports. We also recommend that the Probation Department shorten and simplify the form of the report.

Part IX—BELLEVUE PRISON WARD

Facilities and Personnel:

Defendants are sent to Bellevue Hospital for psychiatric examination and observation to determine their fitness to stand trial; or for treatment of physical illness.

Since the winter of 1969, overcrowding in the Bellevue prison wards has caused a severe backlog of prison cases in court. Only 54 beds are available in the psychiatric division, and the staff is inadequate.

Because of this insufficiency, dozens of prisoners charged with various crimes are detained in the Tombs and other jails awaiting examination in Bellevue Hospital. . . . Prisoners transferred to Bellevue have been returned to jail because of lack of space, without having been examined.

Bellevue has only thirty beds available for defendants with disorders, too few for treatment of prisoners who are suffering from tuberculosis, heart disease, etc. Consequently, inmates are distributed to wards throughout the hospital, thereby requiring special correction officers to guard them.

On October 15, 1970, six prisoners were being treated in hospital wards outside the prison ward, requiring the services of 24 guards taken from a staff of fewer than sixty. . . . A similar problem confronts the New York City police department, which during the first week of October had assigned 42 officers to guard unarraigned prisoners in various medical institutions throughout the city because of lack of space at Bellevue. . . .

Psychiatric Reports:

The poor quality of psychiatrists' reports, filed with the court in recent months, has delayed disposition of cases considerably. . . . These stereotyped reports, devoid of any factual information, offer no assistance to the court or the attorneys litigating the question of competency. . . . The psychiatrists' reports must be upgraded to a level which will permit a court to make proper disposition of a case. Printed form reports are quite inadequate.

Availability of Prisoners:

There is a lack of notification, to the appropriate district attorney, of the admission of a prisoner from a Department of Correction facility. Too often a prosecutor is unaware of the unavailability of a particular defendant until he is told, in court, that the subject is in the hospital. . . . A simple notification by the hospital administration or the Department of Correction to the D.A. could save much time.

Part X—NARCOTIC ADDICTION CONTROL COMMISSION

Treatment Facilities:

The Narcotic Addiction Control Act provides that convicted defendants who are found to be addicts may be sentenced to the custody of the New York State Narcotic Addiction Control Commission for treatment for a period of up to three years in a misdemeanor case, up to five years in a felony case, instead of to prison.

The efforts of this office to have addicts certified to the custody of the NACC have been virtually abandoned. With more and more addicts remaining in jails for many months after certification to the NACC, and resources of the administration of justice heavily overtaxed, the district attorney has been waiving attempts to establish addiction and permitting the sentencing of convicted defendants to regular prison terms.

The fact that there are more than 100 addicts in jail, awaiting beds in addiction centers, indicates the seriousness of the problem.

A defendant facing commitment to the NACC is entitled to a jury trial, a procedure which lasts for an average of three days—a waste of time and resources, considering that a verdict of addiction means the remand of the defendant to jail.

Facilities must be made available to receive and treat these individuals. Their retention by the Department of Correction is unlawful.

Their cases add to the overcrowding in the prisons, and the delays intensify the bitterness of the defendants toward the system of justice.

Medical Examination:

The drain of the Narcotic Addiction Control program on the system of criminal justice is heavy. It is increased by flaws in the method by which suspected addicts are examined for the purpose of determining addiction. The first step in the process is frequently mishandled. In many cases no urine specimen is obtained within 48 hours of arrest, as is needed.

The caliber of the examining physicians is uneven. Although the physicians at the Women's House of Detention, and some of the doctors examining male defendants, are competent, most border on incompetency.

Part XI—PROPOSED LEGISLATION

Many basic improvements in the system of criminal justice can be made at the administrative level. New legislation,

statutory changes, and constitutional amendments may also
be necessary.

Court Administration:

Merger of Criminal Court and criminal terms of Supreme
Court. The New York City Criminal Court should be eliminated and its functions merged with the Criminal Terms of
the Supreme Court. This new court of criminal jurisdiction
should be part of the unified statewide court system, financed
by the state budget.

Merger of all state and local correction, probation, and
pre-trial detention agencies and facilities into one statewide
agency. . . . In this unified system, correctional facilities,
whether currently operated locally or by the state, whether
handling convicted or accused defendants, would come within the umbrella agency.

Grand Jury:

Waiver of Indictment. . . . Because of rulings by the Court
of Appeals, the right not to be prosecuted for a felony except by indictment of the grand jury is the only constitutional right in New York that cannot be waived by the defendant. To reduce delays, without prejudicing the rights of
the defendant or the public, the New York constitution should
be amended to permit a defendant's waiver of grand jury
hearing and indictment in a felony case, subject to agreement of the people.

Tape recordings of grand jury presentations. . . . The
taping of grand jury proceedings would permit instantaneous
review of the testimony, and eliminate delays caused by the
stenographic bottleneck.

Pre-trial Proceedings:

Elimination of preliminary hearings in misdemeanor cases.

Deadlines for Pre-trial Motions:

The filing of such motions on the eve of trial is currently
a frequent cause of delay. . . . Reasonable, specified time
limits should be provided for all pre-trial motions.

Trial Proceedings:

Judge-conducted jury selection. The present practice of jury
selection at trial, by which the defense counsel and prosecutor question the prospective jurors directly has produced

inordinate delays. In many cases, the selection of the jury takes longer than the presentation of evidence. . . .

Elimination of the three-judge bench in the Criminal Court. . . . With the added burdens created by jury trials, it is absurd to waste precious judicial resources by impanelling three judges to hear the trial of a Class B misdemeanor, a petty offense punishable by no more than three months.

Reduction of youthful offender sentences in misdemeanor cases to six months. . . . In practice almost no youths are sentenced to imprisonment for more than six months, although on a Class A conviction he is subject to imprisonment for up to one year. If the authorized punishment is reduced to six months, jury trials will not have to be provided. Delays in trials of youthful offender cases will be substantially reduced.

Probation:

The new Criminal Procedure Law forbids a court to sentence a defendant for a felony, or to sentence a defendant for a misdemeanor to probation, a reformatory sentence, or imprisonment for more than ninety days, unless a probation report is filed. Given present case loads, this would increase the number of reports by many thousands. . . . The requirement should be repealed.

Proceedings After Conviction:

Trial courts and prosecutors are forced to waste countless hours reviewing and responding to frivolous petitions filed by prisoners who seek to vacate their convictions after the normal appellate process has been exhausted. . . . In 1969, 438 *coram nobis* petitions were filed in the Supreme Court. Only fifteen were granted.

A public office should be created to provide free assistance to indigent prisoners. . . . These attorneys would screen out many frivolous complaints, and present the remaining claims coherently and professionally.

Elimination of the Absolute Right to Appeal in Some Cases:

Very few appeals in *coram nobis* cases, or appeals after pleas of guilty, are successful because almost all of these appeals lack merit. Almost 97 per cent of the non-trial cases were affirmed on appeal. But the appellate courts are plagued

with hundreds of such appeals every year. This has placed
a tremendous burden on the defense bar. . . . While the system of justice is collapsing around us, urgently needed prosecutors, Legal Aid attorneys, and other defense lawyers must
be assigned to the fruitless task of examining closed cases,
or cases in which the defendant has admitted his guilt in
open court. . . . Elimination of the automatic right to
appeal in such cases . . . would free thousands of man-hours
of time of defense lawyers and prosecutors for devotion to
more serious tasks.

Contents of the Criminal Law:

Removal of Certain Offenses from the Criminal Law:

a. Public intoxication, prostitution, and Administrative
Code violations should be removed from the jurisdiction of
the Criminal Court and handled by administrative agencies.

b. Penalties for possession of marijuana should be reduced.

c. Amend the law pertaining to narcotic addiction cer-
tifications and commitments, to provide that under appropriate situations the district attorney could defer criminal prosecution, and refer the matter to the Attorney General for
civil certification proceedings.

Creation of Two Degrees of Murder:

Delays in the trial of homicide cases, currently averaging
eighteen months in New York County, are attributable in
great measure to the absence of the degrees of murder in
the revised Penal Law. Elimination of the distinction between murder in the first degree and murder in the second
degree in 1967 has reduced the ability of the district attorney
and the court conscientiously to approve a plea of guilty
to a lesser offense where the defendant is charged with murder, because of the wide difference in the scope of punishment between murder and manslaughter.

Conversely, a defendant charged with murder has little
incentive to admit his guilt of that crime. The ability of the
courts to dispose of murder cases in fairness to the accused
and the public would be increased by a statutory distinction
between the first-degree murder—that which is premeditated

—and second-degree murder—murder without premeditation or deliberation.

Prosecutors:

Permitting law school graduates to appear in court on behalf of prosecutors. District attorneys in the metropolitan area are increasingly turning to law school graduates to fill urgent personnel needs. In New York County, as in other counties in the city, many such graduates are added to the permanent staff every summer (eighteen in 1969, fifteen in 1970), but they may not appear in court until admission to the Bar, generally in January. The delay prevents these employees, who are otherwise qualified, from relieving the pressure on the other prosecutors in their offices. Legislation has been submitted for two years. In 1969 it passed in the Assembly but never came to a vote in the Senate. In 1970 it passed in the Senate but died in Assembly Committee.

CORRECTION—THE BLACK PIT—WHOSE FAULT?

Correction

George F. McGrath, who followed Anna Kross as New York's Commissioner of Correction, many times felt he had inherited the bad press that had for so many years badgered his predecessor. A bad press goes with this job. McGrath quit at the end of 1971. New York now has its first black Commissioner, a fine man— Benjamin J. Malcolm—and an excellent appointment. But already this man is getting knocked around, not by the press as yet but by the State Commission of Correction. Malcolm hasn't tidied up the problems at Rikers Island fast enough.

Anyone can understand a plaintive note in this, his first "introduction" to the public:

"I am shocked the Commission came out with its criticisms before I have had time to make changes. I took office less than two weeks ago."

The poor fellow hardly had time to find out where the men's room was.

One of the State Commission's complaints was the alleged lack of counseling for inmates. Mr. Malcolm said he had just added a psychologist and a teacher to the counseling staff and would add more counselors "when more money became available." Why don't newspapers *publish* the itemizations of our prison needs? And publish the cold-cash figures in identifiable dollar signs? Let the public *see* the hot iron on the anvil and the feeble hammerings that beat out nothing useful?

Where does the bad press come from?

It may proceed from the psychological overhang that is the public's response to the word "prison." Or its response to the image the word "prison" throws up on the screen of the average mind, including the mind of the reporter. And riots do nothing to damp this down, or to clear it.

Prison atmospheres all seem sinister, unapproachable, forbidding; medieval holdovers, mute and stony; the long slow exhale just before death. It is not surprising that most media repeat this dreary monochrome, but it is unfortunate.

It is as if those who run our prisons were the proper target for the scoldings of all the good people who never go near them.

Wardens and commissioners are used to this. If a prison is tight, it is oppressive. If a prisoner escapes, it isn't tight enough.

Commissioners of Correction can't win. They know this. Commissioner Malcolm, in office less than a month, was already finding it out. They know other things: that it's your fault, not theirs. They know they are taking the abuse that should be on your head. They also know they can make a better accounting of themselves, in respect to this toughest of all jobs, than you can make in respect to all your philosophies about it.

They're in the muck of the arena. You're in the bleachers. They're ducking the flung debris while you're home doing your memo. They know they have to do it all alone; that you won't help. You never have.

So they count on you for nothing. America's jailers are never alone, jumping from meeting, to prison, to appearances before boards, to hospitals. Never alone, yet the loneliest of men. It is not the prisoner who is the forgotten man. It is his keeper. And it is you, the public, who has arranged all this; who has set it up this way and who keeps it going this way.

Commissioner McGrath's stewardship of his various New York fortresses was sharply called to account in a New York *Times* editorial (April 12, 1971) titled "Making Justice More Equal." Other press stories hurt his administration. There was a story in the Sunday New York *Times* (Jan. 17, 1971) that hurt the work Commissioner McGrath was doing and seriously depreciated the morale of the men and women under him. The story was titled "Prison Guards: What Kind of Person Takes a Job Like This?" Here are the opening three sentences of the story:

Perhaps the problem is that few of the city's more than 2,500 correction officers wanted to be prison guards in the first place. What they wanted was the security of a civil service job, and the tri-agency examinations for appointment to the Transit Police, the Housing Police, or the Correction Department were a means to that end. The goal for most was to become policemen, not guards.

Some paragraphs later, this sentence:

The city has no problem in recruiting correction officers, only in holding them.

The news writer could have received the exact figures if he had asked the Commissioner for them. That is where I got them. Here they are:

From a full staff of 2,706 (January 1, 1971)
73 Male Resignations   Appointed: 485 Males
Conditions of Resignations:
    2 to join New York City Police Department
    2 to join Nassau County Police Department
    1 to join Westchester Police Department
    5 to join Transit Police (N.Y.C.)
    3 to join Housing Police (N.Y.C.)
    —
13
    5 to become Court Officers
    5 to join Fire Department (N.Y.C.)
    —
10
Fifty resigned for personal reasons.

I consider the omission of this information to be irresponsible reporting.

In the same article there were destructive insinuations about prison guard brutality:

Whatever their reasons [for wanting to be prison guards], it was clear last week that some of them at least should not be prison guards. Last Sunday four guards were suspended, accused of beating a prisoner later found to be hanged in the Manhattan House of Detention, known as the Tombs.

The case is now in the office of District Attorney Frank S. Hogan. To newspaper readers, none of this should have come as a surprise. Almost all prisoner suicides in the city are followed by charges of brutality toward the inmate by correction officers. In every prisoner uprising, there are also complaints of guard brutality.

Most of the time an investigation is called for by responsible city officials, then the suicide and the charges against the officers are forgotten. What made the suicide of Raymond Lavon Moore, also known as Raymond Lavon, different was the newly revitalized Board of Correction—headed by the very energetic and politically ambitious William J. vanden Heuvel, a former aide to Senator Robert F. Kennedy.

Chairman vanden Heuvel responded to the usual cries of guard brutality, rejecting the Correction Department's own investigative results. The prisoner Moore, or Lavon, had been in the Tombs ten months, awaiting a trial on charges of assaulting a police officer. He was found dead by hanging on Nov. 3, 1970, two days after an incident occurred in which guards said he struck one of them with a shoe. "No unnecessary force was used in the altercation that followed," the Correction Department report said.

The Board of Correction kept after the matter, however, and earlier this month another correction officer, shaken by still another suicide in the Tombs, came forth and accused his four colleagues of unjustly beating Moore before he committed suicide.

The whole case raised again the question of what kind of man becomes a prison guard?

Whom do you believe—the newspaper's or the department's report?

Having noted in his news story that the case had gone to the D.A.'s office, the reporter might have pursued it there himself. The truth came out on Tuesday, April 20, three months later, and the New York *Times* (by-line of Juan Vasquez) stated:

GUARDS CLEARED IN TOMBS STUDY
Seymour Discloses Findings of Federal Investigation

A Federal investigation into an inmate's death in the Tombs last year has concluded that there is "no factual basis to support a finding of misconduct" against prison guards.

In a letter to four members of Congress who requested the investigation, United States Attorney Whitney North Seymour, Jr., disclosed that a former guard who said he had witnessed a beating of the inmate had recanted his earlier testimony.

The investigation concerned the apparent suicide last November of Raymond Lavon Moore, an inmate in the Manhattan Men's House of Detention, also known as the Tombs.

Indications of a beating were uncovered in an autopsy, and his death was the subject of a study by the Board of Correction and, later, a grand jury investigation by the office of Manhattan District Attorney Frank S. Hogan.

The Board of Correction report cast doubt on some aspects of the official statements made by the guards. The grand jury, however, said it could find no evidence to support criminal charges against four guards who had been suspended.

In his letter to United States Representative Edward I. Koch, Democrat-Liberal of Manhattan, Mr. Seymour said that "the facts do not support any finding of criminal conduct."

Mr. Seymour said that the study had been conducted by the Federal Bureau of Investigation and that it had been directed by the chief of the criminal division of his office.

He said interviews with "correction officers and other principal witnesses" had been conducted. Among the "salient facts" uncovered by their investigation, he said, was the following:

"Correction Officer Arthur Blake, who was reported in the public press of Jan. 7 as declaring that several officers beat Mr. Moore with black jacks, has recanted that statement in writing."

I would consider this investigation a conscientious one. D.A.'s, grand juries, the F.B.I., congressmen—all had done their best. But like most exonerations, the clearing of the four suspended guards got about half the newspaper space of the earlier story.

The press could do better. With everything boiling over; with everyone rapping, yakking, or latrating, it would restore dignity to a number of America's newspapers if the objectivity of their reporting would harden in direct proportion to the subjectivity of the story being reported. But it works the other way—sensationalisms compound each other. Very few can talk or write or think about crime or prisons or correction facilities without a sudden rush of blood—not to the brain but to the belly.

A bad press can always slow down a good man and hurt his programs. In public issues as critical as these, inaccurate reporting can only exacerbate these crises. But Commissioner McGrath looked tough enough and resilient enough to take the welts and beltings—just as Anna Kross had had to be in the same job in the previous administration. They quickly got used to the fact that newspaper readers would sooner be shocked and infuriated than informed and inspirited. When our public servants do get a good report, they accept it with the surprise and gratitude of thirsty lands for unexpected rain.

In Attica now we are experiencing the same torment over which, in her twelve-year battle to shake out the money to get the job done, Anna Kross collided with the men (the Board of Estimate) who had the money but who would never open their purse to her. It is this same torment of frustration that crippled George McGrath,* an immensely sophisticated man in every phase of prison work. After taking the lash of an unfavorable press during his reading hours, and no money to get the job done during his working hours, the dosage of "masochism" (his word) overwhelmed him.

The pot will boil over again. We are just seeing the first of our Atticas.

George McGrath was a superior public servant in all his areas of energy and the new Commissioner of Correction can be no better. Nor can he know more.

Other things will happen to him: he will inherit the same bad press. He will be proclaimed "ineffective." And he'll be discredited, he'll be fired, or he'll quit. That is all there is for commissioners in this rotten game; all there has been.

Would Mr. William vanden Heuvel, head of the Correction Board, or would Councilman Carter Burden, chairman of the subcommittee on Penal and Judicial Reform, be able to do this job? Or handle the nation's Atticas? I mention them because these two men (in New York) were the most hurting of all the gadflies to

---

* Resigned Nov. 19, 1971; effective Dec. 31, 1971.

bug the ears and eyes of the former commissioner during his thankless lustrum at 100 Centre Street. And these are men of brains, experience, and conviction. But given the job, could *they* get the money? *Would* they get it? How?

No one in the history of any American city has yet charted a way to this shiny rattrap of this country's self-betrayal. It isn't New York. It's every city we have that has a prison problem. Do you know one that doesn't?

While giving his strength and his judgment and his natural resilience to the work he was employed for, McGrath never had the support of the press. As the years mount, doesn't this begin to seem universal? At his departure, his service and his record received a lukewarm sendoff in a New York *Times* editorial titled "McGrath Goes" (Dec. 17, 1971). It was reminiscent of a line by Damon Runyon: "I didn't like this character very good so I only give him a medium hello."

The editorial contained a sentence of bitter if unintended irony: "Perhaps he did not fight fiercely enough for the funds necessary to carry out badly needed improvements." What a stingy valediction that is! In my invincible hope that everything is not hopeless, may I ask the *Times* just how you do that? What weapons? What media? What forum? In this area what did the *Times* ever do for McGrath? Or for any commissioner? How do you get the *money*?

No one has ever revealed this magic to any warden or commissioner or captain of correction officers I ever talked to. If an answer exists, even a scheme, we might have a better world; a setting out of priorities under which able men, who can do effective thinking, can do effective work.

They cannot do so now.

Here's why: Attica needs $16,000 to build some new showers and can't get it. Albany won't give it. But the same men who can't find the $16,000 can find the money to put up the new Mall. And that bill is $1 billion, 500 million.

In the self-perpetuating grind of no-answer-to-the-main-problem, New York's new Commissioner of Correction, Benjamin Malcolm, will have to accept the prospect that his term will be more grotesque, more marvelously unmanageable than that of a general who knows how to win the war but who is issued no battle gear.

Commissioners of Correction, wardens, superintendents must
continue to buck, beg, bug, swear, and importune—what else is
there?—while crime and corruption cross-pollinate, while city
treasurers don't hear, while jails and the men in them slowly
mould and mummify.

Why does anyone think it's going to be different now?

Most people, whatever their information, have fixed opinions
about all these matters, yet not even the sophistication of the
American press appreciates the absolute control that money has
on all these horrid problems. But when an opinion is offered from
a source as knowledgeable as Tom C. Clark, retired Associate
Justice of the Supreme Court and a former Attorney General of
the U.S., it has to be respected. In December 1970, in Washington, he had this to say about courts, crime, and correction. And
money.

It is open season on the courts. The judges are blamed for all sides
of the crime wave, the clogging of court dockets, the over-crowded
jails, excessive bail, short sentences and downright indolence. If I
were called upon to identify the culprit, I would first point to the
fiscal authorities who decide the amount of money the courts receive.

For example, the City of New York spends forty times as much
money on its police system as it does on its criminal courts. The city's
correction system receives less than one-tenth of the police budget
but it must house all the arrestees of the police. The District Attorney,
who must prosecute all of the arrestees, is allowed less than one-
fiftieth . . .

It is clear to me that what the courts and corrections systems need
today are the funds to do their job.

Justice Clark was as alarmed as all other jurists, judges and
lawmakers over the problem of congestion in courts, and the pile-
up of untried cases. The physical aspects of this alone made it
impossible for such considerations as "due process" or a citizen's
constitutional rights to get first notice; or even to get any notice at
all.

"The crisis in courts is so bad," he said, "that no one is even
talking about rights any more. They're talking about backlog.
Until the backlog problem is solved, any more work in rights will
have to wait."

If Justice Clark can name the number-one culprit in the current imbroglio as the "fiscal authorities" who allocate public monies, the New York *Times* also has an identifiable candidate. The most blistering editorial I ever saw, in many years of reading this mighty paper, appeared on June 9, 1971. Here are the opening two sentences:

This was, in all probability, one of the most thoroughly regressive, anti-democratic, anti-consumer, anti-urban boondoggling and backward-looking sessions of the State Legislature in all history. It leaves the state far worse off than before the Legislature convened so long ago in January.

Meantime, somebody had to hold the baby, and with little expectation of imminent relief. Commissioner McGrath was one of these.

He came to New York with impressive credentials.* It would not be possible to improve on the thoroughness of his background, in either theory or realistic exposure.

Because I had been through his jails so many times with his predecessor—and through a large number of other prisons and penitentiaries scattered about the U.S.—I could inhabit, in my own mind, most of the fixtures and frustrations of his inheritance. It takes a strong man to seek this work; a stronger to survive it. Commissioner McGrath seemed both. He's a big man, strong, rumpled, human, interested, listening, and articulate. Sense pours out of him.

"There is something terribly wrong, terribly stupid, about society, about any society that puts sick people into the stream of the city's normal life. And it's more stupid still to place these sick people—and I mean addicts—into the stream of convicted felons. Stupid to lock them up with those who have committed our worst crimes and who will soon go out to do it all over again."

"We have a New York State law that authorizes involuntary civil commitment. Why don't we invoke it? We should get these addicts before a court gets them. Before a jail cell does. The authority is there to do this. But it's not being exercised.

* Commissioner of Correction, Massachusetts, 1959–65; researcher, crime in delinquency (Harvard Law School—1940–59); professor of criminal law, assistant dean, Boston College Law School; assistant D.A., Boston; practicing attorney, prison case worker.

"Right now, right this minute, over fifty per cent of the prisoner population are addicts. Now. Today. May 6, 1971. And we have money to build more jails. But that isn't an answer. Only ten per cent of the total census of prisoners really should be in maximum security. It's idiotic. We don't need more cells. We need more beds. Beds for addicts who have committed no crime. Get them *before* they commit a crime. We can do this, and do do it, with a mental case. Why not an addict? His potential for harm is far more certain. The quality of the harm far more serious."

I had read, as had countless others, the interesting suggestion the Commissioner had tossed out to the State Commission of Investigation: to pick up addicts off the street and force them into facilities of the State Narcotics Addiction Control Commission.

"Do you mean," I asked, "just walking down the street and picking up any recognizable addict you saw and bringing him in?"

"I mean that *exactly*. Exactly. Before they're driven to crime by the cruel cunning of the drug."

"Who should do the picking up of the addicts?"

"We've thought about that, and it's very hard. The police don't want to do it. They say they're not health officers. They say they're not social workers. Same with school teachers. Teachers actually see much of it in their own classrooms, even in junior high. Even *below* junior high. But should a teacher certify that so-and-so is an addict? Should they do this even though they know every addict in their class? They don't want to because it would get around at once: 'He's working against us,' or 'she' is. 'Turning us in.' You'd get an instant boil of resentment. The police feel themselves a body separate from social workers. So do teachers. Yet both are deeply in social work. So . . . it comes down to this: who is going to bell the cat? Who is going to walk up to an addict, touch him on the shoulder, and say: 'Come with me?' But this is the question that has got to be answered. And got to get answered right away."

"Isn't it a proper function of the narcotics authorities themselves?"

"Yes. That would seem to me the right course. Special officers appointed by Narcotics Control to identify and bring in addicts. Reach them *before* they've mugged anyone, killed anyone, snatched a purse, or knocked over a liquor store. We don't need more cells. We need more *beds*.

"The whole country is yelping about overcrowded jails and prisons. They'll continue to be overcrowded until we clear out the addicts. It's not a crime to use narcotics. It's not a crime to *be* an addict."

"How is the detoxification program working out? I just saw Mr. vanden Heuvel's statement regarding this program at the Tombs. He said: 'It has transformed the most dismal part of the prison into one of the most hopeful.'"

"He's right. And a lot of this is his own doing. He's recruited a number of M.D.s for us—seventeen of them up to now—doctors who come down as needed, to supplement the work of our own medical staff. All the volunteer doctors are paid by the hour. With the huge leap in the number of certified addicts, we couldn't manage without this volunteer support."

"What does it cost the city to keep a man in the Tombs?"

"Thirteen dollars a day. It's the worst sort of domestic economy. Purely as a health matter, purely as a civil action, addicts should be lifted right out of the flow of society. Right now we just wait for it to worsen. And it always does. Any addict will commit a crime. He has to. He has no choice. Put him on the Involuntary Commitment Program. Treat him. Detoxify him. Get him work. *Change* him.

"All the New York prisons are designed for maximum security. It's ridiculous. Only one man in ten needs to be under such tight security. We know who they are. All prisons being built now, and from here on in, should be built with only a small wing given to maximum security. All the rest of it, medium or minimum security.

"The whole secret of penological success is in *changing an inmate's attitude while he is serving time*. And medium or light security is the first and best instrument toward effecting that change. Let him know he's a person. Let him know that *you* know it. How do you *do* that? Let him go home for Christmas. Give an occasional ten-day furlough. Make him earn it, but, once earned, give it to him. Let him go home weekends. Let him be with his family for a two-weeks' vacation. What he wants most is to be in touch with *life*, not prison. So make it possible that he keeps in touch with life, with love, with family, with community living."

"What experience are you having with work-release?"

"It's an enormously valuable idea. A great idea. And it *is* working. It is succeeding. Let the prisoner *out*. Open the gate and let him go to work. Let him go to his own job; to feel it *is* his own job. Let him work at it. All day. Same as any other man. And come back to prison at night. But even now, most of the new buildings going up are the old concept. 'Set it up so nobody can get out.' The hell with that. It's out of date. It's dead. It's stupid. It's wrong. It's wasteful. We *know* it doesn't work. It's been known to be wrong for two centuries. Not only right here in New York. All over the U.S.

"We're lucky to have a Mayor that knows the prison situation. John Lindsay knows it well. Usually it's just a great big embarrassment to a Mayor. They'd sooner *not* know. Sooner leave it alone. Not to John. Prior to his getting the big job, Lindsay was executive assistant to Attorney General Herbert Brownell. There is no aspect of the prison system the Mayor hadn't seen and explored for himself."

"Aren't your plans for addicts in real peril because of the cutback in state funds?"

"Indeed they are! Frightful! The money seems to keep moving back and forth. Now a lot of facilities have had to shut down. Think of it! When it's known to be the number-one crime-breeder in all metropolitan living! $30 million has just been clipped. We'll pay for it. In smashed heads and smashed ribs and store windows and smashed futures. We could have a crisis in overcrowding that will make today's riots look pale. With the boys coming back from Viet Nam it will continue to compound. L.E.A.A.* is just now coming in with $7 million for us. And this will help some. I can improve some department facilities. And several of my Correction officers will be attending John Jay College on some of this money. Learn the immediate needs of prisoners. Seeing prisoners every day, they know the needs. But not what to do.

"The Women's House of Detention on Rikers is now up. And the women have moved in. In every way it's a fine facility. Hori-

* Law Enforcement Assistance Agency.

zontal, 600 women. Lots of outdoors area. We'll probably pull
down the old vertical monstrosity at 10th and Greenwich. But till
we do, we could make intelligent use of it. Men who are classified
as 'low risk.' Men who are in for mental observation; low bail;
homosexuals. Men on work-release sentences who can come and
go."

"Shouldn't work-release be introduced to your very youngest
inmates?"

"It should be and it is. You should know what is happening in
Brooklyn. We have a floor for young prisoners in the Granada
Hotel over there. This is new. This is experimental. But it's working. Nobody can be sentenced for more than eleven months at
Rikers. Some of the young men serving time there—fellows from
16 to 21—are being allowed to finish their sentence in this
new arrangement at the Granada Hotel. They've earned the right
through a good deportment record. We started this plan on February 6, 1970. It needs to be copied and multiplied all over the
United States. The boys are doing time for misdemeanors, not
felonies. We're trying to let them have a chance—in this liberal
administration—a chance to do something for themselves. Allow
them to create some of the opportunity to have that chance. They
have the privilege of coming and going. Unsupervised. Unguarded.
They can go out for a soda. Go out for meals. They can go to the
movies. They have to get permission for these short leaves. And
sign back in when they return. But when they're out, they're on
their own and they know it. It's a great elevator of morale. They'll
be here in the hotel for two or three months, however much longer
they have to serve. Some have jobs and this is heavily encouraged.
I'm still talking about *control and change*. This open prison, as it
were, creates a climate in which the prisoner *can* change."

"How serious is the temptation to abuse the privilege? Can't
they just cut out?"

"Sure. And some do. But most of them realize three things:
that they *are* getting an honest chance, something they can't really
bitch about. They also know it would be stupid to risk getting
caught when there's only a couple of months to go, and months
that are a lot easier living than Rikers. And finally, being their
own man, their self-respect begins to return."

"How many are at Granada now?"

"Fifty. We've put 215 through the experiment so far. And we have put up two more such facilities, one in Harlem and one in South Bronx. Facilities for 300 more. In the Model Cities area, and paid for by Model Cities money. But we need fifty of these places, not three.

"All prisoners are different people, just as different as non-prisoners. Different instincts, heredity, capacity to learn, tendencies, reservoirs of bitterness, quality and amount of self-pity, ability to throw this off. A lot of inmates have high-quality intelligences they never use, that the system never arouses. Most men harden as their sentence goes on and on. What else *could* they do? If there's nothing at all to break the monotony. Putting things in his way that *invite* him to use his intelligence—this in itself is intelligent. Putting him in a situation that puts *him* in control of it, or in control of some of it, he begins to feel like a man again. Or begins to feel that he wants to.

"Minimum security, work-release. These are the roads to change. This is the future of correction."

Now before the Albany legislature is Commissioner McGrath's "Prisoner Furlough Bill": weekends for prisoners; keep the prisoner in touch with his family; maintain his morale to the end that when he has a chance to return to society, he very much wants to do it.

Like most everything in criminal justice, it is pending.

The Commissioner is also concerned about prisoner pay. The pay-rate almost everywhere is worse than stingy. It is insulting. He is trying to improve it. Cities are the worst. State prisons are a little better; Federal still better.

In New York, prisoners can work five hours a day and at these rates: 3¢, 5¢, and 10¢ per hour. They can make a maximum of fifty cents a day. But this is so feeble it is non-incentive. He can just about make cigarette money.

In Massachusetts, where Commissioner McGrath comes from, they do better. A prisoner keeps one-third for himself, one-third goes to his family, and one-third goes into a release kitty for him. It is called "gate money" and is never less than $50.

Why can't prisoners make more money?

Unions won't let city prisoners get into a profitable bread-baking business, for example. In New York they bake bread for the city schools but at no profit. State prisons, besides making license plates, often do much of the state's printing, and the prisoners are better paid than city prisoners. In Federal prisons there is definite profit-making, with contracts to make equipment for the Armed Forces, to make clothing of all kinds, uniforms, mail bags. It is run like a business. It *is* a business."

The prisoner pay-rate is one of the great deserts of penological thinking and local do-nothing. The Commissioner has gone after it.

We turned to another subject.

I asked him how often a judge or state legislator ever showed up at a prison, asking to be taken through.

"With so much talk and criticism, a few judges are now beginning to show up. I almost never saw one before. Politicians, no. They just don't come at all. Maybe one a year. Most of my life has been in prison work. And I've always wondered in my own mind how any judge can fulfill his duty as a judge if he doesn't know where he's sending a prisoner. If he has no real notion at all of what it's like. How can a law maker make a law about a crime and the penalty that goes with the crime, and at the same time know nothing about the box into which he's sending the criminal? It should be mandatory for judges and legislators to visit jails and prisons and remand shelters and youth houses, just as it is part of the training of firemen to know how to go up a ladder. How the hell can you put out the fire if you can't *see* it!"

Rehabilitation

On Wednesday, October 7, 1970, Richard W. Velde, associate administrator of the Law Enforcement Assistance Administration, recited some melancholy facts to a Senate Judiciary sub-committee in Washington:

Prisons keep offenders out of circulation for varying lengths of time, but all too often they are unchanged when they are returned to society. Or they are worse than when they went in.

The nation's 4,021 jails, and its 400 major institutions for juvenile delinquents, are typically overcrowded and old. Virtually none of them makes any physical provision for corrections programs.

New York City, too?

Yes. In earlier sections of this book I've reported the vigorous battle put up by Anna Kross, both as judge and later as Commissioner, to erect and maintain useful programs to rehabilitate inmates. What she did was brave, new, and serious. And also pitifully insufficient. She called it pitifully insufficient then, and does now. Many times I personally saw the efforts she had mounted, saw them in all the facilities in which they were being introduced; and met the men and women in whose charge the programs were placed.

They were good people. They were also insecure, and most of them were discouraged. Why? They had been given the money to start the show, but money to keep it going was never put on the barrelhead. Seed-money only, and always used up before it had its chance to multiply. Project after project had to be dropped.

Is the money there now? No. Will it ever be there? Never in practical amount. Is Rehabilitation, then, a joke? Yes, it is. Except for a token and ephemeral existence, it is a cruel and bitter joke. It is a torture of hope. It is a rich harvest in disappointment. It is a soughing back-draft of unheard appeals, aborted energies, and legal and fiscal tergiversation.

Before me are the figures for New York's Criminal Justice Budget for 1970–71. The total figure is $843,208,910.

How much of this near-billion dollars goes to Rehabilitation? Two and a half million.*

That is *less than one-third of one per cent.*

That is the measure of our caring.

Rehabilitation is a word. It is not a fact of prison life in America.

It is your fault. It is not the Mayor's. It is not the Commissioner's.

Acutely, painfully aware of this is Mayor Lindsay himself. The niggardliness of the provision for rehabilitation of prisoners in the 1971 budget he calls "striking," and further points out its futility: "Most of this [money] is for operating costs rather than provision of services.

---

* An increase of $400,000 in the 1971–72 budget, but earmarked for salaries for nurses, chaplains, administrative personnel, as before; nickels and dimes for the prisoners.

"On an annual basis approximately 80,000 detained prisoners and 18,000 sentenced prisoners pass through the institutions of the Department of Correction. While one facility may be operating with fewer prisoners than capacity at any given time, others may have over twice as many prisoners as can be adequately and properly provided for. Prison conditions, especially since the recent riots, have been dramatically described in the media. The caging of any individual necessarily dehumanizes him. . . . Prisoners awaiting trial cannot be ordered to work. . . . Physical recreation is unavailable for the most part. . . . On any given day, less than five per cent of the department's inmates are receiving any formal education, vocational training, or psychiatric services.

"Department of Correction personnel are overwhelmed by logistic demands. Prisoner turnover is enormous. Each must be processed. Almost everyone needs some form of medical treatment. There may be five shifts in a cafeteria for each meal. The movement of prisoners to courtrooms must commence within some institutions at five o'clock in the morning. Up to one-half of the inmates have been habitual drug users. Many require intensive observation for their own protection.

"The daily transport of prisoners to court is a most taxing job. . . . In 1969 the department had to move approximately 1,000 prisoners *daily* to courts in five different boroughs. On an annual basis, the total number of prisoners moved was 215,000. . . .

"The Department of Correction faces the future with great uncertainty. . . .

"There are built-in difficulties to meaningful programs in the Department of Correction:

1. Most of the sentenced prisoners (adults and youth 16 to 21 years of age) are in prison for a relatively short period of time (i.e., under one year).
2. Of the approximately 5,700 sentenced prisoners in department custody, about 3,000 have been transferred to state institutions out of the city; another 2,200 are needed for routine maintenance duty in city institutions (food services, cleaning).
3. Most of the youth are upstate.
4. Over one-third of the sentenced population have been habitual

drug users who require intensive treatment in any positive program.

5. Overcrowding leaves little space and few personnel for rehabilitation efforts.

"At present, the department has a total of seven inmates on work release, and fewer than sixty in one pre-release center.

"The community correction programs of the department have proceeded very slowly. While this effort proceeds, there must be programs to undo years of criminal life-style and reinforcement of that experience in prison.

"The approach must first focus on joinder of prison and aftercare programs. The transition period upon re-entry into society is crucial to the future of every offender. . . . Only by extending a program and opportunities after the end of a jail sentence will an attempt have time to become something greater. . . .

"Only by getting away from institutionalization can rehabilitation programs hope to be successful. . . . This does not mean that rehabilitation programs within existing institutions will be ignored [but] for sentenced offenders within the prisons, CJCC's* main goal is the provision of decent living conditions."

Through the Criminal Justice Coordinating Council, Mayor Lindsay has set up a series of Action Programs, some in force now, some waiting for money to get going.

Project Manhood—
This is a placement program for people returning to the community from state and city correction institutions. The program has served approximately 1,000 men and women each year, and has placed them in jobs, training programs, or educational programs. The project is being extended into other areas of the city and will be servicing approximately 2,500 persons a year.

LIFT Project—
Funded in late 1970, this project identifies leadership potential in a selected number of offenders, trains them while on work-release status, and places them in group counseling positions upon release. Help to offenders carries over into, and through, the first months after release.

* Criminal Justice Coordinating Council.

Correctional Services for Women (CSW)—
A non-profit organization to provide extensive services for females involved in the criminal justice system. Services to include residential and boarding facilities; counseling with which would lead to training programs; income assistance; followup to prevent recidivism.

Columbia Teachers College Board of Education Project—
Specially trained teaching students will work in the school at the new Women's House on Rikers Island, tutoring, providing courses in dance, drama; and to serve as role models who will be available to ex-offenders in the community upon release; the college to provide follow-through for the women.

The Fortune Society—
A group of ex-offenders, organized and funded to provide three special services: counseling of newly released prisoners; training for parole and probation officers; public education.

The Mayor's comprehensive plan (120 pages) has this to say of Rehabilitation in general:

Rehabilitation is a long recognized need that has never received any real public funding or commitment of support. The deficiency here is enormous. The Criminal Justice Coordinating Council's funds are just a first step in the development of meaningful rehabilitation programs. . . .

A final word of caution is appropriate here. Experts and researchers are finding that different kinds of existing rehabilitative programs do not produce much variation in recidivism rates. This finding emphasizes the need for stressing an element not now included in most rehabilitative programs; i.e., intensive follow-up and after-care for offenders released into the community. Also to be emphasized: the elimination of most disabilities imposed by law on ex-offenders.

Exactly what is meant by "disabilities imposed by law on ex-offenders" will be garishly, frightfully clear to the reader in the next two pages. I would doubt any reader will ever forget the unimaginable frustrations and turn-down calmly recorded by this ex-prisoner in seeking honest work following incarceration.

The following is a great monument to contemporary American idiocy:

WHEN THE EX-OFFENDER COMES HOME . . .

(By Melvin Rivers—printed here with the permission of
Mr. Rivers and the *Fortune News*)

Even though life in prison teaches you more crime than anything
else, I still never met a guy coming out who didn't have one thing
going for him at the beginning, and that was the will and determination to try to go straight. The forward thrust in the mind is to get
a job and settle down or, if he's a parolee, to keep the job he had
to find in order to get out. But it's tough. You really run into problems.

When I got out of prison in 1962, I had a "can opener" job, a phony
offer from a cousin of mine that satisfied the parole board's requirement and let me out. I had intentions of getting a barber's license,
because I'd been the institutional barber in the prison and had a
slip of paper that *certified I'd spent 2,400 hours barbering*. But when
I applied at a barber shop, I had to start as a shine boy, even though
I told the boss how much hair I'd cut, and showed him what I could
do. He said he couldn't put me on a chair until I got a license. But
the license never came. I got a note back saying the city *couldn't give
me one because of my record*. The boss said to reapply, and I did,
but the same thing happened again.

Later I worked in a real estate shop, but I couldn't get a salesman's
license. A little later I found out that the guy working with me was
also an ex-con, but he was using another man's broker's license and
later got into a complicated mess. He told me he was submitting my
application for a license, and I could work as a salesman while we
waited for it to come. So I did, and was renting apartments for
about five months until I got wise and asked him what was going on.
Eventually I found the application in his drawer—he hadn't even
sent it in. He said, "I'll tell you the truth, man, you can't get a license.
I didn't want to tell you because I didn't want to hurt you, and I
liked your potential." That's when I found out he was an ex-con, too.

I stayed on there a while anyway and made a little money, but then
I cut out. I was going to go to nursing school, my Parole Officer
thought I'd be good at it. (He was the one Parole Officer who really
helped me in seven years of parole.) He sent me to a nursing school.
I asked about the course, and of course I had to tell them about my
record. They said they were sorry, but they wouldn't be able to
accept me.

Then I went across the street and applied for a security job at
King's County Hospital, and again I told the truth on the application. The guy came out and said he was sorry, but it was against
city policy to hire me.

Then I worked at Downstate Medical Center for a while, and this time I didn't tell them anything. I got a job in their supply place, where I had to be bonded. But they *ran a check* on me, and I got fired.

Then I worked a year as an usher in a movie theater, and they had an opening for manager in the same theater, so I applied for it and the bonding sheet went out again, and *I got fired*, even though I'd worked there a year, and they liked me.

There was a construction job, too, but the man said I couldn't get *into the union because of the record*, so I worked "off the books" and got paid in cash. But when my Parole Officer found out about it, *he made me quit.*

I worked in a laundry, too, for a while, but some *baby clothes* got *stolen*, and when the manager asked me if I had a record and I said yes, he *fired me*, even though I told him I wasn't married and couldn't have any use for the stuff.

Then I worked in a car place, and one day I turned a car on that had been left in gear, and it crashed into another car. But they didn't fire me for that—*they fired me because* a bonding company said I had a record and I guess they figured I might steal a car, even though nothing was on my record about ever stealing a car.

I had a lot of trouble getting a *driver's license*, but after *three years* I finally got one. . . . I applied for a bus driver's job, and I got very good scores on all the tests. But the city of New York informed me it was exercising its rights to choose only *one out of every three people* who applied.

I had a job driving a gypsy cab for a while, and it's a funny thing, I thought it was a parole violation to drive one of those cabs, because we all stopped to pick up people even though we weren't supposed to. So I never told my Parole Officer until I applied to get off parole. He said it wasn't a violation to drive a gypsy cab, but it was a violation not to have told him about it. So I had to serve two more years of parole.

One thing I'd always wanted to be was a singer, and I did cut a record. I even sang with a group for a while, but they had to let me go because I couldn't *get a cabaret license* to sing anywhere they sold alcoholic beverages.

Eventually I gave up, and went back into crime. I'd spent about three years trying to go straight, and it just seemed it wasn't going to work. And in prison I'd learned how to graduate from snatching pocketbooks and mugging to armed robbery, living off women, selling stolen goods, and dealing in reefers and cocaine. So I started a second criminal career.

But I wanted to breathe easy. I really didn't like it. And then one time I was watching TV and saw some members of the Fortune Society, and I've been with them ever since.

November 1970

Where Law Enforcement Came From

Earlier pages have suggested some of the arboreal tangle in our courts and police structures in all our big cities. Our "inheritance" of these courts and services, in fact the entire police idea, is little looked into, little known. The fact is that it is quite recent, and a few pages regarding its origins will be of interest.

We didn't invent it here. Its provenance is London. It was quickly born, and, considering the public convulsions in which it appeared, surprisingly able to deal with a problem never met before; a problem painfully suffered and publicly acknowledged, yet never sensibly confronted nor waded into.

Now we have all these problems here, right down the front of our shirt. If it's a different time and setting, it's the same in all its major lineaments, roots, and provocations. Crime, like war, is picturesque only when it has become history or fiction; when the shock and pain of it is borne not by you but by another. Because there came that day when Englishmen would take no more, we have our own police services now.

Evolution of Law Enforcement

Most Americans know very little about this subject. Law enforcement is primarily an English product. Though its true origins go back to the Magna Charta (1215), its "modern" outlines were first seen five centuries later, in 1749. That was the year a pamphlet appeared bearing the title: *"An Inquiry into the Cause of the Late Increase in Robbers."*

Its author was Henry Fielding, an English magistrate with a court on Bow Street, and remembered today not as a magistrate but as the author, among other classics, of *Tom Jones.*

In the middle of the eighteenth century, London was protected by 2,000 watchmen, beadles, and constables. Sheriffs also served, both in the city and in outlying counties. The men were poorly paid, poorly trained, and bribable. Bribery was common, too, among magistrates and justices. Liquor was sold inside London prisons. Gin cost one English penny a quart.

Fielding's paper hit fed-up Londoners where they could feel it; the same way residents in American cities today can feel it. Instant public support of Fielding's report and plan brought the Bow Street Runners into being. It was England's first organized law enforcement agency. And it succeeded. Public support helped. Tough training and regular pay did the rest.

The pay, which seems pitiful today, was respectable money then: two shillings and sixpence per night—about sixty cents. Tours of duty ran from 10 P.M. to five, six, or seven in the morning, depending on the season, the weather, and the degree of daylight.

What Henry Fielding had first organized was a foot patrol, but it grew each year, expanding from a beginning unit of five town patrols—the City of London itself—to thirteen county patrols. Five years after it started, a horse troop was added and this enormously increased the effectiveness of the Runners—giving them mobility and faster communication, much as prowl cars, radio, and helicopters do now. It made the commission of a crime more difficult by increasing the risk of detection.

Much of this was effected by giving to pikemen, who guarded all the main roads leading into and out of London, descriptions of "men wanted," of stolen merchandise, and suspicious vehicles.

To enter or leave London at night, all travelers needed a pass. If such was in order, the highway pikeman guarding the gate turned his pike, permitting the traveler to pass. (Hence the word "turnpike," in the opinion of many.)

But here all suspects were detained, for the Runners of eighteenth-century England held what is equivalent to today's Stop and Frisk law. And used it.

Henry Fielding is the first significant name in the long struggle to improve police techniques, and the first anywhere—in terms of crime deterrence—that *certainty* of punishment was more effective than *severity* of punishment. Unfortunately for London and English law enforcement, Fielding died in 1755 and for some years the effectiveness of the Runners lapsed. Without the effective "carry-on" of his blind half-brother, affectionately known as "The Beak," it would have died out.

In 1770 London had the first and worst of many riots. It was led by a nineteen-year-old Scot—George Gordon—who objected to Parliament's easing of restrictions against Roman Catholics. He was a fanatic, but he was eloquent—a born leader of bad causes. He defied the new laws and assembled a mob of 60,000 who for eight days fired and ransacked shops, warehouses, and private homes. Half of London was burned down. (Charles Dickens has written vividly of this in *Barnaby Rudge*.) London called out the military but it was too late. The damage was done.

Some of the destruction wrought by the insane Scot, George Gordon, was mitigated by another Scot, Patrick Colquhon, 25 years later. In 1795 he confronted English citizens and the Houses of Parliament with the size and reality, and the *cost*, of the corruption all about them. Nothing reaches an Englishman (or an American) faster than a threat to his money. Colquhon pointed out to Parliament what the figures were and reminded England once more of a great but simple truth: when the courts are weak, the police are powerless. His speech soon appeared as a pamplet, extant today, and titled: *A Treatise on the Police of the Metropolis*.

It had some immediate results. One of these was a revival and extension of the horse patrol of the earlier Bow Street Runners. And this in turn was improved and extended, in 1805, by Sir Richard Ford. Mounted troops were now to be found all over London's main roads, spoking out twenty miles in every direction from the center of the city to all high-roads, where highwaymen had been robbing private citizens and holding up coaches for a century.

Under Sir Richard Ford, the concentration was on putting down the marauding of highwaymen. He and his mounted troops stopped them cold. They were exceptional horsemen, most of them being retired English cavalrymen. They were tough. They were expert in the use of the cavalry sabre, and they carried sidearms. There were 52 patrols of fifty men each. There were remount stations, and the men were well paid.

(Here a note of more than passing interest: compared to today's volume of clerical work expected of America's police, the

500 men in the horse patrol of 1805 had only two inspectors and *one* record clerk.)

But English crime sprang up anew in the cities. Transporting criminals to Australia and to Oglethorpe, Georgia, did nothing to stop the birth of new criminals. Parliament once again took notice. The presenting drama was the Peterloo Massacre on August 10th, 1816. In England there is no such place as Peterloo but the irony was clear and the name has stuck: the massacre occurred one year after the Battle of Waterloo and occurred in St. Peter's Field, in the city of Manchester. Sixty thousand farmers, yeomen, and townspeople, peaceably assembled under one Henry Hunt, were petitioning Parliament to repeal the Corn Laws. Magistrates ordered the cavalry to charge. Which they did. And disgraced themselves, chopping down everyone in their way. They had forgotten that the military had done nothing to stop the Gordon Riots. And now this. The military always made everything worse.

Sir Robert Peel introduced into Parliament a bill *dispensing* with the military for any peace-keeping purposes and providing, instead, for a professional, permanent, paid police force; a force to be smartly uniformed and sharply trained.

The training took place on the grounds of a large field, which during the eleventh and twelfth centuries had been the site of a palace where the Scottish kings resided while making their annual visit to London to pay tribute to the English kings, a yard known, for the reason given, as Scotland Yard. And it has been romantically, if incorrectly, called Scotland Yard ever since. The proper name is the Metropolitan Police.

Sir Robert added one more dynamic to the armamentarium already put together by his predecessors. Like many other great ideas, his was remarkably simple, almost primitive: *instant contact with any disorder and the instant handling of it.*

The success of this platoon, men who were high in character and hard in muscle, soon spread to other English cities where their skills and methods were adopted. Presently the idea of the "new police" jumped the English Channel and became the model for police organizations in most of Europe's principal cities. And from there to our own shores. The police departments of most American cities, in their main outlines, can be directly traced to the blueprints drafted by Robert Peel 140 years ago.

Dangerous Holdover

Think how stubbornly, though, some of the oldest ideas still cling to police custom and observance. I shall cite only one. It relates to rape. We all know the expression "hue and cry." It was perhaps effective in rural England—metropolitan England, too, when a girl called for help while being chased by some bumpkin who wanted to head her into the barn. Or, being surprised there, could scream. Most rapes in America are unreported. Those that are all testify to its unpleasant increase. It is an experience that only a woman can fully comprehend—one of terror, shame, and total victimization. I know two women who have been through this. Neither reported it. In the matter of rape, both law and custom (and psychology) leave women very poorly off.

They don't report it because it is too "private"; they are too embarrassed. Many don't wish it known to anyone, even to a relative. They doubt if they'll ever again see the rapist, so doubt any chance of identification. The police "attitude" is not very helpful. They are men with men's feelings, not women scalded with hurt and outrage. And they know that irrespective of the evidence, or strength of corroboration, the chances for conviction are very small.

One day in a gathering of police, while I was taking courses at the New York Police Academy, I suggested that many women would be less reluctant to report a rape to another woman. New York has 360 policewomen. The suggestion got nowhere. "It comes under hue and cry," I was told. "All they need to do is set up a hue and cry." I told this officer that hue and cry is *900 years old*; that the world has changed and that any woman in any American city today has as much chance being heard—given the opportunity—as a talking doll in a rock festival. And with a knife on her, what woman is going to be foolish enough to scream?

During the '60s, rape increased faster than any of the crimes committed against the person—93 per cent.

New York State laws aren't 900 years old but the laws pertaining to rape are over a hundred. Bills urged on the legislature, four years running, have failed to pass. An interesting account of this foot-dragging appeared in The New York *Times* (June 15, 1971) written by Angela Taylor. What do these laws say?

"Rape laws are tremendously prejudiced," Miss Taylor quoted Assemblyman Constance E. Cook, a Republican from Ithaca, one of the three women in the Assembly. "The law discriminates against women and children, who are the victims. No other law requires such corroboration."

"The present laws are a disgrace," said Assemblyman Fred Schmidt, Democrat of Queens, who helped sponsor one of the current bills. "It's tough to prove rape. And a rapist can get off with probation."

Jack R. Litman, an assistant district attorney in New York, explained the current laws:

"In order to get an indictment, you must corroborate every element of the crime, including identity. You must prove penetration: a doctor's testimony that there was recently deposited sperm in the vaginal vault, or a ruptured hymen. It's very important that force be *proved*. Force is what separates rape from fornication, and fornication is not against the law in New York State."

Assemblyman Alan Hochberg, Democrat of the Bronx (Miss Taylor reports), sponsored legislation to amend the old laws in 1970 and again in 1971. He had previously been a Bronx D.A. "When I was a district attorney, I often had to tell parents that I couldn't convict the man who raped their daughter. I think sex crimes should have the same degree of evidence as a mugging."

Both Assemblywoman Cook and Assemblyman Hochberg stated that their colleagues argued for retention of the old laws because "a spiteful woman could bring false charges. Prosecutors say there are cases where women go along with a seduction and then suddenly report rape."

What do most women do in this emergency? Here's the story of Jane M:

I had been having dinner with friends and I took a taxi home. Because of the one-way street, I asked the driver to let me out at the corner. I was at the mailbox in the vestibule of my building. The man suddenly appeared from nowhere, put a knife to my throat, and asked for money. I had only $10 and that made him mad. He ordered me to take him to my apartment. I thought I could fool him by going to a neighbor's door but in the elevator, he changed his mind and took me to the roof. On the roof he slit my clothes into strips and tied me up. It occurred to me to yell but there was no one to hear me.

He said he wouldn't kill me unless I screamed and he kept asking me, "Do you think I'm good?" Believe me, I said "Yes." Then he carefully put everything back in my purse, told me not to move till he got away. I got myself untied, put on my coat and shoes, and ran to neighbors on the top floor. They called the police. They asked me if I wanted to go to a hospital, but I couldn't face it. I went to my own doctor.

Later she went through police files but her assailant's picture was not there. Her attitude was more philosophical than that of most women:

After all, I wasn't a kid or a virgin. I was just glad to be alive. The police asked me if I'd appear at the trial if they caught him. Of course I would. If this had happened to a young girl, it could destroy her life.

"Roof" rapes are hard to prove: no evidence of a wrecked room, no one to hear, no signs of disturbance. And wherever it occurs, women hate to face police questioning; hate the raw details. But the women are beginning to gang up on this outrage, and the outrageous lack of physical and legal protection provided them. Most weapons are illegal. "Kick him in the groin" is about the only police suggestion ever made. (Suppose she misses?)

The radical feminists are vocal about what is happening to their sisters, supporting legislation in many states. And they are screaming at police departments to set up a "rape squad of women officers" to interview victims. But it's just as hard to see how any police service can quarrel with the sense of that as it is to see why they still invoke hue and cry, which was in England when William the Conqueror got there. In too many police services, the physical equipment is as up-to-date as the philosophies are ancient.

PART FOUR

Attica

"Are those black doors the cells?"

"Yes."

"Are they all full?"

"Well, they're pretty nigh full, and that's a fact, and no two ways about it."

"Those at the bottom are unwholesome, surely?"

"Why, we *do* only put coloured people in 'em. That's the truth."

"When do the prisoners take exercise?"

"Well, they do without it pretty much."

"Do they never walk in the yard?"

"Considerable seldom."

—Charles Dickens
American Notes—1842

Some Thoughts About Attica

PRISON GUARDS have had a bad press for as long as we've had prisons. I've seldom seen—nor have you—a feature story about guards in any American newspaper or Sunday supplement that didn't set forth, or at least insinuate, that this special fraternity was a cadre more depraved and sadistic than the inmates they were hired to control.

I do not believe this to be true, either at Attica, or in general in other prisons.

By this time I know a large number of these men; what they feel on the job and off it, how they live, what they make, what they think, what provocations and rewards they live under; what the risks and pressures really are; where, and how long, they went to school, and why they sought this work for a livelihood.

I've fished with them, played cards with them, eaten their prison food, met their families, slept in their homes, danced with their wives, played with their kids.

It is my belief that prison guards are normal males, behaving well in abnormal settings; responding to the danger, confinement, boredom, and vicissitudes of prison life very much as you and I would respond were we there.

I know the "feel" of Attica, the prison; and I know the town. I had been to both and had been there years before the uprising that shook the nation so severely in the dreadful days of September 1971. And I will go back again, to talk to prisoners there, if the service that brings in outside speakers is reactivated.

The popular and the publicized concept that prison guards are socially dislocated loners—seeking the main chance and not finding it and winding up in prison work in lieu of something else or something better—is quite false. Prison guards are first of all family men. And local men. They grew up in the community they serve in. They live in it, marry in it, raise their families in it. And remain in it after they retire.

Nor is it a floating population. In prisons located in rural America, there is almost no turnover of guards. (Previously I've brought out the turnover rate for the Tombs.) At Attica it is less than one per cent a year, and it relates to young guards only, and to their earliest days.

Another misconception: the public never thinks that prison guards have honest gripes of their own. They do, the same as the prisoners do, though the gripes themselves are quite different.

Still talking specifically to the point of Attica, I shall mention only one here, though it is common enough in others. It is the request, through the years, for three pieces of equipment they don't have: hard-hats, gas-masks, and walkie-talkies, and you may decide whether you feel this to be trivial.

Through their union—#82 of the C.I.O.–A.F. of L.—and through direct representation, this has been urged on the Albany Assembly for years and consistently bypassed. Yes, of course—no money for such. Yet in the instant case, this has unusual meaning and tough significance. Before the insurrection, the guards knew it was coming. At Attica there is an idiotic, antebellum lack of simple communication, withheld for budget reasons. Had it been provided, it would have positively prevented, in the opinion of the officers, the slaughter that occurred there.

Almost every police service in this country today has a dependable intercom system. Prisons don't, and Attica, by nature of its architecture, is really not one prison but four, each block a separate entity, independent of the others, physically partitioned from the block adjacent by walls, gates, and individual locking systems.

This lack of a rudimentary communications system at Attica had the charnel result we've read and heard so much about. Though guards, captains, and the "P.K." (Principal Keeper) knew that serious trouble was soon to explode, those at the very flash-point of its origin were not physically able to alert their command. There was not a walkie-talkie in the entire acreage.

"You go along with a situation for years," John Cosgrove, an Attica guard for the past 26 years, said to me, "and all of a sudden there's trouble. And it's too late. And it's always the same reason. Equipment costs money."

Is that not a fiscal stupidity to stun any layman? Nonetheless it is another fact of prison life in America: primitive equipment in an age of communication marvels.

Even Boy Scouts have walkie-talkies. They cost fifty dollars.

Prison guards have other headaches. Consider them. They hear little from inmates but complaints. They get used to it, tired of it, inured to it. So would you. You read about prisoners' complaints all the time. Prisoners complain about prison food. They will always complain about it, and in all prisons. There is a good reason, too, yet in nothing I've read in newspapers, social-study books, magazine articles, or ever seen discussed on television programs, has it ever been brought out. *Is* prison food really as awful as all prisoners, in all prisons, say it is?

Here is a truthful statement about food, not in prisons throughout the country, just the food at Attica. Prisoners don't like prison food because it isn't the food they're used to. At Attica, when I was there last (June 1971), the prison population was 2,200.* Ninety-seven per cent of these men were big-city prisoners. Eighty-five per cent were blacks or Puerto Ricans. Almost all of these men were street-oriented. They were sandwich-grabbers and coffee-jumpers. What is such a man going to do with a tomato salad?

* As of June 25, 1972, Attica's prison population was 1,226, and for the first time in many years, more whites than blacks. At this time there are 18 black guards and one Spanish-speaking guard, coming in from Rochester and Buffalo, none from New York.

The Attica diet regularly includes salads. Most Attica prisoners never had a salad before. They don't like it. They don't want it. They don't eat it. So they complain.

From a dietetic point of view, the Attica meals are well balanced. Half the food comes from the prison farm. And meals, for all the state's prisons, are scheduled by a professional dietician. It is good but not glamorous, no more so than Army food, but its nutritional value needs no vitamin pills as dietary fortifiers.

Attica inmates get a lot of spaghetti and meatballs; cooked cereal twice a week, fresh fruit and sweet rolls only once a week. They get a lot of pork (from the prison farm). They complain that they get too much, the Black Muslims especially. It is a justifiable complaint. Moslems don't eat pork (though it is interesting to note that pork, for blacks, was as popular as chicken, before they became Moslems). I remember a comparable problem when, as a young man, I was teaching in a university in a part of North India that is now Pakistan. Here we had to have *three* kitchens: one for Hindus, one for Moslems, and one for "Europeans." American prisons can't maintain three kitchens. They can handle only one, the same as a ship in the Navy. I remember another problem, quite recent. A new restaurant, a good one (the Camelot) most agreeably appeared on the ground floor of a brand-new high-rise across the street from my own apartment. It was, and is, heavily patronized. It serves New York's best roast beef. I took friends there one night only to find all the kitchen help on strike. You know the reason: within four months, "the hell with all this roast beef."

There will always be complaints, many of them valid, about prison food, but the lay reader hearing about it throughout his life never puts his own mind to the exercise of inquiring into the life-style of prisoners-before-they-became-prisoners; that their eating habits were bad and that these habits are hard-set; that many of the younger men lived in rooms, alone; moved often, snatched food at the sorry counters nearest them, wolfed it, developed a fixed appetite for a few special dishes and stayed with that.

The food at Attica is better than the food they had before they got there—better food than the guards', say the guards. Guards don't eat much better than inmates. And all hate the pork. The pigs from the Attica pig farm are just too fat. Prison food is unappetizingly served. This is the fault of the prisoners who are responsible for keeping the trays clean.

They complain, too, because it's traditional to complain. I've many times noted, though, that all the meat they are given—ham, lamb, beef, veal, or bacon—is stamped with the seal of the state inspector. Their hotdogs are put up by Wilson. It is military food, prepared to feed large masses of men, 600 or 700 at a sitting. It is well cooked. And you can stay healthy on the Attica diet.

What about the Attica hours, in and out of cells?

There is too much lock-in, all agree, including all the COs. We've seen few reports on *how* an Attica inmate spends his time when not in his cell. How is it spent?

About 400 prisoners work in the Attica metal shop, about fifty in the laundry. Other shops—paint shop, roofers, electricians, plumbers, shoemakers, spot-welding, tailor, and clothing shop (pants and shirts only) account for 500 to 800, depending on prison population.

Probably the metal shop at Attica is the most "sophisticated." They make desks, lockers, and hospital nightstands. The equipment is complete and modern, the instruction good. In all the shops there is opportunity to learn a skill or trade. Any prisoner who applies himself in the metal shop, for example, or in the prison garage, is qualified for an outside job as a machinist.

Most of these opportunities are resisted. Before finding their way to prison, most inmates did little work, so they have poor work habits. Most have a hostile attitude toward work, as such, of any kind. Their job records are spattery. Many never worked at all, don't know what it is. It was not part of their street life, the only life they knew.

If an inmate is interested, he can be assigned to any prison shop or task, from making safety devices to repairing conveyor-belts. It is only the exceptional inmate who seeks this chance. (And conversely, it is always his own work area, in the destructive frenzy of riot, that he smashes first.)

Except for their special hustle, most have been unemployed, in the conventional sense, through most of the years of their lost and spotted lives. Most are young. The educational and intelligence level is low. So is the emotional level. Most guards feel the emotional level is that of ten and eleven-year-olds. I've never heard it estimated above the fifteen-year level.

For Attica inmates having a fifth-grade education or less, class-room instruction is compulsory. Beyond that it is elective, though few line up for the limited courses available.

The depressing effects of claustrophobia on prisoners have been explored in many studies. The depressing effect of claustrophobia on guards has been ignored. Nonetheless, it is very real. And damaging. In prison management work it can't be ignored. In its stealthy creep, it takes hold of young guards in the first few weeks of their service, and it can turn them quickly into psychiatric casualties if it is not relieved. Those seen to suffer with it, those who don't or can't adjust, are usually moved to wall positions, where the unbreaking monotony of terrain, the endless openness, sometimes induces fears of its reverse; of agoraphobia.

These men don't stay, but the dropout rate is very low, and most who can't get used to the prison climate are COs doing duty in their first or second year. If a CO stays for five years, he'll stay for life; or, barring accident or illness, till he retires at sixty-three.

Among the guards at Attica there is a sense of kinship. Most of these men have known each other and members of each other's families from early days. Most have passed through pretty much the same life experiences from infancy on, whether in the town of Attica itself or in its few factories or in the long, rolling farmlands —dairy farms and orchards mostly—that are the central feature of all these western New York counties. This is a part of America well known to me. I went to college in it and have returned every year since, often for many months.

Having the same backgrounds, including education, and making the same or nearly the same money tends to breed a stable and homogeneous society, essentially, irretrievably "small town," if you wish; and this is the setting for the pool of prison guards who do, and who will continue to, hold these jobs in all our prisons, state or Federal, that are not located in or near big cities; that are located—most of them invisibly—in areas remote from metropoli-tan contact. Attica is ten miles from the larger town of Batavia, forty from Buffalo, about the same from Rochester.

In terms of raw economics, the town of Attica subsists on the prison. And the prison is the core of both its civic life (Attica's Mayor Richard Miller, for example, is an Attica guard) and its preoccupations.

Attica was a "nothing" town before the prison, newly built, was dedicated in 1931 by F.D.R., himself not long in office. It drew the biggest "house" the town had ever beheld, until the riots forty years later. Now it is a prison town and little more, featureless, close to dreary in any weather, authentically so in autumn rains or April slush. But it's a "good" town of church-goers, Christian canvasses, and pinochle-but-not-bridge. It is the center of New York's mighty snow-belt. Its climates are extreme, cruel in summer, unbelievably hostile in winter. (On June 10, 1972, a hard freeze, worse than a frost, killed all of Wyoming County's tomatoes and early beans.) The weather and the land, the prison and the farms, have stabilized the citizenry here, a town, an atmosphere, a community that changes little as the generations move up. The only new sight anywhere is a proliferation of Ski–doos.

Thus Attica's officers are country boys. High school diplomas or "equivalency" certification is required before applying for work at the prison. There are tough physical and agility tests, easy to pass for most men with such outdoor backgrounds as theirs. Defects are screened out early. The new guards come in with strong bodies. Eighty per cent have had military training somewhere, a good plus for such work.

From my own acquaintance with this austere and cheerless facility, the most valid, most pitiable complaint that inmates make is that there are no black guards and no Puerto Rican or Spanish-speaking guards. This is an important and persistent complaint, for these are the ethnic preponderances that make up Attica's main population. Superintendent Vincent Mancusi during his six-year service there, had endeavoured to correct this, without success. Probably it cannot be corrected. And for a simple reason: blacks and Puerto Ricans don't want jobs there. In a way, it's related to complaints about the food. It's too far from "home," too far from surroundings they know and respond to. It's 400 miles from Harlem. When off duty, black guards have nothing to do, nowhere to go; no tinsel, no "life," no women, a bar or two only. Very few black families have ever settled in any of these counties. Nothing up there for them.

Attica has three motels—the Stag House, the St. James, and the Attica House—each accommodating about fifteen guests. The town has one poolroom, one factory (a Westinghouse foundry), and no movie theater. There are no blacks in the schools, not one black family in the town, very few in Wyoming County at all, and since the Erie Canal days there never have been.

Yet Attica *has* had black guards. One stayed a month, the other two months. Puerto Ricans are also non-receptive and for the same reason. No prejudice is involved in any of this. But it is a serious and conspicuous lack. And it has no remedy.

There are many black guards in Sing Sing but the prison is only a 35-minute trainride from Harlem. Most Sing Sing guards live in Harlem, and commute.

What do Attica guards think about such things as work-release, inmate instruction, inmate security guards, lock-in, an honor system? All of them support the penological recommendations we read about. They know they'll have a better prison, and that the prisoners will, if any of these germinal plantings are allowed to send up any shoots. But these improvements, universally recognized as morale-builders, recognized as incentive generators of proven rehabilitative value, never get well started. Or never get started at all. It is the same experience, at Attica, as it has been and is now in the Tombs and Rikers Island in New York: no state money to support new projects, and such Federal money as is intermittently appropriated is short and temporary.

Thus work-release, which in theory does exist at Attica, does not exist in practice. The inmates who have benefited by it are a pitiful few indeed: six, the last I knew, which quickly went down to three. Why so? To drive these men to work required a state vehicle. This cost $25 a week. The prisoners worked in a pre-fab factory (Sterling Homex), a respectable and profitable firm. They could keep the money they earned ($90 a week as carpenters) and were glad to pay for their own breakfast and lunch. Three of these six prisoners were paroled, which is good. But six out of 2,200 is worse than a poor showing. It is a public disgrace. It obliterates the purpose of work-release. It is the exact situation, in a huge upstate facility, that has mocked and stultified all comparable programs in New York City's prison jungle for fifty years, and of which you've now read, in earlier pages, the scorn poured out on that city's fathers by Anna Kross.

It is tokenism of such exquisite attenuation as to be comical.

Where Should New Prisons Go Up?

The American public is "on record" for prison reform. It is also on record for being against it. Consider the public's reaction in the matter of the *location* of prisons. No American wants any prison anywhere near himself or his family. Relax security? Sure, we like that, too, provided the prison is in another state or county. They are "your" prisoners, never "mine."

When Attica was built, penologists were unanimous that this three-tiered fortress was going up in the wrong place, that prisons should be constructed in or near large cities. And for good reasons: easier for inmates' families to visit; access to work-release opportunities; availability of more diverse and professional manpower for staffing these facilities.

Attica went up in a rural county anyhow, and its staff is drawn from the 30-mile farming radius around it. That was forty years ago.

Has it taught the public anything? Not much. Ohio is just finishing a huge prison at Lucasville. Where's that? It's close to the Kentucky border and "just about as far away from anything else as they could have gotten it."

An important new facility is going up at Steele, Missouri. Where is Steele? It's an obscure village close to the Arkansas line. New Jersey has a new prison going up at Leesburg, a prison widely acclaimed for the modern practicality of its design. Near a city? No. It's in the farming and truck garden part of extreme south Jersey, as unrelated to metropolitan contact in New Jersey as Attica is in New York.

In 1966 Maryland put up its state's "correctional training center" in Hagerstown. Was that, is that, a good place for it? Not in the opinion of Maryland's former Commissioner of Correction, Joseph G. Cannon. "You couldn't get anybody to go up there. You couldn't staff it professionally. You end up with people—

God bless 'em, they're good hard-working people—but for one thing, they don't understand the blacks."

Doesn't this sound like Attica all over again?

What does it do to work-release? It kills it.

Once again it is *money* that keeps putting up our prisons in rural areas. It's cheaper. But you can't have work-release programs in rural areas. Why not? No work to which an inmate can be released: no industries, no factories, no commercial centers.

Work-release is a vital part of rehabilitation. We don't have either one in America. We just talk about it and approve of it, and don't do it. Work-release was an innovation when it came into being in Wisconsin, in 1913. The ensuing years haven't taught us much beyond proof that it's an excellent thing: good enough so that nearly 40 states have adopted it by law. And let it sit there. It has an almost prehistoric viability, somewhat like the armadillo, surviving despite man's indifference, living in solitude.

Some sad but interesting figures come to use from Walter H. Busher. He was director of a work-release study at the Criminal Justice Institute in Sacramento, California. Of 200,000 prisoners (scattered over the whole of the United States), 5,000 were participating "in some form or other" in work-release. That is one out of forty, and better than nothing. Better by a good deal than the Attica figures—6 out of 2,200. But most of these one-out-of-every-forty were involved in work-release in only four states: North Carolina, Florida, Maryland, and California.

Why not the others? Most states—37 in 1971—have laws that support work-release. Yet many of these same states disqualify any inmate from participating in the programs if his crime involved violence, drugs, alcohol, or "sex." What does this condition mean? It means that it virtually bars them all (all but sober swindlers or eunuchoid check–hikers). So what does this mean, in sum? It means that work-release, though fertilized, is an embryo close to stillbirth.

It's working in North Carolina. Why is that? There are two reasons: North Carolinians are accustomed to *seeing* prisoners at work in road gangs, outside their prisons. North Carolina adopted it soon after Wisconsin invented it. The other reason: the only inmate *ineligible* for work-release in North Carolina is the man doing a life sentence, less than 4 percent of the total prison population.

What about the domestic health of "halfway houses," another hopeful breakthrough. It is very bad. Halfway houses are limited in number—today there are about 300 with a floating population of 4,500—but the public, again approving, is, by its response, disapproving. They want them. But they don't want them *in their community*. (They want them in yours.) They don't want to be in the same block with a halfway house. And it is feared (by home-owners) that they hurt property values. A Louis Harris survey (1967) confirmed this; that Americans wanted them but didn't want them in their neighborhoods; "and knew their neighbors didn't want them either."

In somewhat the same mood of indifference is the case, in New York City, of an empty facility, on Morton Street, which the city wanted to use as a treatment center for drug users who had been jailed. Morton Street residents howled. Not in our block! They organized a committee and petitioned the city to keep it empty.

Mixing in-prison labor with in-prison vocational training has its headaches. The director of "state use" industries (license plates, in this case) complained that it was hard for him to meet his quotas because his best workers were always being called away from their machines "for one goddam class or another."

How can the prison win? How the prisoner? Who cares? Americans don't care. They just claim to. Correction officials all over this country agree on one basic item: that our prisons have the *lowest* priorities of any other public responsibility. This is a dis-tinction universally challenged by the superintendents of all our insane asylums. I've been through fourteen of the latter. And I'd call it a photo finish. Americans, a most compassionate race, *do* care about the invisible mumbling wrecks in all these horrid places, but care about them on only one condition: that our con-victs and our insane be kept permanently out of sight.

So that is pretty much what we do. We don't want to shock any-body on Morton Street. God forbid.

Once more the physical location of prisons brings up the hoary paradox: work-release exists. But it doesn't. The last work-release effort at Attica, funded by the Federal government, lasted only three months. Then the money ran out.

Everything costs money. And this is where the public drags its heels, without knowing how to lift them. Perhaps it is better to say this is where the pressures on budget priorities in all of America's boards of estimate are largely unseen by the voting public; largely withheld from scrutiny or free debate, open to all.

Attica prisoners complain about the showers there. What *about* the showers at Attica? There are eighty of them. Half the inmate population can take a shower every day. They don't complain. What about the other half? They can shower, but only once a week. They complain. They're dirty. They stink. They don't like to stink. Why can't *they* take a shower every day? There aren't enough showers. Nor enough guards to escort them there. Showers, like breakfast or the milk-run or paint-spraying, require supervision. Men. Money. Always money. So Attica has only these eighty showers, and some inmates smell better than others. When you're near them, you know who has showered and who hasn't.

Prisoners complain about being beaten. And they get beaten. The polarization between guards and inmates has been known for some time. When it hears of a prisoner being beaten, the public response is the same everywhere: "How awful!" The public never knows in full who did what. Nor who did what first. The public did not inhabit the scene, nor did the men who reported it.

If you have a system of control, mandated and paid for by society, is there any known way to control violence except to meet it? Violence anywhere is awful. To me it is the most hideous thing in all living, a direct denial of the primordial right to be safe in one's person. In prison as well? Yes.

This also includes the right of a prison *guard* to be safe in his own person, in his own prison.

A few pages back I mentioned a name—John Cosgrove, an Attica guard well known to me. He is more than a personal acquaintance, he is a close personal friend, a friendship beginning in the early '50s. I believe I know his chemical and moral quality within two or three per cent of its exact value. His wife's, too. She is head nurse on the night staff at Wyoming County Hospital in Warsaw, sixteen miles from Attica. I've seen these people many hundreds of times and will continue to see them, to seek them out, through remaining years. They are that kind of people—open, giving, serving, uncomplicated.

I had long talks with John and other guards after the riots. "I've never clubbed a prisoner. And I've never seen a prisoner clubbed," John said. I believe him. But does it prove anything? No. Over the years, though, I've seen many Cosgroves. If you find weapons in a cell, you have to take them out. If you find weapons on a prisoner, you have to take them away from the man. If he uses his weapon first, you have one to use, and use it. No guns. Just the club. Almost all collisions between guards and inmates are provoked by the inmates, who are provoked by the rotten circumstance of their life, the unresponding muteness of corridors, the dull special meanings of all the clangs and clangor, the retreating shadows of parole.

The Emotional Charge the Prisoner Carries

It is difficult for any layman to reconstruct or even to guess at the day-to-day and night-by-night entries in the diary of a young man (were he to write it) in a big city, in his knockabout relentless progress through the city's slime and alleys that ends in a crime for which he's caught and put away, a crime that is not his first, a prison not his first. To him, prison is a wasting stopover between trains. His return to old scenes, his picking-up of familiar operations will resume when he can move again.

But he's here now, in this prison, and coming in with him is his culture. Nakedly stated, it is this: you do the things acceptable to your particular neighborhood.

None of this is acceptable in the prison that now receives him. The shock is painful, the resentment electric. Opportunities to retaliate are limited. Frustrations multiply. The dividend of resentment, never a "dividend," builds or diminishes according to the intelligence, malleability, or adaptive skill of each man, as prison routine engulfs him. But the resentment, big or little, remains, and seeks any lightning-rod down which it can dump its mammoth rage.

This conduit has to be one of three persons—an officer, another inmate, or the prisoner himself—for during his days he sees no others, and he has no "nights." ("I've been here seven years," said an Attica prisoner, "and I haven't seen one single star.")

He's an unstable person, crammed into sudden mechanical stability, but at the same time into emotional, functional, and social instability of large dimension. He may be and often is physically audacious (riot leaders), even courageous; cunning, too (riot planners); and he is gang-bred, gang-oriented. He's vicious, and though he doesn't carry his own detonator, he does carry his own charge. It goes about with him, inside his skin. The guard is the detonator. Or the food. Or a bad call in a ball-game, the colliding points of his life.

It would strain the imagination of any sociologist, any penologist, to create a climate of propaedeutical improvement in which the inertial drives as inhere in the average prisoner could be reversed; a climate in which such a man could *really* be remade; in which such a man would wish it. But for such an objective the American prison is a poor incubator, for it is the fortuitously calculated opposite.

A prisoner brings other things, other reactions, immediately dangerous to COs and to the atmospheres of prison routine, prison stability. Whatever his age, he brings in a lifetime of instant gratification. Instant gratification of all his desires: sexual, recreational, social, physical. This, and what it means, is seldom thought of. They may be large, they may be limited, but they are his and they are basic. For his own needs, before incarceration, they are instantly available or soon made to be; cajoled, appropriated, or forced. What he needs, he takes. When not on the beat of his hustle, he's been raised in front of a television set where instant gratification is delivered free to him, with some quick food in his lap and a beer sitting on the floor.

And he brings his vanity. Each prisoner is his own hero, self-declared, self-admiring, as Henri Charriere is in *Papillon*, without realizing that we, the reader, can re-work the portrait and limn in what he left out. And appearing not so noble as he'd have his reader think. Whether an inmate really "made it" on the outside— and most haven't, and know it, and know it of each other, and hide it in the big talk in the yard, or in the garish, autistic reveries of the cell—he tries for the bad-dude, big-shot disguise; he picks up the colorful new words in the polyglot and patois of the block;

an early coaching in, and sharing of, just who's who around here. But it's all false and phony and inside themselves they know it. They see through the tatters of their own charade.

A captain at Attica, Frank Wald, in earlier days at the Clinton State Prison (Dannemora) near Plattsburgh, had piloted a diagnostic treatment center there, which had, among other innovations, the acting-out by prisoners, in sessions of socio-drama, of the crime that brought them there; the acting-out of this, plus the needs and urgencies that had brought them to the crime's commission.

These socio-dramas, conducted by a physician from McGill, Dr. Mark Senick, were enthusiastically joined in by inmates and very often brought out, for the prisoner's own first moment of self-recognition, *why* he was hostile. Socio- and psycho-drama is emerging as something a good deal more than parlor entertainment, and psychiatrists are making valuable therapeutic use of it, though its creep into prisons is certain to be slow. It has not shown itself in Attica at all, so self-knowledge by inmates there, at least through this technique, is largely unformed: society is still their enemy (as they see it), not they society's, and what they did to society had it coming. The common attitude of prisoners everywhere.

Captain Wald was an Attica hostage, hospitalized for two weeks after his own ordeal, still under treatment after seven months. He was struck down and beaten, blindfolded, dressed in prison clothes which were then saturated with an inflammable liquid (paint-thinner, not gasoline), and saved from being ignited because rioters could not get a flame to his clothing in the huge commotion in which he was first knocked over. This occurred in the wild melee following the herding of hostages into the yard. The saturating of the clothing of all the hostages with a highly volatile liquid was part of the set plan to incinerate them all, though the plan, as we know, was never effectuated.

Captain Wald has been in prison work his whole life. His retirement, after 35 years of service at Attica, coincided with the uprising there but was not influenced by it.

At the time of the riots he had already bought a property in Warsaw and was building a house there. He bears the inmates no resentment, no bitterness.

"I don't know who beat me and I don't wish to. I was blind-folded a good part of those three days and nights. The sanitary conditions were pretty make-believe, but we were fed, and given coffee, and untied so we could eat. I don't hate anybody. In the yard, as a hostage, I talked to the men, knowing we might be dead any moment. You do some good thinking with a knife in your neck. I asked them what good they'd get out of wasting a bunch of us educated fellows, and it got some hoots, but it also got some big laughs. Much later, after the shootings and killings, the guards who hadn't been killed were all still lying down in the yard. In prison clothes it was hard to tell a guard from an inmate. I was real glad to see a state trooper looking down at me. He was the biggest trooper I ever saw. There was a CO with him, going over the ground to identify the hostages. It was a relief to know we weren't going to be set afire. I was hurting pretty good by that time. I took a good mauling but nothing I needed very much was busted. I was lucky." He crushed out a cigarette. "Many weren't so lucky. It's a tough way to go out. Tougher on the families. All the waiting. Then all the bad news. We all lost some mighty good friends here."

Thirty-five guards, younger ones, resigned after the Attica riot. Thirty-one needed psychiatric help.

We were sitting around a kitchen table having coffee.

"What does a prisoner respect?" I asked.

"Fairness. Fair treatment, and a chance for their grievances really to get an honest review. And they respect the authentic big-shot, whatever his bag."

"Like who?"

"Like Willy Sutton, the bank robber. No violence in him at all. And he never carried weapons on any job. He was the most popu-lar prisoner I ever heard of, not only with the administration but with the prisoners themselves."

John Cosgrove came in: "I was on night duty in the prison hospital a few years ago. Willy Sutton had been operated on for an abdominal aneurism* the day before. It was four o'clock in the

---

* This extremely complex operation was performed in the Batavia Hos-pital and cost New York State $5,000. Willy Sutton did his convalescence, a complete recovery, at Attica. Willy Sutton is alive and well and living in Fort Lauderdale, Florida, where he is writing his memoirs.

morning. I didn't hear a sound but I saw a slip of paper slide under my office door. I knew no matter how fast I got to that door, I'd see no one. It's uncanny but it's true, how messages can be transported around a prison—Devil's Island to Dartmoor— and never seen. I picked up the paper. It was a 'Get Well' card for Willy and it was signed by every inmate in his block."

"They loved him," added Wald, "and he really was a lovable man. Inmates are sharp assessors of the skills and courage of others, and secretly aware of where they themselves made the big blunder. They'd like to be the world's most renowned safe-cracker or counterfeiter, too, but most of them messed it up in their apprenticeship. Went too fast. Got too cocky. Took on too much, or double-crossed somebody. In America's prisons you see very few of the really successful criminals, and Willy Sutton, as you may recall, really got fingered by chance. The Attica inmates admired his cunning, and of course they envied his great success. And they overlooked—they always overlook it—the fact that bank robbers and big-time gamblers all wind up broke. They get it quick, then blow it. But with Willy, all the inmates at Attica knew the real thing was here among them, that he'd beat the so-called system time after time, in one coup after another, in one masterful disguise or another. No shoot-outs. Just good planning and steady nerves. He was really worshipped here. He was no trouble. He read all the time. He was the most well-read man I ever met in a prison. But you're right about the image that most bring in, the image of themselves. They know they're losers but they try to hang onto something, so they pin a few decorations on themselves. It's ego support at a very elementary level but they all need it."

I'd seen it before—all of it false and phony, and inside themselves, known to be such.

If prisoners come in with these forgivable, inevitable pantomimes, they leave others out, and those left out—most of them in the "instant gratification" category—both hurt and cripple. Left behind are the flashy clothes, the city lights, and the girls.

The sudden impersonal cut-off of the sex life of prisoners, many at ages of greatest sexual activity, carries a biotic certainty of violence. Young guards are fearful of the unprovoked flare-ups that any mechanism—even in a pacific nature—can unloose, such as a handful of feces* flung through the bars; always a defeating and demoralizing encounter for both sides. (What else can an inmate throw at a guard? An inkwell? He doesn't have an ink-well.) But as these rages immediately reverse themselves, the question of just who's who around here is now cleared up. Overt assault is a round the prisoner can never win; a round he can never be *allowed* to win, any more than it can be allowed or condoned or "understood" in a military establishment when a private knocks over a captain. Yet the rage engendered by sexual starvation is, in the opinion of most guards, the trigger-inciter behind most attacks by inmates upon guards. Often the inmate is not aware of this. He's aware only of his colossal discomfort and his suffocating cramp; the paralyzing sameness of days, the vast uneventfulness of night.

Every month or two there is an episode like the above in any large prison, crowded with young inmates from large cities. Their crime profiles, like their heritage, life-style, domestic privation, and lack of schooling, are largely similar, at least in their principal contours. Prisons in America bring them nothing of what they want, little of what they need. We never put up the money for it. Nor do prisons set up opportunities for self-help or self-discovery, opportunities that are offered with enough psychological persuasion or attractiveness so they can *see* they want it.

Is the rouine at Attica altogether hopeless? No.

At Attica—and this has been much ignored—there are athletic schedules that make sense and that are popular with prisoners. There is quite a variety.

About 150 prisoners play football, about 700 play hand-ball (two courts in each of the four yards). Weight-lifting is big and manly, so it not only draws many participants but always a good audience. There are fourteen horseshoe-pitching pits. Baseball and softball are very popular, about 300 inmates favoring one or the other.

* According to Dr. F. L. Rundle, chief psychiatrist at Soledad, throwing feces is "a last act of desperation. A man has been stripped of every other weapon. It's the only thing left to do. It's humiliating to him, but it's the ultimate humiliation to a guard. The prisoner is just trying to say: 'I'm alive. I'm a human being, even if I don't act like one.'" Of the guards, Dr. Rundle said, "They're like the prisoners. They're almost as helpless. These places don't change. The citizens don't want them any different."

The principal athletic director is a CO. Beyond that, all the officials, trainers, referees, coaches, and instructors are themselves inmates, with uneven skills in the sport they support or follow. There are no gyms nor swimming-pools. All prisons could use both. Few will ever get them.

Men who are tired through healthy exercise don't get in trouble. Skippers of training-ships all know this. They keep their apprentices busy all the time, making and taking in sail, cleaning equipment, rotating the ship's chores from vegetable-paring to deck-hosing. And they turn out good sailors.

Frictions exist in any establishment that operates on a basis of absolutism, but when these frictions ignite, it is almost never a veteran guard who is involved. It is almost always one of the young guards, a first- or second-year man. In this area, part of the blame may be traced to their insufficiency of training. Attica guards are trained at Mattewan, as are the guards for all of New York State's prisons, but they are trained during a period of only three weeks.*

When these young men come on duty, they are not guards. They are nervous young men in unaccustomed uniforms. Though many of them are the sons of other guards, have heard all the "talk," have lived close by the looming walled mound of Attica, they are a long way from being professional. These are the men who make the mistakes, some through early zeal, some through the infecting haze of apprehension. Most guards, of middle-age, report the back-of-the-neck feeling they experienced in early duty. The younger men have not learned how to look back into the hostile glare of strangers' eyes with a returned steadiness that makes no response, that communicates nothing, that is totally non-provoking. In these early months they have to do some camouflaging. All know they are being watched and tested. This can produce unexpected, unwanted self-consciousness, even in the phlegmatic.

In the formidable library of prison literature by psychologists, psychiatrists, and sociologists, there are some omissions. I have never seen, for example, a profile of a correction officer; never seen an accurate run-down on who he is, where he's from, what he

---

* The training period for guards has been raised to three months.

knows. We've had no pokings into his character, background, or motivation.

Although the correction officer is not excluded from this body of inquiry and surmise, the scantiness of attention he receives amounts to exclusion. We are informed that these officers are poorly paid and poorly trained. That is all. It is not enough.

Thus he appears, as he has all through the century, as a crepuscular shadow, hooded, retreating, stealthy, impassive, mute, impersonal, crafty, and, of course (everyone *knows* that), cruel. The-poor-prisoner-and-the-brutal-guard-who-beats-him.

In terms of fairness and intelligence, the condition, position, background, and stance of correction officers has surely earned, by now, an objective evaluation. I deprecate the poor notice these fellows have been getting and I'd like to turn it around a little; not the full circle but enough for focus.

Their use and goodness is everywhere ignored. Their character is everywhere suspect. Not to know him is to my mind a most significant and crippling neglect, since a prison guard, like the prisoner himself—like men everywhere, whether lighthouse tender, shepherd, or delivery man—is, unto himself, a unique entity. His life, however little, is a matter of extreme subjectivity. It is exquisitely personal. Yet no such person as a prison guard, nor even a prototype, emerges from sociology's delvings, a search that is prosecuted by the same people who would make meaningful revelations to us, the unpunished public, about the men we punish.

A correction officer is not a part of that punishment. The prison is, and you, the public, put the prisoner in it. You put up the walls and pay for them. And you put the guard in there to see the man does not get out.

The men we hire to manage our inmates either should get better billing or better examination. Today—1972—they are anonymous and amorphous. And they are anomalous, too, as I think you'll presently sense. Surely they are all so set apart from the vivisection of other dismemberments as to be invisible.

You can't name one prison guard. All you can name is the movie actor who impersonated one.

It would make an interesting book indeed if a university sociologist, unknown to any authority including the prison itself, were to serve two years as a correction officer, and to serve those two years in the block and not in the office. Such a sociologist would have much to tell us. And to tell other sociologists.

The disparity between a concentration on a single case or person (by social workers in family casework, for example) and the same output of energy by equally serious researchers exploring our prisons is an alarming disparity. They will explore an individual prisoner but never an individual guard. Thus, to the many probes and needles of penological inquiry, the correction officer seems untouched. Or if touched at all, it is once-over-lightly, each finding not being a revelation at all but a repeat of another's study, an echoing conjecture, a guess, an assumption. No depth study of a prison guard has ever been made, at least none I know of.

One moves gloomily through the dusk of this endless journey, fanning for air but breathing only swamp fog. Guards are men, the same as the inmates are men, but from the fishings of sociology they are not brought to the surface this way. Instead, they are moved into slots or positioned on quintiles on some expensive, foundation-funded "pattern of variables." And though the chart remains, the *man* escapes. Similarly, though he never runs, he has not yet been caught. The prison screw is still the public's villain. And sociology's orphan.

This is a rich area, never profitably penetrated. It must be conceded that for many reasons it is an area difficult for any sociologist to get into; not to get into physically but intellectually. His visits will be accompanied by the effect of his school or schooling and they will be pre-edited by this. By other factors, too: his own prejudice, present though unseen; the unsettling shift of atmospheres, the social scientist's own non-prison conditioning, his inexperience with frightful smells and sudden bells.

If these can be dismissed as "surface" things—and I'm sure they will be—others can't be. If a prison is disturbingly unfamiliar, it is also a place where the searcher is not much wanted; where responses will be "careful"; where self-consciousness is epidemic, educations dissimilar, purposes indistinct or withheld, prison theories both fixed and confused. And since all prison personnel is itself in the survival business, a prison is a place where most answers will be protectively deflected.

Any prison administrator can and will show to any researcher his policy code, yet few of these men are the authors of what they show. Most of what they have has been inherited from a predecessor, or from the state. How much of it *is* his? Any of it? How does the researcher know? He does not know. He must trust his own insight, acute in many, and trust his observation for the rest, a period that is limited, pre-arranged, and usually brief.

The university presence in most prisons is suspected and unwelcome. It's a disturbance and a nuisance. The mere fact of its being there at all suggests dissatisfaction from outside; perhaps from powerful influences outside (all outside influences are "powerful").

Prison officials are suspicious of sociology's vocabulary. They have a right to be. They are suspicious of the nature and motivation of the man or the committee they are receiving; of the pertinence (or vagueness) of their questioning; of the uses to be made of their answers.

Prison officials are on the spot, never anywhere else. They're used to this. Being on the spot is the truest part, the most conscious part of their work, their responsibility, their life. It goes with the job. They know it, accept it, and deal with it. To deal with it, they have their own techniques; what to hold back, what to show. Being in charge, they can assert these and do assert them. This is a hard-earned prerogative you or I would exercise were we to occupy the same office.

Perhaps these headaches are normal enough for any executive. Within the same edifice, however, the condition of the correction officer is somewhat different. His frustrations are real. And they are multiple.

He is a man under a hard authority. He, like the prisoner, must conform. His regulations, though different from the inmates', are as restrictive as theirs.

He is required to report any break of regulations by inmates: work details, refusal to take orders, fights, theft. But if he is overzealous and reports everything, and some do, he does not go through his career this way. It will presently appear to his superiors that the officer can't manage his block; that he is too informal with prisoners, too close to them; that he is too arbitrary; that he lacks leadership; that he's setting a bad example. In short, that he isn't handling the job.*

Most young correction officers feel unequipped for the work given them. And they are quite right—they are unequipped for it. They feel they didn't get enough training. And they did not. They feel, too, that their jobs are more demanding than people know. When it is pointed out that over the years little ever happens, the officer will point out in his turn that this very thing is a problem by itself. Crises and disruptions, escapes, fights, plots, contraband— these are the exceptional peakings on a graph that for months running shows little rise or fall.

Whatever their personal feelings, guards must remain emotionally neutral. They feel superior to the inmates, who in turn feel superior to the officers. And the officers know this, too. Officers come to know the men in their blocks; they grow to like certain prisoners more than they like others. They'd like the special few to get along, get a break, and to help them toward it. But they can't. This is an acute frustration. They have many others. Consider this one:

Correction officers are aware of the existence of and the real need for prisoners to have status. They understand the peculiar apparatus by which this is achieved; understand their own need to recognize it. Since it relates to the management of their own block, they know how to use it for control purposes. They appreciate the

---

* Governor Francis W. Sargent of Massachusetts has initiated prison reform plans for his state but, like governors everywhere, is at the mercy of the legislature. Among Governor Sargent's recommendations: repeal the "two-thirds law" (which bars parole for those convicted of violent crimes until two-thirds of their sentence is served). The legislature killed it. Killed also was the Governor's proposal for "halfway houses." Pending: a nonprofit prison industry corporation that can contract for work and pay prisoners the minimum hourly wage—$1.75 per hour. Two of Governor Sargent's proposals, through administrative prerogative, are now in force: improved training for correction officers; recruitment of black and Spanish-speaking correctional staff.

An excellent appointment: for State Commissioner of Correction, a black—John O. Boone—formerly head of the largest correctional institution in the District of Columbia, "a dynamite guy," "a fantastic man." But a Walpole prison official found one conspicuous omission in the Governor's recommendations: "Nowhere along the line does the governor come up with what we should do with the incorrigible and repeater inmate. Nobody has an answer for that." (Boston *Globe*, December 22, 1971)

sense of this since it relates to the main goal—stability—of the whole complex. Correction officers tolerate this curiously anonymous inmate—a fixture in most of our prisons (call him the "manipulator")—pretty much because they have to.

Who is the "special" prisoner and why do guards have to deal with him, have to use him?

Prison inmates respect only him who by his actions rejected society outside and who, by his attitude, now brings his rejection inside. Penitentiaries have few penitents (prisoners don't wish to be forgiven) and correction officers thus deal with an agglomeration of non-repentants, a reverse of the outside notion that a penitent prisoner gets the best jobs. I am not talking about the trusty. I am talking about the noticeably impenitent, the flagrantly contemptuous—it is he who is looked up to by other inmates. He has status.

In a tight though fluid congeries such as a prison or a military cantonment, such men are automatically invested, by their peers, with status. It comes about in many ways: through the strange though unmistakable chemistry of charisma; or status secured through cleverness, salesmanship, or subtle yard control; through political cunning, through personal manipulating. It comes about also through overt contempt for guards and through steady devotion to the prison caste system.

It is from this pool of attributes that a few men, in every prison, find their way, little by little, to such things as commissary jobs; or to the privilege of peddling purchasable commodities to inmates; to jobs as file-clerks or assistant foremen in the prison shops. They are crafty and maneuvering. They are never disruptive, and, out of self-interest, they are dependable.

Removed from his comic setting, Sergeant Bilko would "make" it in any prison, while Gomer Pyle would never get off the ground.

The more canny ones become the prison's "manipulators." (Many sociologists call him the "politician.") All play for keeps. The manipulators never rat on inmates. Their hatred of officers is no pantomime. It is rich and real. Though not a sham, both know it is a surface thing, a control mechanism helping both sides, an operational necessity that serves to hold the balance. Manipulators never organize riots and never participate in them. They would and do discreetly and indirectly report any beginnings of one. Any ruckus would flake out the man's usefulness.

His contempt symbolizes and epitomizes the inmates' contempt, and inmates like to see such a "worthy" wearing so much of it and doing so with impunity. They applaud his cunning and, though envy is there, they are not openly envious of his preferments. Though these preferments might seem meager to us, they are immense to him, and he must protect what he has won for there are others who will take it way from him if they can. And who try.

The manipulator takes credit when it's volunteered, for things he didn't do, such as the removal to another block of a pesty or snoopy or unpopular inmate. And he takes credit as well for things he has himself managed or arranged. He has the cherished possession of *movement,* not much but more than the others. He's cautious, imaginative, and self-controlled. He never shoots off his mouth, and lets others build his reputation. He is basically cold and calculating and is in it for himself alone.

Though not a listening-post, he's thought to be one, and he does hear much the others don't. And never forgets what he hears nor who said it. If his work is in an office, he may over the months hear much.

There is no flamboyance in him at all, and he counts on his protective coloration—meditative preoccupation with filing, with pushing the corridor wagon, with clerking or copying—to make him a familiar yet invisible fixture there.

He decides what use to make of what he knows. He decides what has been planted so he *would* hear it, and what he has come upon that is not for his knowing. These overtones are delicate and hard to catch, but the rhythm of prison life and his slowly accumulating knowledge of the men about him all help him in these translations. So does his own insight and his poker-playing instinct.

Though not a deep one, he is a repository of special information. He is respected, too, for what he doesn't say, the acceptance of his special skill and privilege giving him the advantage to be thought to know when he does not. All is close to the vest, dealt with precision, the top cards being held back till they can be played when they matter: dismissal, transfer, or promotion of a guard; the exact condition of any hospital patient; any shift in work details; news of special interest from out-of-town papers, the pending arrival of lawyers or agitators, or their failure to get a clearance; the name of the next movie, the location spot of the warden's vacation, his means of travel and who's going with him; price changes in purchasable merchandise, editorial changes in the prison paper, and what's for Sunday dinner.

He knows the group that is smuggling contraband, where it comes from, its handle and its going rate. Where guards are involved, he knows who they are. He defuses fights before they ignite, arbitrates inmate gambling quarrels, gets letters out, recognizes tensions, and disperses pressures.

And he largely keeps to himself. A necessary part of his congenital shrewdness is self-containment. Many of these men would make good military officers. He never blabs or over-talks. Though untrustworthy, he is trusted by cons within the prison code, for he is undeviatingly pro-inmate. And trusted by the employees for his contribution to prison stability, the basic imperative. No manipulator could keep his job in a setting of frequent turmoil.

The manipulator has the quick eyes of a croupier, taking in much in swift review. He knows who's ahead and who's behind, knows how and to whom to feed his precious disclosures and his warnings; when to expand or to diminish their meanings. To himself he is Number One. He's in the survival business and no other. His modus operandi, while not one of stealth, is one of secretiveness and unacknowledged collusion; a life of personal discipline, good memory, and of instant recognition of any threat to his privilege and the instant handling of it.

There is great practical use in this man, and no brag at all. All businesses, including banks, churches, and advertising firms have such men. And use them. Very often they are the company's president. They are aloof, cautious, and hard to quote, for they say little, all of them managing to seem informed when often quite empty, through use of the primitive techniques of putting off questions by raising other questions. The dead-pans who managed the merger and collapse of the Penn-Central are good outside examples of these same mechanisms. So is any swindler, caught or uncaught. They are beyond surprise, embarrassment, or feeling.

But the manipulator keeps his job by helping to keep a balance all prisons must maintain. Though such men are never recognized on the operation sheet by name, number, or function, they are a big cog in the social and disciplinary circuit of any facility.

For the correction officer there is an ambivalence of feeling here—approval-disapproval—but they go along with it, a fixture they did not invent but inherited. They aren't staffed or situated to do anything else. They hate the odor of complicity; they hate to rely on the manipulator, but far more, they hate to *have* to rely on him. Without him, they could function, but with him there's less trouble. It tends to make the guard's own job that much more imprecise.

A frustration of a very different kind and quality, but one afflicting all correction officers, is this: having to maintain that some sort of better life is waiting outside if the inmate will accept the benefits of the prison's pre-release conditioning (the official attitude recommended for guards in our so-called "treatment" prisons), but knowing these opportunities won't be there when the prisoner gets out. This knowledge throws a frightful sense of hypocrisy into the very center of their work; into the center of their own potential usefulness in that work, because correction officers know the score here; know the figures for these same inmates who have had these same admonitions and encouragements inside the prison before but who are now back, three- and four-time losers.

These are the recidivists who come back, often to the same block, and who report that "prison promises" don't work; whose return proves it, proves it at least to the marginals who are now about to have their own chance to test it. "It didn't work for him. Why will it work for me?" Parole candidates have a right to wonder about this.

What's-the-use frustration deadens the air in all our prisons. It is not the fault of correction officers. Nor is it management's fault. It is our own.

The smell of defeat is in the air all these men breathe, the same air for guard as for prisoner. Most of those who would like to see sense brought to all this penal nonsense never realize it smells the same in the corridor as in the cell. The sense of defeat is punishing to the morale of any correction officer. It is especially punishing to those involved in the rehabilitative exertions of their own house—

even at the baseball-umpire level (in those few prisons in which guards are allowed to do this); punishing to know that even such little good as they can bring to the life circumstance of the men around them—that this all vanishes as soon as the men leave.

It necessarily adds a layer to the sediment of his cynicism to realize he will probably see this fellow again. It adds to it because he *does* see him again. Though the rehabilitative programs are almost everywhere lamentable or unstructured, the correction officer knows that more is offered in the pre-release schedules of prison life than society will provide in post-release.

No money for it. Little enough here inside. None outside. If it is now being conceded here and there that we never learn, may it not be also suggested that we don't want to?

A frustration felt by all correction officers, though never reported (at least I've never seen such), has to do with parole. More than any man except the prospective parolee himself, the correction officer knows this man. The Parole Board knows the record, and knows the Parole Officer's recommendation. But it does not know the man. The correction officer knows the prisoner himself. He *alone* knows him. And despairingly knows (for he sees it) which candidate, who should not make it, will do so; and which, who should, will not.

They understand the "recital" distress of these fellows; the nervousness and the psychic semi-paralysis that afflicts many of them at the moment preceding a parole hearing. A guard knows the emotional exactions put on these candidates; the importance of his physical appearance, his speech, neatness, self-conduct, and the way he presents himself and lays out plans for his own redemption. Guards know that little of this is likely to favor a "sensitive" prisoner or favor the real trier. Often a prisoner's expectable nervousness comes through in the parole report as "motivational insecurity." But it is exactly here that the correction officer, and not the Parole Board, knows the good risk from the bad; the real from the phony. A bad risk can put up a good front.

The resources to comprehend and to measure the regeneration risk an inmate presents to society and to himself are right there in the prison where he's doing his time. They aren't outside. They're here where the man is, and they're wasted.

In most prisons the correction officer has seen the prisoner daily, and over a period of years. The prisoner's previous experience, in crime, is well known to the guard. His accommodation to prison life is intimately known to him. This same officer carries assessments of great value. Yet all this is thrown away. It is never consulted. It is as if the correction officer were never there at all; or knew nothing of the men he guarded.

His opinion as to the success chances for any parole candidate should be sought. It's the best opinion the convict is going to get.

It is not being argued here that correction officers ought to supplant America's Parole Boards. Nor is it argued that these officers, were Parole Boards to be doing their work inside the structure instead of outside, should even be a part of such boards. At the same time, their judgments have solid empirical validity. In terms of continuous observation over long periods of time, they are sophisticated judgments.

A guard's memorandum concerning the potential of any inmate would have entries known only to himself. It would enjoy the quick respect of his own lieutenants and his warden, for they also know that *he* knows. It would serve to reduce the everlasting complaint most prisoners raise on the score of grievances; on the score of an honest opportunity to be heard. Inmates would come to know that final verdicts on whether they stayed in the can or not were being influenced by men who really knew; by employees who were locked up, too, however free they might be legally; by men who in the sense of monotony, contiguity, atmosphere, and food (guards eat little better than prisoners) were coming from their peers.

A system of parole that was moved from the outside to the inside could dispel much of the miasma of defeatism that now demoralizes the work of all correction officers in all prisons. But these men are left out of these deliberations, as if without humanity or intelligence.

Equally with the inmate, the correction officer must accept the rejection of the society he seeks to serve. He knows it does not serve him now, though such is never noted by the public nor clearly seen by sociologists. And he knows that beyond his pay and his pension it never will. So he settles for that. He has to.

On the job, correction officers aren't bitter, just sad; in retirement, laconic and reticent. And they never go back, as an old grad goes back to his school. Why should they? They know what's there. They know it will so continue. They also know it could all have been so different had the money been there to make changes.

For many guards their bleakest remembrance is this: that incoming prisoners (the new fish), exposed to the institution's orientation process and urged to help themselves by way of such rehabilitation schedules as are there, that such do not make it. They know that the socializing equipment to steer them to the possible beginnings of a turn-around of attitude is too sleazy, too intermittent; that the recommended routes to eventual community acceptance and to jobs they can handle are roads to nowhere. The older inmates know it, too, for they've been over these same roads and know them for what they are: their own matriculation to recidivism.

Correction officers know that society never celebrates the "recovered" con; that he's never seen as a private triumph, only as a public curiosity.

There is something else, a severe wasting the public never thinks about at all, and it is this: spiritually both the prisoner and the man who guards him are each other's captives. Physically both are in the same box, both doing time; the guard, in his own way, doing life. Thus the spiritual anomie and sense of apartness that seeps into the battered consciousness of the prisoner equally infects the correction officer, for there are no fans or ventilators to blow this away. Plans are there. Plans are always there, but not the equipment, never the equipment, and never the people to run it.

Through the years there has been generous foundation money for theory, state money for inspection, Federal money for pilot studies, grants-in-aid for motivation studies. Some of this money offers partial solutions, on paper and in theory, to special or compartmentalized problems. And most of them are academically sensitive. Many are seriously considered, and much lucubrating has gone into them all. Then why don't they help more than they do?

They don't help because most are written not for public digestion but for the smaller company of their own colleagues; for university sponsors and foundation backers. Or they are written out of the cold professional necessity to appear in print, a necessity that is one of the exactions of their discipline. Publication is as necessary to their rating as it is for college teachers who want to be department heads. "What have you published?" Publication is primary, subject secondary, readership an also-ran.

Too many prison sociologists would sooner publish something than cure something. Too much is written to be published rather than written to be effective. To be effective they would have to be simple. Often it takes courage to fight one's way through their vocabulary to get to their point, a vocabulary often used to inflate a small meaning, or, as we sometimes see, to conceal a larger dubiety.

To the acknowledged need to "change the man while he is serving time," there is never any money. A paper on *why* the money can't be steered to the prison that needs the money would make a good subject for social inquiry. Political inquiry has failed altogether. Sociologists know little about money beyond knowing they are functionless without any at all. This in itself might be a point of sympathetic kick-off, since it's the fundamental problem through the whole penal system and always has been. And is now. The years 1971 and 1972 have witnessed a fine burst of talk, but it will end as talk.

Social inquiry goes deeply into recidivism, as we all so wearily know, and there gets deeply mired. If a focus on money were mounted; if libertarians, idealists, and theoreticians were shelved for a year or two and if a concerned sociologist were to produce nothing but a cost-sheet to support his argument, he might have a trophy instead of a thesis. He'd certainly have a novelty.

For fifty years these cost-sheets have been submitted to legislatures all over this country, then upon submission either trimmed, castrated, or enucleated entirely. Then signed by the governor. Whereupon the bill, now pale and exsanguinated, becomes another Nantucket sleigh-ride with nowhere to go but the stone fence, the same road that returns the parolee to the stone wall of previous incarcerations.

It would be wrong, certainly ungenerous, to say that over the past fifty years the labor-force of sociology, in seeking cures for the disease of our prisons, has been wasted. It would not be wrong to say it has been ineffective. For what has it effected? Over this same fifty-year period you could throw out most of what's been explored and written and prisons would look the same, contain the same, think the same, and graduate the same end-product to the inviting prospect of all our happy towns and fun cities. The labor-force of sociology has made a dent on the public. It has made none on the jail, the jailed, or the jailor.

Most correction officers, whatever their education (Attica's rating here: eighty per cent high school graduates or "some" college, ten per cent college graduates) are reading men. They find that whereas much is being written about prisons, nothing is being written about *them*, and that little ever was. They feel a further rejection right here, a sense of incompleteness, of incertitude, of dismissal; of being the large unknown and uncared-for in the immense sprawl of penal literature and all its diligent fossickings. No one knocks on their door to ask how they feel about things. No lawyer comes. And their unions can't get them hard-hats. They share the same bad press their warden does: the sad innocent prisoner, the subhuman guard with his quid, his club, and his taunt.

This is a lie and a slander, and we are the subhumans who perpetuate it.

Correction officers need help, recognition, respect, honest profiling. No one has ever defined their problems, and their problems are deep and disabling.

Like the prisoner, they are seeking answers for their own isolation. Like the prisoner, they never see society and are never seen by it. With peculiar accuracy they understand the social rejection of inmates because it is their rejection, too. This has never come to the public's notice. And it has this further sting: no one at either the social or structural level appreciates their situation—appreciates in the sense of comprehension, not thanks. The guard's awful dilemma never to know for sure who he is, never to know exactly what is expected of him, has never been the subject of sensitive inquiry. If he's there at all, he's a footnote. Can there be such a thing, for example, as esprit de corps in such a company? No, there cannot, and he remains, even to himself, a shadow in a long tunnel of other shadows. And for him, there are no known ladders to success. There is no known way, in any prison, for a guard to advance himself, to get ahead, to lead, or to grow and expand as a person.

Their anomalous situation, their invisibilizing uniform, their mandated neutrality, and the gradual grinding *mechanization* of the man through early obliteration of any idealism, individuality, or enterprise—these are the real sources of his number-one problem: an acute sense of non-being. Just as truly as the inmate himself, the correction officer also must fight off the ultimate destroyer: self-rejection.

Most guards are reading men, as has been said, hunting for clues as to what they are, hunting for clues to survival. But they dismiss, as do their captains, most of the university literature they see. They've been into it and have turned away from it. It has no meaning for them. It's addressed to another audience. The concepts are remote from any of the realities before them. The sentences are too long. The basic themes are obscure, minute, or unresolved. To them, sociologists describe a situation, then walk away from it, brushing their hands over a job unfinished. They've put the patient to sleep, then left the hospital without operating.

It raises an interesting question as to sociology's readership: *can* this audience act? It is hard to see how. In this tumble of caveat, of quick inspection and laborious output, though the work of prison sociologists is often motivated to do much, it is implemented to do little in the practical sense of initiating change. Publication seems its own right for appearing at all, the accompanying credit the author receives being its real objective. He is now a Reference. And so remains. Though safe and sanitary, he is stale and stationary, uninvolved in the main problem. Yet prison guards are a persisting part of this main prison problem, and they know this.

They also know they will never be brought into it. They will be brought in only when they have to subdue a prisoner. Or when a prisoner suicides. Guards don't drive prisoners to suicide by beating them. Drugs drive them to suicide; the sudden cut-off. This is the most abject spiritual necrosis in today's society. If you recall what Anna Kross found when she was administrator of New York's prisons, the punishing extent of drug abuse thirty and forty years ago, you know that "cold-turkey" is not new. I've witnessed the pitiable agony of it four times, a very disabling convulsion that engages the entire human mechanism, hard to watch, sickening to think about, unbearable to go through. It is not the guard who drove the prisoner to hang himself. Drugs drove him to it. The mercy of methadone was not known in Anna Kross's time and is far from universal now. Prisoners commit suicide because they can't stand living another instant. The suicide rate of imprisoned addicts is *ten times* the outside rate.*

But the correction officer is always blamed for the suicide, and this is another inequity that deeply hurts and scorches.

No correction officer can ever rebut a newspaper story about brutality. No forum exists for him. No. A.C.L.U. zealot saw the action. He got his replay from the prisoner. Prison guards are sick to death of having to wear the phylacteries of the brute and the bully; sick to death with the newspapers for tatooing them with such a humiliating wound. These stigmata hurt them all, blind the public to their own use and goodness, and smut their character. Their position as Hitler's boys is just as safe in American mythology as is that of the "cruel stepmother."

Guards have other headaches. A severe one is agitators. The reason prison personnel dislike agitators is because they agitate.

There can be no doubt that these agitators fanned the Attica fire, Kunstler in his familiar, self-memorializing posture of hero, idealist, and rescuer. What vagrancy of mind was it that urged him to dangle the hope of amnesty to his mob? He was a lawyer and knew it couldn't be done. But he raised it and when the empty promise came back for what it was, he had to shuffle his way out, earning the public's wide contempt, and being disowned by two of his own committee members, Alfredo Matthew of New York City and David Anderson of Rochester, both of them school officials.

They, with Kunstler, were fellow-members of the observers' committee, but Kunstler's hortatory excesses were so much sand

---

* In the opinion of other sources, this figure should be raised even higher. Calvin J. Frederick, assistant chief of the Center for Studies of Suicide Prevention, in a hearing in Washington, D.C., informed his audience that the suicide attempt rate among young heroin and cocaine addicts was "at least 15 times higher than the non-addict rate in the same age group." Additional independent corroboration came from an official of the National Institute of Mental Health: "Among addicts sweating out their habit, one in five expected to meet a violent death." (Miami *Herald*, April 1, 1972)

in the journal-boxes, and so destructive of any chance of progress that Anderson and Matthew had been struggling with before Kunstler got there, they were glad to see him go.

"Kunstler heightened the expectations about getting amnesty," said Anderson. "The idea picked up and put the inmate leadership we'd been dealing with before Kunstler came in a precarious position.

Once the word "amnesty" got into the talk, it ran up the prisoners' list of demands from 28 to 30, number 29 being: amnesty from any court proceeding; number 30: quick passage to a "non-imperialistic country" as free men. Kunstler knew this was legally impossible and Attica's guards knew that he knew it.

No matter how many blacks he hugs, one has the feeling Kunstler is propelled not by love at all, but by vanity, and that if they'd turn off the television cameras, he'd be seen no more. Or that if he'd get his glasses off his fontanel and over his eyes, he could see better.

He backed away from the amnesty miscalculation and bumped into another. When he called Rockefeller a "murderer," Congressman Louis C. Wyman of New Hampshire sought to get New York State and the American Bar Association to disbar him, and said of him: "This man's repeated incitations to violence and hatred are a continuing disgrace to the Bar."

A prison guard's contempt for the agitator can be quite as personal as the New Hampshire legislator's:

"Agitators," an Attica guard said to me, "are men who sit at the bedside of an injured prisoner, taking notes. They never take notes from any of us while we're getting our own cuts closed, in another hospital." It has never entered an agitator's mind to do this. It has never been his intention. It has never broken the surface of his curiosity, any more than it did Tom Wicker's, of the New York *Times*, when he flew up to cover this dreadful devastation. But these men cover one-half only. They do not intend to be fair. They do not recognize the existence of guards or perceive their burden of accumulated provocation. They do not want to hear about it. In all the public screaming that is now going on about Angela Davis, her insistence upon a change of venue (and getting it), in her charge that she will never get a "fair trial," she has conveniently ignored the recent history of blacks in American courts and has enjoyed such a frontage of advance publicity that few realize this woman, whatever she did or did not do, has already *pre-judged her own case* to her own advantage, and if she is convicted newspapers have already guaranteed her "martyrdom." No one *wants* to wait for a trial. She has already tried herself and exonerated herself.

In their complaints and grievance lists, prisoners have received enormous help from agitators, not to get at the truth but to get them out. Yes, the correction officer did subdue the prisoner. The prisoner first split the guard's head with a Stillson wrench, whereupon the guard struck the prisoner with his nightstick.

"Unnecessary force?" Who is to say? In any sudden physical encounter, who is to measure the foot-pounds of any blow, given or received? Or measure the impulse that released all the steam and brought on the action? Who will measure the provocation and its period of boil? But this is not the point. The point goes beyond the collision and it is this: the encounter is initiated by the prisoner. The guard is under orders to stop it. This is never reflected in an agitator's report, nor press story, nor is it ever seen or acknowledged in any A.C.L.U interview.

Guards don't tour these dim corridors knocking over prisoners for the fun of it. In all fairness, consider now, just for fifteen seconds, that in the same assault—in any assault—the guard did nothing.

A curious request, new in these times, is finding its way to the lengthening list of prisoner grievances. They, who never treated any member of the public as a human being, now wish to be considered such. They who had no dignity now wish it. They don't seek it— they demand it. They demand it, not knowing, beyond its being a cessation of indignity, what its true quality is. Nor how it's come by. (Should we treat them with dignity? Surely it should be tried.)

Very few prisoners can assess their status as prisoners, and relate any of their present circumstance to any past action of their own.

Felons forget their felonies.

The public forgets them, too. There is nothing on Edgar Smith's conscience for having destroyed sixteen-year-old Victoria Zielinski. He's free. And celebrated. The fact that Victoria, being deceased, has more time to serve than the fifteen years Smith did for murdering her is of academic interest to Smith; the lingering pain of the family who reared her, of no interest at all. Such are many of the merciless men petitioning us for a new issue of their social wardrobe.

The public pushes it all aside—the nature of the crime, the perpetrator, his wild instinct to cut down and rip open, his enthusiasm to take what is not his, his aboriginal delight in savagery. This the public pushes aside, or, more commonly, knows nothing at all about. The public never saw the criminal in action. But the prison has to live with these tailings. The guard knows what the inmate did. And it is the guard, and not the public, who also knows the victim; knows him to be, next to himself, America's most anonymous and neglected citizen; knows that if he's still living, he is still hurting. There are no constitutional anodynes for the victim, any more than there are for the guard. The victim, if living, has to repair the damage to himself, his body, his family, or his business, in any way he can manage. So also with the guard.

In the matter of demanded dignity, an Attica guard put up a good question in the summer of 1971: "*How* do you invest a prisoner with dignity?"

A prisoner cannot see, for example, that a quality of forbearance is something to be sought. A prisoner's concept of dignity (a new word to him) equates with merchandise a customer can buy in a store. He had no acquaintance with dignity outside, as an operating but unapprehended criminal, and since the attribute of dignity does not seem to descend upon him in prison, he presently feels it is being arbitrarily withheld; that correction officers, or his own prison clothes, are keeping it away from him.

That dignity is of the man himself, slowly earned through habits of restraint, of control over his impulses, that it is earned through honest perception of another's gifts and rights—all this is quite foreign to him. His search for dignity, as something suspended on a hook, is hung to the wrong lanterns. He won't enter the darkness looking for it himself, nor even cross its beam. He feels it is something that can be suddenly bestowed, with no doing of his own; a testimonial, a decoration, a hit in the numbers. Something coming to him, now that other privileges have been taken away.

Having spent his life in a gross denial of dignity to all he met—whether jobs, people, concepts, opportunities, money, duty or schooling; having robbed it, raped it, struck it down, burned it up, then sped past the wreckage without seeing it, he now finds himself, by this quaint prearrangement of society, the *recipient* of this same denial. But prison gives him no awareness of his crime, no curiosity about the condition of his victims, especially if he, as a violent and thieving man, has scored many times unhurt. Now, as inmate, the prison gives him only a magnification of himself as victim. No identification of himself as criminal. And his demand for dignity is not rooted in a purge of previous wrong-doing, or any present urge for self-discovery. It comes from intense self-pity.

The "Political" Prisoner—Is He Really That?

There is a new presence in which this growth is now incubating. In prisons today a new lenience, not of conscience but rather an improvised ladder to sudden self-regard, is reaching its way to the odd rescue of bomb-throwers, murderers, and gun-smugglers. It is a "reinterpretation" that serves to sanitize and legitimize their conduct, however frightful, by having it defined (for the prisoner, and by him) not at all as criminal but as "political." It is especially welcome to the worst elements in any penitentiary. Their stabbings and burnings and explodings and shootings were a matter—it now appears—of "protest." And many prisoners, among the blacks especially, are rejoicing in these readjusted classifications.

Suppose *you* were the warden of a large prison, one that held 2,000, of whom four-fifths were blacks? Can you envision the tension build-ups that the "crusading" of Angela Davis must bring to such a place? Indeed she is the voice of blacks everywhere and, in or out of prison, plans to continue to be. And will.

She is audacious, brainy, and beautiful. She is young and fiery and beset. She's articulate. Photogenically, she's the best face that Communism has ever had. Most Communists seem bug-eyed, unbathed, warty, and shrill, but Angela Davis is authentically bandbox. Whatever your age or color, you'd like to date this girl. She exudes vitality. She coruscates a powerful urgency of mission, of noble pursuit, a spirited, energetic quest for the Grail; Harlem's

Florence Nightiningale, California's Maid of Orleans, and Communism's Carry Nation. She is quite a bundle, no doubt of it.

She has vowed to work for the release of "all political prisoners."

"It is a victory all right"—her first comment to the press upon being released on bail on February 24, 1972—"but a larger victory, even in my own case, is yet to be obtained. There are many, many thousands of sisters and brothers all over this country who are forced to live their lives behind concrete and steel. We have to free all our brothers and sisters."

A reporter: "How do you feel?"

"I feel fine. Better than I have in sixteen months. The real reason is that now I am able to give much more of myself to the struggle to free all our sisters and brothers. . . . This has been a people's victory. . . . It has been a victory in the sense that abolition of capital punishment is very closely related to all the struggles conducted around the prisoners in the last two years, related to the murder of George Jackson and to the massacre at Attica."

Any black, imprisoned or free, has to be stirred by this. And indeed there may be and there probably is very real nobility here. Surely there is intense feeling, as well as an appealing, even haunting, puissance in the unexpected demureness of such a person in a role so formidable.

What has she done by this? What has she won? It is not what she thinks. She has "exonerated" multitudes of blacks—and many whites among them—of all the wrong-doing that brought them to where they are; of crimes somewhat different and separate from those she calls "political." She has expunged their records, a bravura mechanism of exculpation which transfers, to those who do not have it, her own nobility, whether this nobility is real, confused, or spurious. A Communist is obliged to ignore any truth that happens to be in the way. So we do not know, for example, why she hid for so long if she had nothing to hide. Nor do we find any record of her appreciation—if she felt any—of such American freedoms as she herself has enjoyed, one of them being the privilege to teach philosophy to American youth in an impressive university. This is hardly the mark of a "repressive" society. Communists never say thank you for anything. Nor has Angela

Davis. Nor will she. Yet it is hard to fault, wherever one's sympathies may lie, the American legal procedure that has, for the time, closed about her.

She is a good complainer. She complained about an earlier defense staff and got a new one. She complained that she could not get a fair trial in Marin County (and probably couldn't), and was again accommodated. She gets a good press. She takes a good picture. She gives a convincing interview. I do not doubt in my own heart that she, in her heart, feels a Great Cause, one she truly feels she has been brought forth, somehow, to deliver.

There has been some masterful stage-managing through all this, and having a quick sense of the theatrical, she has made good use of it. She has every right to do this. Others have, others will. During the actual conduct of her trial, Angela Davis appeared on a national (NBC) television show and implied that, were he alive today, Martin Luther King would have supported her revolution. Did she have a right to insinuate a philosophical turnaround of a man who is now among history's immortals for practicing and proclaiming the absolute reverse of violence? King is America's Gandhi.

Now that her acquittal has returned her to society, now that her national tour (including a Madison Square gala) has occurred, I would like Miss Davis, sometime in her private meditations, to consider this: supposing instead of being a dedicated Communist, she were a dedicated anti-Communist; and suppose she had been judged by a Communist court on the same charges of murder, conspiracy, and kidnaping that brought her before the jury in California. What can she truthfully feel would have been her chances in a Communist setting?

But she has also most cruelly intensified the burden of the very people she wishes so passionately to liberate. All prisons are now infected with her fevers. It is epidemic. Costly, too, as was Kunstler's chant for amnesty. It is having its own backlash. It has been poured white-hot into a pot already boiling and has frightfully compounded the "inmate management" problem throughout the full prison structure, for no inmate any longer feels that he should *have* to feel like an inmate. He's a "political" prisoner now, pure and aggrieved, exactly as was Nehru under the British.

It is as welcome to prisoners as it is fearsome to the authorities we pay to contain them. And there are no techniques for the handling of this. It's too new. We should expect the worst now, for we're going to get it. And many will die, including many Angela Davis would like to save, or to free.

Who's in charge of this horrible mess? Who's *stuck* with it? You, the public? No, no more than ever before. It is the guard, as before—America's most anonymous citizen—who has to run this show all alone.

This multiplies the hazard of prisoner control all over America. It was and is acutely present in Attica. Correction officers, living with the reality of dangerous men, don't recognize these distinctions. *They know the man.* They know the accomplished ferocity he carries, the ferocity he can at any time discharge. Many of our most predatory inmates aren't and can't be sequestered. There isn't enough money to make enough room, so they mingle with the general prison population.

These men have brought a new animus to prison atmospheres very hard for guards to accommodate, for they do represent a new kind of elitism. It is a contagious and contaminating influence, a laboratory culture-medium in which agitators, skilled or Kunstler-warped, can proliferate. And in which they do.

It is this element that correction officers do not properly know how to handle; nor wardens nor superintendents either, for it is altogether new. So is the public's response to it, some cheering, some holding their breath, the rest wavering, waiting, and uncertain. The public never really had to think about prisons before. Read about them, yes. Think, no. Now they have to. And the explosive risk in so many penal facilities today is not the risk of Rahway or Raiford fallout. It is all over the country now. It was totally unknown fifteen years ago.

On this one point prison guards are of one mind, very old-line in their attitude, a unanimity rare for them: the problem began to show when Earl Warren's "permissives" began to come in; when the ghetto was found to explain everything; when prisoners' rights presently appeared on street banners; when society-is-the-villain was proclaimed, when no-man-is-guilty was discovered. The problem worsened as the phrase law-and-order, though overuse and overcartooning, lost its meaning, probably forever. Though the need remains, the impulse to keep it alive is gone. Quite suddenly in American life it is unfashionable to be decent.

Prisoners don't want to be "rehabilitated." They sought what they had as criminals, and preferred it. They want to get out so they can operate. They aren't out, so they operate within. Most of these men are extremely violent. They accepted violence. They sought it as their own personal life-style and wave of the future. They are afraid of no contest. They have been in crises before and survived them. Their potential for disruption is very large. Society's protection of them, through reformers, lawyers, constitutional interpretations, and agitators is also large.

These three sentences most powerfully impressed me:

We should develop sentencing techniques to impose a sentence so that an inmate can literally "learn his way out" of prison, as we now try to let him earn his way out with good behavior.

Those who would disrupt and destroy a penal institution must be separated to protect those who are trying to learn and to prepare for the future.

We should make certain that every inmate works, and works hard.

Such are the thoughts of Chief Justice Warren E. Burger of the U.S. Supreme Court.

I'd like to quote one more, this from Judge William B. Bryant, district judge of the District of Columbia:

In the business of rehabilitation, if the prisoner is aware that the navel cord which connects him to the human race hasn't been severed, there is a chance the prisoner can still be reached.

These remarks are right on the nerve center. See how in their various ways they relate to Attica.

Attica prisoners are out of their tedious lock-up from ten in the morning till five in the afternoon. Work there is not compulsory. Neither are classes, except for those whose schooling never got past fifth grade. Most Attica prisoners resist both opportunities. While out of their cells, the time on their hands is therefore of their own choice and doing. They'd prefer to do nothing than to do something, an extension of the way most of them lived before imprisonment.

It is the conviction of many that this policy should be reversed in all prisons. Inmates should be compelled to go to classes; compelled to learn a trade. It is not the prison's fault, in any state, that inmates arrive with little sense of their own being, little hope they could someday be useful. But it is society's fault that they are permitted, to the end of their time, to continue in the deep freeze of this social pointlessness. It is society's fault that they emerge, upon release, into the same twilight that stunned their sunless days before they were put away.

"Had there been enough money," said Rep. Claude Pepper of Florida, "much of this tragedy [Attica] could have been prevented. Because of inadequate financing, all of us are responsible for what happened here."

In truth, it is our own American society, including its lobbies, that turns its back on reform, and the McGraths, Mancusis, and Anna Krosses are the chosen victims of this rigidified apathy, just as the new wardens, the Malcolms and the Montanyes, mentioned before, are now being set up to be its next.

May I modestly suggest that the true beginnings of a new order in all our prisons can come about through a redirection of prison guards? (And please note that I say the *beginnings* of a new order.) And I do not see such a turnaround as an impossible transfiguration in contemporary prison patterns.

The potential of the CO has never been tapped; his potential as something more than the caretaker he now is, the hard-hearted herdsman who conducts lost sheep from one area to another during the day and who steers them to their proper pens for the night.

A guard is better educated than his charges. He knows more, cares more; is himself rooted, home-oriented. Though shied away from by strangers, he is respected in his own community.

Among other qualities never mentioned, he has surprising industry. He doesn't make much, so he moonlights. He has skills and enthusiasms. He is a lot more than a forty-year-old walking about with a stick. He is very much a person. He is very human. And he is decent.

Most guards have skills but skills of which the prison, in the current stance of most, does not or cannot make use.

What skills?

In the rural facilities I have visited over the years, I've found most guards to be good mechanics. They own machinery. They know how to repair and maintain it. Being farm-bred, they're good men around gardens and animals. With many it is these very activities to which they return during time-off that helps to keep them sane; that refreshes them for their endless tomorrows.

In his time off, the CO works at other things: he's part-owner of a filling-station or carwash. He's a house-painter. He owns and rents out a truck. He's a silo erector, he operates a cider-press, he keeps bees, sprays fruit trees. He's a crew member for town snow-removal. He's in freight-forwarding, motorcycle repair, printing, road construction, trenching, reforestation. He's handy with tractors and earth-movers. He's a volunteer fireman. He belongs to the Grange. He bowls, he has a hunting license, an outboard, and a four-year-old Pontiac. He plays clarinet in the town band. He's a church member, and he sends his kids to college.

These are some of the activities I've seen prison guards, off-duty, engaged in. He's no bully. He's no bum. We put the black marks on him that we make him wear. He's done better by us than we by him and if he chooses to ignore the society that has brought him nothing but slander, he has certainly earned that right.

It is an expanded and broadening use of these very men that I would like to see bringing a bit more light to the dark tunnels they work in. And more light to prisoners.

Of his meaningless uniform, take it off and throw it out.

The very physical appearance of the guard carries a minatory and punitive shadow. Guards should appear as any other man in the street, in the same garb—a suit or slacks—that will be the same familiar scene the prisoner knows and remembers, the same to which he will one day return.

Split the guard's time between custodial care and teaching, no guard to apply for prison work unless he has a teachable skill the prison can put to use.

Turn the prison into a college? No. Turn it into a high school, and a junior high, with deliberate emphasis on a job-range that has reference to employment opportunities in the cities the prisoner will go back to.

What things? Basically simple things: truck repair, painting, mechanical drawing, blueprinting, press-work, typesetting; simple math and basic English; shorthand; cleaning and dyeing, pressing and tailoring; wallpapering. History taught to blacks by blacks. Linotype, welding, garage mechanics, engine-assembly, airplane mechanics, electronics, air-conditioning, food freezing, lawn-care and landscaping, tree surgery, bus-driving, commercial art, hospital work.

Nothing arty and nothing very advanced. Practical occupations only, teachable, and needed by the world. Prisons should be Y.M.C.A.'s.

Wouldn't the farm skills of guards in our rural facilities be wasted? Yes, they would. But this doesn't empty the reservoir. Four-fifths of America's COs have had military service where they acquired skills at government expense, skills they still have but no longer use: radar, navigation, marina work, corpsmen, signaling, computer work, warehouse supervision, storehouse inventory, first-aid, code-reading, radio. In most prisons the service background of any guard is part of his record of application: good pages to turn over in any census-taking to measure the teaching power that is now unused but that is present in any large facility.

The emphasis should be on the incoming applicant. A higher standard should be set for the educational background of all guards. One cannot expect a sudden conversion to college levels from present high school levels (though city police are going this way) but it is not illusory to think of the quality of response, in any recruitment campaign, that a pay raise, from the present $10,000 a year to $15,000, would produce.

In my own wanderings among our prisons, the most unhappy of this nation's prisoners are always those who are either isolated (because of disruptive behavior) or those who by their own choice serve out their sentences unprogrammed. Men with nothing to do, nowhere to go; prisoners who shun the shops, who bypass the classrooms. And this, sadly, in the code of so many, is the approved thing to do. They come out as stupid and useless as they went in. They feel they're getting some sort of revenge against the system, albeit a negative one, by shunting aside all the "improvement" stuff that's offered; that there's something sissified in any prisoner who wants to "get on."

Prisons have to insist that these men, however hostile to such meager benefits as may be there, be obliged to enroll in them. This has been urged before, and the cry of "forced labor" goes up. "Indentured slavery." "Unconstitutional." You've heard this. Everyone has. But if it's unconstitutional, this has not come to the notice of the Chief Justice of the Supreme Court, whose phrases of a few pages back—"make certain that every inmate works hard" —that "he learn his way out"—will return to the reader's memory now.

No, it is not unconstitutional, and leaving the matter open to the judgment of the individual is the purest insanity. It is cruel to the inmate himself, whose self-judgments are often infantile. It is cruel to the facility for immobilizing the guard, the only ameliorating influence it has to offer. It is destructive of society for so mindlessly spilling back upon itself the same barrel of rotten apples it has already paid so heavily to get rid of.

In many prisons, inmates of 30 or 40 can't bear to face classes that include inmates much younger. It would be found out at once that they can't read. They could not bear such humiliation, and feel all their status would collapse.

Sending prisoners to prison schools, even over their protest, is no different from sending six-year-olds to first grade. We all managed to survive it. So will grown men.

But in many prisons the authority to *make* them go is not now here. Thus we have the absurd, wasting spectacle of prisoners sulking in their cells and souring in the yard: "Make *me* go to school! Get lost, brother!"

This glacial drift to their chilling impassivity is correctible. The drift to the self-exiled can be reversed and set in motion with simple enabling legislation, and made to go the other way. In a month the men themselves would be happier, more self-respecting, and tractable; less in-looking; healthier-minded. And they'd know how to read.

The very word "work" actually terrifies many prisoners. They never did any. Their contempt for it is rooted in their ignorance of it. The terror diminishes in rough proportion to the adequacy of the teaching, and to the suitability, for any individual prisoner, of the job itself and of his natural bent to its mastery.

Not big jobs. Simple jobs, simply taught.

When prisoners begin to respect something else and when they begin to do this through their actual comprehension of its use, precision, complexity, and function—for example, the equipment that seals tin cans—their own respect for themselves can be born in that comprehension. They find that in the free man's world, the world of commerce, they aren't derelicts and dummies after all. They find they *can* learn. It's quite a discovery, and here and there I've witnessed it. I've seen it. Never before had they known this about themselves: that they had employable magic in their own hands. Now they have it.

No man ever insults his own proficiency.

Many years ago the Hawaiian pineapple industry ran off its pineapple juice through a ten-inch flume from the canning factory, and dumped it all into the Pacific. This dumping went on for eleven years. One day it was pointed out, by a grocery retailer who was touring Hawaii on a holiday, that such juice as remained in the can was also consumed along with the pineapple, according to his customers, and that maybe consumers liked the juice as well as the more solid fibers of the fruit. The industry thought about it, then began to divert and to package the juice, too. They've done well with both.

I feel this way about the guards in our prisons; that they represent half of the business and they're only half-used.

The turn-around of prisoner attitude toward the guard could be very immediate, when it got through to the prisoner that the guard was not working against him but for him. I've never talked to a guard of whatever rank—new man to captain—who saw anything but good in such a rearrangement. "Even the mere projection of the idea would change the mood here," a captain said to me in New Hampshire.

Are these two phalanxes—guards on one side, inmates on the other—so polarized now as to be emotionally and chemically immiscible? I've not discussed it with prisoners, but guards feel such a program, if seriously structured and candidly presented to prisoners for what it really was, would work. All agreed it would have "beginning" troubles, and agreed that its components, before the full program got rolling, should be handled one by one: limited schedulings to start with, then let its benefits, as they developed, find their own way to the prison population, by its own "good mouth."

No forcing. And no big claims. And no promises.

Guards also see an improved status for themselves *among* themselves. And they see a steady upgrading of their image as guards, before the inmates as well. They agree the teaching staff would have to be absolutely sure of its subjects, and that initially all courses should be at elementary levels, simply delivered, patiently repeated, and with much visual illustration.

Guards know something the public doesn't: they know they don't deal with adults. They know that our prisons are full of children.

An incentive to attend and to keep coming—whether mandatory or voluntary—will be sharply stimulated when "learn your way out" becomes an observed factor in parole decisions; when others waiting their turn see their first "graduate" getting out two or three or four years ahead of his ten years' time.

We're tough in our prisons but increasingly, it seems to me, we're tough about the wrong things. No one at Attica—and in many hundreds of other holding facilities—has to work if he doesn't want to. Daily classrooms should be compulsory. And a prisoner's response to the work conducted there should be an important part of his parole sheet. It is his proof of a steadily advancing improvement in the schooling assigned him, and this should steadily advance the day he can say goodbye to the big house.

Most inmates are dropouts, the first short-cut to any prison. And most aren't very bright. The intelligence levels for all of them have never been quickened, and the intake levels for most of them—their inherent capacity to learn—have never been taken. Prisons are warehouses crammed with the unschooled and the uncaring.

A graduated feed-in of correction officers who have something usable to teach; a higher standard of education for them; an appreciable hike in pay; an emotional capacity to split their time between the classroom and the cell-block; a gradual though deliberate breaking down of the traditional polarizations that now exist —this to my mind is the only direction under which the painful conversion of the anti-social man to the useful man can occur. If a prisoner can't become useful, he's bound to come back. You know the rotation. You've spent your life looking at it: most men came into prison not knowing how to do anything. And they go out that way.

Vincent R. Mancusi, superintendent at Attica when the insurrection broke out, is now deposed. State Senator John R. Dunne, who was chairman of the State Crime and Correction Commission at the time, said only: "I'm surprised." When told the identity of Mancusi's successor—Ernest L. Montanye*—he said only, "I never heard of him," even though the senator had visited every correction institution operated by the state.

We now have another example of the rocky way these things go: if there's trouble, fire the warden. Put in somebody else. The upheaval in New York City in December 1971, with the replacement of McGrath by Malcolm (also an unknown), was followed by the same at Attica only a month later, in January 1972.

No one has any confidence in anybody.

Mancusi was knocked around from the start. He was superseded by his superior, Russell Oswald, hence immobilized by him. He remained impotent during the rebellion. His humiliation continued even after it, for he had to take orders, in the aftermath of the rioting, from those directing the state's investigation. Could Mancusi have stopped it?

On the stand in Washington, before the House Select Committee on Crime, he said: "I would have moved in immediately with force. I would never negotiate with prisoners so long as they held hostages."

For the committee, Mancusi listed fifteen causes for the Attica tragedy. Here they are:

1. Lack of funds for staffing and equipment
2. Fiscally starved correction services

---

* Ernest L. Montanye, new superintendent at Attica, was born in Elmira, N.Y. Education: New Paltz State College and St. Lawrence University. Majors: psychology, criminology, administration, sociology. Sociology lecturer at the Correction Department's training academy at Beacon, N.Y. Career began at the State Department of Mental Hygiene, then guard at Napanoch (1942), institution for male mental defectives and delinquents; 1950 nominated "Correction Officer of the Year." Subsequently, sergeant at Walkill Prison; 1965, lieutenant at Sing Sing; 1968, director of four correction camps for young offenders in four different New York State counties: Schuyler, Schoharie, Chenango, Madison.

3. Outside conditions of unrest and violent protest
4. Abuses of correspondence rules
5. Increased influx of radical literature
6. Wish of special segments in the prison population to destroy the system
7. Increase of militancy
8. Channeling of known trouble-makers to Attica from other prisons
9. Federal court decision exercising authority in state prisons without responsibility for the results
10. Failure to transfer inmates identified as agitators
11. Insufficient staffing, both custodial and supervisory
12. Distorted complaints of inmates
13. Inadequate facilities
14. Impatience of young inmates for immediate change
15. Doctrine of permissiveness in society: freedom without responsibility

Those are tough handicaps for any warden to have to operate with. Especially note the first two. They are typical. And they are universal.

What support did Mancusi get? Not much. One member of the committee sarcastically observed that the warden had brought a lawyer with him. (Who wouldn't bring a lawyer?) Another member, not impressed with Mancusi, did acknowledge that "a warden can't do more than keep order if he doesn't get the financial support from his governor and legislators." This was Rep. Jerome R. Waldie, Democrat of California. Rep. Charles B. Rangel of New York, the only black on the committee, was hostile to Mancusi, saying Mancusi "opposed the reform measures that Oswald supported," a charge Oswald quickly rebutted. "It is pure nonsense to expect to change the thinking of the 7,000 members of the Correction Department in less than a year," he said, and reminded the committee that "these patterns have been here all through the lives of the full staff." And he backed Mancusi in his claim that he had asked to transfer some of the more troublesome Attica inmates to other prisons a full two months before the riot. This request had been turned down.

Let us concede that these are all good men. Let us concede that they are good men in rotten jobs; that nothing good will ever come from these weary post-mortems until everyone stops talking about the life-or-death exigency of more money, and goes out and gets it. There is no aspect of prison reform in America today that makes any sense at all until the money is there to effect it.

George McGrath noted that in times of prison uprisings everyone tended to become an "instant penologist." A good point. And most of us, as I've said, never act. We just react.

With such an unexpected parade going by as Attica presented itself to his own sense of the perfect setting, William Kunstler puffed his way to the cameras and press, stirred the kettle again, and went off accusing Governor Rockefeller of being the killer of the 43 sad wretches who so sadly and wretchedly died there. Seldom in the history of prison riots has one man done so little for so many. It wasn't Rockefeller—one of the finest men in American public life today—who caused those killings. It is my own belief that it was Kunstler.

Aren't We Too Soft on Addicts?

It is commonly believed that the drug-addiction problem in this country is our greatest crime-breeder. (Actually, alcoholism is.) But the severity of the drug problem, the hard facts of its being under poor control, and the harder facts of the speeding spread of it, have set many millions of us into direct conflict as to how to manage it at all.

Mention the "British system" and whatever group one may be talking with is instantly split in two. Perhaps the reason Americans will continue to reject the British system is because the system makes sense. Either way, Americans aren't having any. Why not? We're informed that "conditions" are quite different in the two countries. Or that the British are different. Perhaps so, but if so then someone should inform heroin about all this, for heroin, if I may speak for it, has always felt its precise pharmacopaeia to be marvelously parochial, pleasing to all users from social arbiter to Chicano. Heroin does the same in London as it does in Miami, and it does not care at all whose arterial system is host to it. But once there, it very well knows what to do and very well does it.

Should we subsidize the Turks and urge them to pull up the poppies and plant hyacinths? Give heroin away? Sell it in drugstores? Sentence all non-addicted pushers to fifty years? Educate school children with films showing the agony of withdrawal?

Force cures on addicts, whether jailed or free? You know the list. No doubt you could add to it; and no doubt have your own preference.

I'd like to suggest one more: new legislation that makes it a felony to *be* an addict.

We are presently to come to something quite as harsh. There is no abatement in sight. Except at what we might call the "Synanon level," few current programs are working, and all programs are spotty. Sensible programs get started, then the money is cut off. "Meanwhile, back at the Establishment," so Congressman Charles B. Rangel* tells us, "the state has slashed funds for narcotic programs by 65 per cent." Sensible ones, well funded, get started, then don't know how to manage their own money, as has been seen in the sad story of Phoenix House, carefully examined by Abraham Beame, New York's comptroller.

We don't think enough about *becoming* an addict. We start forgiving at the very beginning and we continue forgiving to the end. Becoming an addict is often a matter of teenage daring, of peer-group acceptance, of initiation, of titillating high-tension experiment. We all know the ritual. And we all know the consequence, including the immediate consequence. Heroin is the world's fastest known way to turn a clean kid into a criminal—first a thief, then a killer. He *has* to steal. And whatever his nature, he must thereafter be accompanied by a weapon. There are no choices here and ethics, if once present, are perforce jettisoned and stay there on the bottom as any other torpedoed hull.

Were it to be known to the young, while still clean, that a pattern of needle-marks was strong suspicion of addiction and urine specimens were proof of it; and if it were known to the young that this automatically meant a three-year sentence as a felon, there might be some second thoughts about first go-arounds. And the same to apply to the "older" young—the college group and beyond—the hard knowledge that there is nothing in it for them but the Bleak House.

Is this not a direct invasion of personal privilege? It is. Another threat to the Constitution? No doubt. But we are up against this

---

* Charles B. Rangel represents the 18th Congressional District in New York City—roughly Harlem and Spanish Harlem.

choice: lose another slice of our loaf of Freedom. Or lose the whole bakery.

Too many who fuss about constitutional amendments don't read them. Most amendments expand, clarify, and secure our freedoms, not cut them down. And most come about when public revulsion finally gets to a legislature.

Such a law—that it is a felony to be an addict—might delay the first prick. While it is true that many can experiment "safely" with drugs of many kinds and potencies—and millions do—it is also true that not one person in ten thousand can take the first four shots of heroin and then voluntarily back away from it. It's the most enslaving drug on earth.

But fear can instruct any man. And certainty of instant punishment can reach the young. It is his certainty of *non-punishment* that provides his present bravado.

Today it is not a crime to be an addict. I am suggesting that it should be.

For all addicts, their personal decision to take "horse" is the one decision they most bitterly deplore, for they quickly know that it annihilates the entire personality. And the "fun" doesn't last very long. It's only fun on the rise.

Compulsory hygiene in most of our public school systems has for many years required periodic inspection of scalps (for lice), throats for infection, eyes for reading perception, ears for abscesses. You remember this from your own school days. I suggest we add two more: urinalysis, and a look for skin punctures.

For in truth no one is compelled to become an addict. The only exception being the pimp who indoctrinates a prostitute to keep her manageable. For most teenagers, no one tied him up. And no one beat him up. Peer-group pressures are surely there, but basically it was, and is, a voluntary action. He, the addict, *learned* how to do it; learned how to split, how to cook, how to distend a vein, and (not too well) how to clean. It was a virginity-loss against which his best struggle was never put. It was willing. And it was sought.

And ruinous altogether.

The saddest thing I ever saw in my life—it was 31 years ago—was in the Old Slip police station at the very foot of Manhattan.

Peter Terranova took me through this sink. I spotted a young boy in a cell down there, a boy too young even to shave.

"What's the matter with this kid?" I asked.

"Professional purse-thief. He's on the needle."

"How old is he?"

"He's eleven."

It wrung me dry. And Peter Terranova, too, who had given his life to the drug problem.

Drugs are ruining what's left of our civilization in America. Drugs have already ruined New York City, and are pulling down your own city, too, wherever you live in America. Harlem is an oubliette.

"Heroin has destroyed the functioning of our school system," Congressman Charles B. Rangel informs us, and he lives there.* "Young girls shoot up in locker-rooms," he tells us. "Thirteen-year-olds buy dope from fifteen-year-old pushers." And later: "The most demoralizing experience I ever had in Harlem was being pan-handled by a twelve-year-old junkie."

Why don't the pharmaceutical companies, he asks, put money behind the development of a non-addictive heroin substitute? And he answers: because there's no profit in it for them.**

All of us are getting to know the feeling of the nearness of drugs. We are physically right next to it wherever we go. Five years ago at the invitation of Dr. Robert Baird, who with his own

---

* "Do You Know Any 12-Year-Old Junkies?"—*The New York Times*, January 5, 1972.

** Successful testing of a chemical to prevent abuse of methadone, the widely used heroin substitute, was revealed (April 23, 1972) by Representative Paul Rogers (Democrat, Florida) in a report from the Pharmaceutical Manufacturers Association. Representative Rogers is chairman of House Subcommittee on Public Health. Also reported (by Dr. John Adams and Dr. Irwin J. Pachter of the PMA) was the potential of a new drug called "naloxone," now in experimental stages with addicts in the Federal Drug Treatment Center in Lexington, Kentucky. Its aim: heroin immunization. The drug would be injected into the addict after he had gone through withdrawal. If or when he used heroin again, he would feel none of the effects. "We are hopeful it could be effective for one to three months," said Dr. Pachter. "In animal tests we are successful in blocking the heroin desire for several weeks."

"The most encouraging report I've seen yet," Representative Rogers told a news conference in Miami. "It indicates that private industry is coming into this problem, as we have been urging."

money had founded HAVEN, an acronym for Help Addicts Voluntarily End Narcotics, I went up to Harlem to talk to one of his
groups. I remember the sight of the hall on 117th Street where the
junkies were presently to come. It had once been an uptown Democratic club and had a small stage at the far end. I was told to
come at midnight and I did. No one was there. By 1 A.M. they
began to drift in. By 1:30 there were about sixty present—blacks
and whites—all trying to find a way out of the trap; all fighting off
the worst struggle of their lives—45 men, fifteen women, one of
them veiled.

"Why is the one woman veiled?" I asked Dr. Baird.

"She knew you were coming. She didn't want you to know who
she was."

Knew *I* was coming? "What the hell of it?" I asked.

"She's a well-known actress and she made a TV commercial in
your studios just last week."

You are now sitting next to it in office meetings, whatever your
business, wherever the office. It is your companion in school. In
church you share a pew with it. It has left the pool-halls and the
stairwells. It is as pandemic as Asian flu, sifting under the doors of
our worst people and our best and it has tapped your own family.

It rasies a tough question: when we're all junkies, who's going
to tend the store?

Let My People Go?

In the "prison" literature that you and I have seen, not many
really spell out what they think ought to be done. They merely
deprecate what is *being* done. Which we already somewhat know.
I am as sick of these taut, impassioned goings-over as you are.
They've become so common today that they constitute a repeat of
the very things they castigate: a ceaseless and largely empty piety.
They don't care either, really.

They attack, prick, haggle, and tsk-tsk, but they build nothing.
They never go near a prison. They read the newspapers and are
hurt, stunned, or outraged, and they grab a spear. But the spear's
tip is a pencil, not a piercing spicule that can probe its way to the

true source of this awesome paralysis: *why* don't prisons get the money they need? And prisoners the benefit of the money?

The public's sense of frustration over the prison crisis is deepening so quickly that more and more we are seeing the blunt advocacy of such desperation ideas as: tear down the walls; prisons only make them worse; let them all go; they didn't do it—we did it.

How do *you* feel about all this? Give it a try? Out of purest idealism?

Certainly the consequences of such massive manumission would not be without interest. To anticipate the involved consequences of any action (this being, we are told, an index of the quality of our intelligence) would suggest the following:

-That were our prisons suddenly to spill their content, there would be no such thing any longer as a criminal

That no police force would be needed for any function beyond tow-away duty and crossing guard pools for school children

That anyone may have a weapon and freely use it

That courts would hereafter attend to property and domestic matters and no others.

If we were to empty our prisons overnight, it could be assumed that certain elements among the released might not make the best use of their new freedom. Some of the idealists grant this but add at once: "What of it? We've got to try it."

It's a bold risk all right, and I'm game if they are. But being alone in the world and having little to lose, my situation is not theirs. What do *you* have that you want to keep? Who is near you whom you love and wish to protect? What plans could you make to do this? And what would you do *first*?

You know, we all know, what you'd do first. Isn't it past time we called our own bluff on this one? It is naked nonsense. In a week, you couldn't get halfway to the A & P.

The idealists can be briefly brave in their grand posture of Jesus Christ Superstar. But they can maintain the pose only because the fence is up. Take the fence down and the posture becomes what it always was, a mokus, ninny-headed strut. It was never anything else.

The idealists who would empty our prisons can think only halfway through their entelechies; only through the actuality of prisoners being safely where they are now; not the potential of their being suddenly out. It is a methane eloquence that belongs only to the vapid and is subscribed to only by them.

It would appear by now, after two centuries of what to do with our prisons and two centuries of not knowing, that it is psychologically necessary for the public *never* to know what to do about it; that the public, in its grandly helminthic subconscious, needs the blessed scapegoat of all the bad people being somewhere far off where they can't be seen but where they are known securely to be.

On a comparable basis it is akin to the blessing that we, the wicked, feel while our children, with folded hands, are seated in Sunday School. "How can *we* be wicked?" Obviously we can't be wicked; and at once feel less wicked. Our children right this minute are in Sunday School celebrating God Almighty for Christ's sake. And it was we who saw to it, we who sent them.

(If you don't like the Sunday School reference, change it to Sesame Street.)

These self-coronations are present everywhere: *we* are good—*they* are bad—and the obligation to know or to inquire who "they" are has been so enthusiastically shunned as to become the great intellectual luxury of Today's Enlightenment.

It suggests this: that the American public does not give a damn about prison reform but at the same time has an egregious need to *think* that it does; and that this need is satisfied in incessant talk, in signed letters, in committee chairmanships and spasms of television huddles. We *must* be good. See what we're saying. Note where we say it.

This surface exercise of the subconscious has firm results: it keeps alive a strong sense of personal goodness. It shores up all the scantlings of our leaning Christian ethic. It validates love-thy-neighbor—a dime on the tambourine. Having so many in prison, and quietly uncomfortable there, makes possible the rationalizing of all our own misconduct, all our basic misanthropy. And securely hides this from us. "Me? Nonsense! Him. Look where he *is*." Since we took care of "them," we never have to know "us."

Consider this: Attica was there, chill and stony, *before* the riot. But did anyone go? (Why should anyone go? There was no riot.) Now, with the riot, everyone has "been" to Attica. And now, as

before, *is* it everyone? No. As before, it is no one. So we return to
our graceful preprandial cheese-gratings, our blessed child-rearing,
and our personal, polite, civilized Christian thievings again and
become Ourselves.

And it's so nice. *We're* so nice.

The scapegoat, God bless it, is still there. And many, without
knowing, plan to keep it so, for the mechanisms of guilt, expia-
tion, and transfer are the most convenient public utility we have,
old as Eve. And not taxable either. What a coup!

These are the people who can't help. And they are most of us.
These are the people who make waves *only* because of their trust
in the tides of history to make the waves self-leveling; only because of their expectation that history will soon return all our
felons safely below the surface, "where they belong." They are the
people who, in this abominable preadamitic injustice, cannot operate at a conscious level, the level that a horror so ancient and so
nationwide and so visible requires of the beholder. In America we
put aside the prison problem with the easy hypocrisy of Germans
burying Buchenwald: the same *gemütlich*.

Though these people are "most of us," they are not all of us.
There is much genuine (cold-blooded, if you wish) humanity outside our prisons. I should like to see it move inside. And once
there, let them see the whole of it. And report it.

An interesting question, with an even more interesting answer,
comes up to us now. The question: *why* do we never know prisoners' needs till too late? My answer: because *wardens aren't allowed to talk to the public.* That is the essence of it. And why
aren't they? Because their jobs are political; appointive, not elective.* To whom *does* the warden talk? He talks to the Commissioner and is answerable only to him. To whom does the Commissioner talk then? He talks to the governor. What does the governor
say? He says he is "studying the situation." And no doubt he is.

But nobody ever talks to *you.*

It is wardens and guards, never prisoners, who could tell the

* The top three superintendencies, in the New York State prison system,
are won by civil service examination. Superintendent Ernest L. Montanye
came in second; Vito Ternullo came in first, so had first choice. He preferred Elmira, which pleased Montanye who preferred Attica.

whole of it, and who wish to. But they never have been allowed. They are more muzzled than the inmates, pitiably silenced, gagged by tradition, gagged by threat of removal. *They* can't tell you how bad it is, though they know, because it will make the Commissioner look bad. And the Commissioner can't tell you, because it would embarrass the governor. You are not to embarrass the governor—he's elective.

It is the same at lower levels. The most larcenous Mayor any American city has ever had—including Jimmy Walker—was Frank Hague of Jersey City. "I-Am-the-Law Hague" took $50 million from Hudson County. He put 88 of his friends and relatives on the payroll and did so with the most economical of briefings: "Don't embarrass me."

Who's embarrassed? No one. The South Mall is going up, day by day, in Albany, and it will be mighty pretty. But its cost, a billion and a half, would take care of every prison problem in New York State right through the end of this century. Of course it was a "crisis" budget—there was never any other kind—and of course it was met. All fiscal crises have to be met. But where did they find the money? Same as before: reallocate. Take it away from somebody else.

And thus, with the "lessons" of Attica so cruelly learned only thirteen weeks before, Albany clipped *$22 million** that was earmarked for New York State prisons.

Was there a public convulsion about this? No. There was public acceptance of it.

I believe a visible structure for correction—practical, sensible and humane—has been present for many years and is present now. I believe it has largely failed and will continue to fail because the money to get it going and keep it going is never there. It is not there and now and it is not going to be there. So it would appear, not as shocking but as inevitable, that what was said earlier about rehabilitation not being a fact of prison life in America today is the truth.

---

* For an exercise in pure fiscal alectryomancy, as it relates to the shuffling about of prison moneys, see the paragraphs (Appendix 3) of reporter Brian B. King of The Associated Press, from Article IV in his fine series "Attica Revisited," published June 8, 1972, in the New York *Post*.

Capital Punishment

There are many who feel (and who do so without realizing it) that "to be against capital punishment" is a sure way to a seeming magnanimity; assertive people as a rule, inflexible in their conviction, but people whose sincerity and whose knowledge may be doubtful.

For one thing, they all say the same thing and say it the same way. And keep saying it. For another, they all stop at the same place; which is to say, they stop at their conclusion, pushing aside any enthymemes that might be inconvenient to the argument. For still another, they never bring to us a thought that has been painfully fashioned in their own mind. Emerson has remarked that "We are of different opinions at different times" but urges us, whatever the differentials, that we should remain "on the side of truth." Those who would abolish capital punishment have no doubts of their own "truth."

So from all these good people we get little but quotes from others' minds: "Maybe he didn't do it." (Or she.) "Cruel and unusual." "Legalized murder." "Murderers have the lowest rates of recidivism." "Sacredness of human life." "Inhuman." "Two wrongs, etc."

But how rare is intelligent comment about the life of the killer after he's escaped the chair. Or the noose, or gas chamber. At the same time, it raises a plausible question: now that you've spared him, what are your plans for him?

It is silly to keep pushing the "deterrence" argument at us, for we all know the figures, and we all accept the premise they show: that killing the killer has no effect on the killer-to-be.

That is not the whole of it. If the killer's right to go on living is given him out of the generosity of the American heart, the heart's obligation is not discharged so quickly. It has a journey to make, a journey to the head, to the mind, to reason, to hard reflection. Few take this journey. Few can. Few will.

We abolish capital punishment and at once walk away from it, much as we do with "rehabilitation." We use the word and abandon the process.

To my mind this is very much on the same thought-level as all the other reform pieties that require no action or, most of all, require no inconvenience. "I am on record," they say. The implication—"You take it from here"—is also present, but they don't have the courage to say that, nor the self-inquiry to perceive it, not having the courage to think on into the immediate area beyond. They've "signed the petition" and that's all. But that isn't all, for you have let the man live. Then what? It comes down to this: these are the people who don't want to be bothered. They want you to be bothered.

This show of righteousness is similar to a public stance by which many Americans (and those over 55 will remember it) dignified their persons and blessed their homes by wearing a decoration called the White Ribbon, a swatch of clipped silk that pronounced the wearer to be a teetotaler. My grandmother, who was the founder of the W.C.T.U. in North Dakota, tucked one of these things in my buttonhole. I didn't know what it meant and would have preferred a trout-fly or a small picture of Home Run Baker. I was eight years old. (But at least I was an eight-year-old teetotaler.) But right here, having invested me with the New Order, my grandmother walked away from my drinking problem and never thought of it again (though some decades later came a day when *I* did).

We don't know what the abolitionists plan beyond abolition. They don't either. They have their own white ribbon right there in their buttonholes, and the markings of the hyssop on their front doors. With such sanitary symbols as these, they can easily show they are the beautiful people, and they use them this way, like a quick flashing of the "V" sign.

Do you know a therapist who can tidy up Charles Manson? Or a group of them who can reassemble Richard Speck? Study his double-Y chromosomes? There is a gentleman in Southern California waiting to know what is going to happen to *him*, and he should be somewhat concerned, having killed 25 men and having made random disposition of their remains in his orange grove.

We felt briefly sorry for some of the victims in these awful cases because some were famous or rich, or because the Chicago nurses were pretty, or because the orange grove victims were so numerous. Corona's victims were nameless and faceless, poor and sad (most victims are poor and sad and nameless); and most of the orange grove victims, when exhumed, did not appear well enough nourished to have done their best work.

These savage killings horrified the world. But then, as it always does, the odd turn-about of public feeling at once set in: victims forgotten (dead and buried), the public mind turns now to the horror of the gas chamber. And there it stays, the abolitionists trying to ram the door shut with their foot, while semaphoring the public to put these relics of medievalism once and for all out of modern life. The victim goes into the dead files of statistics, not being invited to tell what really happened, and the public mind focuses on the accused and tries to save him.

Odd questions come up: why *didn't* we flag down Richard Speck a long time before his three-hour prowlings through the nurses' dormitory in Chicago? We know he had 23 arrests, four for felonies, before he was twenty-one. That is not a promising profile.

There is another question: why do we know so much about executions? We know because we love to read about them. We love to inhabit the horror of it all while being at home reading about it all. We can attend the whole of it without moving.

Because these improving spectacles make us gasp, we are careful to see they are well covered by the media. We dramatize the killing of the killer. We do plays about it, and movies. We wouldn't dare dramatize the killing itself but fortunately no one is ever there with a camera, and the lighting for most murders substandard, but were it to happen—were a sudden convulsive identification with the *victim* ever made—the puff would leave the balloon and it would come down.

Here, in this sudden transfer of humane feeling, we reverse important identities. Consider what we know about the condemned man, for example—any condemned man. Because we send photographers and reporters to the iron floor where the execution is to take place, we walk the "last mile" with him. We know what he ate—we saw the whole menu—and what he wore. We know the fee ($75) the executioner is to get. We know the condemned's last words—"protesting his innocence to the end." We see the priest, the prayer. We see the bent huddle of the killer's family. (The victim's family is in its own huddle somewhere else and has been there a long time.) We surge at the rumor of last-minute reprieve. We wince when the lights dim, for we know its sinister meaning.

All America gasps. Actually, all America thought it was just great and can enjoy it with self-approval, having so fiercely protested it all.

In its curious way it has all been a reenactment of the crucifixion of Jesus Christ, a fitting into today's myths of an ancient, semi-legendary drama in which our religions germinated. The parallels are sharp and distinct: the trial, the betrayal, the brutal guards, the Last Supper, the agonized walk to Golgotha, the Romans, the ropes, the nails, the weeping, Veronica at the Ninth Step of the Cross, Mary, at the end, looking up, and Christ, looking down, still alive and speaking: "Mother, behold . . ." "Father, forgive. . . ."

But here the parallel ends. We aren't in the Holy Land. And it isn't 33 A.D. It is somewhat later. The killer before us is not Jesus, the Supreme Court is not Pilate, and we are not the Romans.

Here we have a sepulchre called the morgue.

In it you may see what the killer did to the killed. No one ever does this. "Who weeps for the victim?" asks Governor Reagan of California. No one does. None but the nameless family, and the question "Who weeps for the victim?" will never get an answer, for it doesn't ring in the ears of conscience, nor nibble the nerves of memory. By conscious neglect, we have betrayed the victim, and because he is thus betrayed we *must* dismiss him. And that is what we do.

It is a conscience burden that we all shun. We would have to rearrange too much if we thought about it. Or saw it. But once the killer is convicted, we instantly move to his side. We didn't see his crimes and don't know what they were, so we don't have to think about them at all. We would grant absolution not through total knowledge; we would grant it through total ignorance.

I suggest that all citizens, in their lifetime, make one visit to the city morgue. Few could survive it: the long delay, the disinfected catacomb, the sliding out of the slab, the pulling down of the muslin sheet, the question: "Is this. . . ?" It would alter some fixed attitudes.

I suggest we quit all the sentimental kickshaws of equating executions with the Passion Play, for the man we condemn in

America today led a life somewhat different. It is not a modern-day Jesus that you would spare. It is a man who began as a punk; a man who fiercely pursuéd, then professionalized, his punkery; who paved his own *via dolorosa* with his own knife.

Two years ago I saw a TV panel show discussing crime. One member of the panel was a minister who, with magisterial benevolence, said this: "I don't know what a punk *is*." An effusion of goodness (he hoped) oozed out of the man and spattered about the studio floor, but it left me unconvinced. All ministers (and I know the fraternity—my father was one) should know something about sin, besides merely being "against it."

I know what a punk is and can define him, and will: a punk is a teenager of any race and of either sex who is not looking for work but looking for trouble, and carrying a weapon.

Our prisons are full of vicious men who have committed vicious acts. And who began as punks and dropouts. We should remember that and begin with it. I remember it when I talk to them. Our prisons are not full of innocents who were "trapped by an uncaring society"; nor by luckless men who survived the unspeakable horror of the "middle passage" on the bare boards of slavers. They have made their own passage. Of course, prisons are full of the disadvantaged. They are also full of the self-disadvantaged, though I've never seen it mentioned in sociological literature.

I have some understanding—limited but real—of their agony and confusion. Life has run over me pretty hard at times. But I am also acutely mindful of the *antecedent* actions that brought them to these dreadful holes. Sometimes it's been hard for me to find my way; hard for you, hard for us all. Few men are lonelier than I but I have no self-pity about the circumstance, and have more control over it than prisoners have over their own. I have pity and recognition to extend to them, pity I truly feel for them but pity I never reveal when speaking before them; to any of the poor wretches I see, in small groups or large, and whom I will continue to visit. For to show pity can only brim the tanks of their own self-pity that came along, full enough then, when they began to do time, and that have been self-flooding since. I go because I think it's right—no other reason. There's nothing the matter with Christianity if those who profess it would only practice it.

I share a certain understanding with prisoners, this especially: that they have met many defeats. So have I. In fact, I have been defeated by nearly every life-riddle I've tried to unravel; defeated by all but the last one: I have not yet been defeated by defeat. Nor do they have to be.

And so with those doing their five-to-ten or their twenty-to-life: any hope? Some. At least, that is what I believe; and that is what I try to encourage them to think. In their present situation, though the climate for productive thought is poor, the time to do the thinking, God knows, is there.

About a few things, I am, as others, sentimental. But there is nothing sentimental about a prison, and in the purposes and motivations that go along with me when visiting inmates—whether jail or asylum—there is none at all. They're bad off and need help. I try to bring them some. And it is surely not very much. But whatever it is, it is always tempered by my honest belief that *no man's life is any more sacred than he considers yours to be.**

Many of these men are reachable, and though most aren't reversible, most are nonetheless redirectible. We just won't pay for the mechanics to make it happen. Other priorities always get there first. About the money, can't we at least make a beginning by being honest? By getting better acquainted with the men and women who speak for us in our legislatures? Then demanding of the people who now decide where the money is to be spent, that it go where it ought? We can still talk. And we can still vote. We can still demand to know how *they* voted. If they don't get the money on the barrelhead, we can vote them out. And if they go through their heckling quadrenniums, capitulating to lobbies that overload us with roads—the oil lobbies and the automobile lobbies—throw the bums out. The gangrene is in our assemblies, but you hold the knife that can cut back this infection; you hold the power to put in the showers for all of Attica's blacks.

The shame of Attica is in Albany.

* See Appendix 2.

APPENDIX 1

AUXILIARY POLICE

At a time when German U-boats in the North Atlantic were effective enough to threaten the world (1916–17), a counter-measure, known and used before, was invoked. It was called the convoy. It came just in time. Without it, we would have lost that war.

By the time of World War II, we were well rehearsed. But without convoys, we'd have lost that war as well. And didn't miss losing by much.

To my mind, American cities today face the same vulnerability as did the cargo ships in 1916. Crime is sinking them. We all know this. We see it, we read about it every day. And do nothing. We hear the sirens or, once in awhile, a pistol shot split the night.

It is cruel and myopic to tell anyone, any longer, that crime doesn't pay. It pays so well many of our brightest people are in it. And intend to stay in it. And will. Why not? They don't get hurt. Or caught. They just get rich. It's the quickest, safest way to get ahead in America, and thousands in every city subscribe to crime as casually now as they ever did under Boss Tweed or "Nothing-Is-Lost-But-Honor" Jim Fisk.

In the view of many citizens and a growing number of police officials, we are neglecting our best weapon. In all our cities, large or small, we have the energy and the man-power to help push back, help stop the encroachment of crime that is imperilling the safety of private families; crime that is chasing us right into our own apartments, double-daring us to come out. In response to this, 1,300 American cities, from cities of 5,000 to 25,000, in size, have invoked the muscle of their own communities to do something about this.

What is it?

It is the trained, volunteer, uniformed Auxiliary Police Force. The reader, whether man or woman, should know of this.

In every community where this service exists, its effectiveness is in direct proportion to three factors:

1. The professionalism of its training
2. The support of its community
3. Its acceptance and practical deployment by the regular police

American cities have now reached the stage where they must call in this "convoy." They have reached the stage where they may go under if they don't get it.

What can an Auxiliary Police Force do for your city that its present police force is not able to cover? Quite a lot.

Auxiliaries can stop and are stopping vandalism in churches, schools, parks, playgrounds, and synagogues. The vandalism committed against public schools in New York City alone—in wrecked rooms, smashed equipment, smashed windows, flooding, and fires —cost the city $6 million in 1971.

How can Auxiliaries stop this? By having the premises, all its rooms and corridors, patrolled; patrolled all night, every night of the week; patrolled by trained volunteers with arrest powers.

Auxiliary Police can't stop muggings on the street but they can stop muggings in apartment house lobbies and in all self-service elevators. How can they do this? It is the custom of Auxiliaries to work in pairs. In the matter of apartments, one officer to stand in the lobby and check all entrances, the other officer to man the elevator. Self-service elevators are any city's easiest trap, not only for muggings but for rape on roofs, and for access to any floor in order to burglarize it. Self-service elevators, to the rapist or the mugger or the thief, is as soft a touch—and as safe—as leaving the bank door open and the cash-drawers exposed. Self-service elevators advertise themselves. They invite violence.

Do this patrolling all night? Yes, every night, all year. Ten P.M. to daylight.

We lose much effectiveness of our police services by confining a trained cop to the wheel. Most Auxiliaries are car-owners and, being city-bred, good drivers. Let these men take the wheel of the cities' prowl-cars, releasing the regular driver for unimpeded observation and for the unrelenting radio duty. There is another advantage: almost invariably, Auxiliaries live in the precincts to which they are assigned, the regular police almost never. Auxiliaries know their own neighborhoods and know them cold.

In the frightening figures seen earlier and relating to the vanning of prisoners from jails to courts, the decimating drain on the manpower of police and correction officers can be stopped by giving these jobs to Auxiliaries. A seeming discrepancy in the figures shown by Mayor Lindsay is explained by the fact that many prisoners have to be vanned many times; a trip each morning and evening being repeated until the trial is over. Every city complains about this. So does every police and correction service. It is an enormous waste, and here the attrition on manpower is for transport service only.

Much of the van work relates not to prisoners at all but to supply and maintenance. It's extremely wasteful to put regular police or elements of trained correction staffs on a job where the logistics are limited to the hauling of food, laundry, traffic stanchions, parade barriers, and milk cans. It's a chauffering job, nothing more, with very little risk.

Another waste of police power has to do with traffic. Auxiliary Police, properly trained and detailed, can assume *all* of any city's traffic control, except that which is handled by computers, from traffic-towers or control-boards. It's an outrage to city budgets to see a member of the regular force spending the day waving cars through traffic at tough crossings. This is a job for Auxiliaries, for citizen police.*

Auxiliary Police in any city where their uses are employed with any sophistication can and do take care of the nuisance of ticketing cars for parking violations. This is a clerical tedium that robs all cities of good men. Give the job to Auxiliaries. Let them tie on the ticket. Let them make the "book" entry.

In this same area of municipal waste are the lost man-hours exacted by regular police in the everlasting drudgery of the tow-away crews. Why should this take an armed man? It takes a little muscle and a driver's license, nothing more. Why not give it to the Auxiliaries?

* Although New York City has never taken adequate (or even sensible) note of the great potential that exists in Auxiliary Police, an encouraging story, headlined "Auxiliary Police Making Comeback," appeared (page 66) in the New York *Times* of June 4, 1972.

The gradual transfer to Auxiliaries of these "non-police" services will in most cities yield a thirty per cent increase in the redeployment of regulars into areas where their training and their skills are cruelly needed.

Who is eligible to join the Auxiliary Police? In most cities, able-bodied men—women, too—ages 21 to 63. Education? High school and beyond, with college preferred. A military service background is an excellent qualification. Today this represents a huge man-power pool. Twenty-seven million Americans, under the age of 63, have now been in uniform, at one time or another and in one service or another. Whether they saw combat or not, this backlog of trained reserves is accustomed to weapons, uniforms, and orders; to tough hours, bad weather, bad food, abuse, boredom, risk, disappointment, darkness, rain, and fatigue. All have been through the grind and gravel of taking orders, and many, of giving them.

I saw a bit of this, and respected all of it. Its potential for *practical* community safety kept emphasizing itself every time I went out. For three years I served with the Auxiliary Police Force in New York City, two nights a week, patrolling Central Park and clearing its 830 acres at 11 P.M. of all visitors, directing the lost to exits, shooing out the steady stream of cars that poured out after the band or symphony concerts on the Mall, or the Shakespeare plays at Belvedere Lake.

Every city in this country, besides its own massive police problems, has a lot of little ones. I am appealing to the sense of municipal survival that the massive problems be handled by men who give their lives to it; appealing to the hard sense of the argument that the "little" problems be taken over by volunteers. The argument not only has to do with returning regulars to assignments where their need is critical; it has also to do with money. Auxiliaries get no pay.

In Central Park no commercial traffic, no trucks, are allowed through the roads at any time, yet many drivers, not knowing this, come in anyhow. Among such, there is an occasional stolen truck. We stopped them all and in any suspicious situation took the driver and his crew to the desk-officer of the Central Park precinct, the 22nd (known as the Two-Two). We had other duties: lost children, sick people, drunks, disabled cars, vandalized equipment (comfort stations were and are a favorite target), accidents, light poles with dead bulbs—all such were dealt with, noted, reported, taken care of, or brought in.

We used our own cars. But we also did a lot of walking, hundreds of miles a year and no fun on a March night. No fun any time actually. There's little exhilaration in police work on any level, in any command. And few heroics. If you're looking for adventure at the Auxiliary Police level, stay out.

With these known disadvantages I nonetheless found the Auxiliaries in this unit to be loyal to their work, dreary though most of it was. And I find this same feeling of loyalty, of personal involvement, of the burden of making a *regular* appearance, to be shared in all the other Auxiliary Police services I've had occasion to see in this country—about fifteen in all.

These men, and these women, all serve because they *wish* to serve. They sense the need. They live in it. (So do you.) And they respond to it. The uniform has nothing to do with it. Most who have never before worn a uniform are embarrassed at first, as I was.

Why do they want to serve? Because in these past twenty years they have come to know their own lives, and homes, their own children, are in constant physical danger; that there aren't enough police any more to protect us all. And never going to be enough. They know that their city—whatever its name—is truly beleaguered; that the relentless crawl and constriction of crime, of assault, of break-in, of getting slammed flat on your own sidewalk, is happening everywhere; that this constriction is tightening night by night and month by month; that it *is* going to be your turn; that it can strike anyone, any time. And that it does. And perceiving this and wishing in some direct way to act, they volunteer their own time and their own bodies in order to release better men—the regulars—to the jobs Auxiliaries can't or shouldn't handle.

What *is* the training for an Auxiliary? Most must attend the police school or academy in their respective cities. In New York we took courses once a week, twenty weeks a year, at the East 20th Street Police Academy; basic courses in police science, crowd control, the rights of arrested persons, the use of allowable force, the more effective use of restraint; observation and memory drill; and the complete grid of the New York Police System, line and staff. We also had term papers to prepare and to deliver. For advancement in rank, these courses were and are compulsory. Most take them.

On the night of the blackout, I was especially impressed with the response and the behavior of the Auxiliaries. At home in my own apartment, after warning flutter, all services winked out one by one. No phones, lights, television, or radio. No elevator service. I turned on a small transistor set, heard the first alarms and confusions, moments later a report of looting. I got into uniform, walked down fourteen flights to the street, and reported. All but two of our platoon of 48 Auxiliaries began showing up, some in uniform, some in business suits. It was about 6:00 P.M. Many had run up from work—no taxis—and were out of breath. But they all knew—once they "heard"—where they belonged. And came banging in.

The regulars were glad to see the showing. They could use us. And did. We were dispatched to bridge approaches, tunnels, and tough traffic intersections to keep cars in motion that were trying to leave the city.

I was assigned to Lexington Avenue and 59th Street, untangling a jam that would still be there had there been no one with a strong flashlight, good lungs, and a whistle. I served seven hours, with only one ten-minute break. No heroics. Except for one hideously smoky and stalled subway, there was no panic anywhere in New York that night. Not a single dented fender that I saw or heard, no crash of a delicatessen window going in. Hotels and bars couldn't serve liquor, and this helped. New Yorkers kept their cool, something oddly bred into them, perhaps because normal New York life is so close to ferocious. The weather (early November) was merciful, the night mild. And there was a full moon.

Stranded, frightened homebound shoppers and office-workers, with the subways dead, bummed rides over the bridges. Most drivers accommodated, anxious to talk to somebody, anybody.

What the Auxiliaries did that night was not very much, to be sure. We were well officered, were quickly set down at specific spots, with precise orders. Then on our own to do the job from there, until relieved. I got home at four in the morning. By then I had had two years of regular duty with these remarkable "private citizens in police uniform" (Auxiliaries wear the regular police uniform), and though in no true sense a cop I was an able-bodied male doing an uncomfortable job on a bad night that could have become quite awful, quite suddenly.

How did the Auxiliaries start in America? And when?

They came into being in 1950, mushrooming rapidly when our fear of an A-Bomb strike by the Russians was very real. In the 1,300 cities where this service is organized, the Auxiliaries are an adjunct of the regular force, wherever platooned. As such, they are therefore a part of the Department of Defense. They have been a national force ever since the Russian scare, some growing larger, others shrinking, many phasing out. In New York 86,000 men and 4,600 women have been trained during these intervening 21 years.

Auxiliaries are constantly asked if they are weaponed.* They carry a nightstick (for prodding, never for hitting), handcuffs, often a billy, never a blackjack. But officially they are not armed with a hand-gun. Only about fifteen per cent are permitted to carry guns, and a "Carry" permit (called a "Straight Carry" by the police) is such a tough permit to get in New York City that it is honored throughout the entire state. If an Auxiliary does have a gun, he had to secure it independent of his service in uniform. He had to get it as a private citizen. It took me five months. Very little of your personal record, public and private, is unknown to the police before you are granted permission to carry a hand-gun. And only 22,000 New Yorkers, including gun-carrying Auxiliaries, have "Carry" permits. These weapons are seldom misused. Your permit and your guns are forfeited at once, in any such case. You also lose your permit if you lose your gun.

Quite properly, the police don't want anyone to have a "Carry" permit unless he thoroughly knows how to use a gun, and thoroughly respects it. He is expected to spend many hours a month at the pistol range, under severely controlled conditions and under the constant scrutiny of experts. Those Auxiliaries who had guns also had superior instruction. Through the years New York has frequently held the police pistol team championship of America. Among regular police services this team is rarely defeated, though

* For some additional editorial comment on gun ownership, see Appendix 2.

they have been defeated by the incredible marksmanship of the F.B.I. team. I've seen men, from each of these two teams, in exhibition shooting, actually split a bullet against an axe-blade set in a block of wood, and shatter two clay pigeons, one on each side of the blade. And do this six times in seven shots, at seven yards. This takes uncanny steadiness.

In no sense am I, nor was I ever, a weapons-conscious person, but having gone this far with a police service I felt I should go the distance. I soon found that all the disciplines of pistol shooting are exacting. And fiercely time-consuming. But I also found that the practice is good for the nerves, for the eye, the hand, the arm. And found, too, that those who were first to become proficient at target-shooting had been proficient at something else before then, whether fencing, billiards, or the playing of a musical instrument. These hard-won skills had produced a habit of intense concentration, indispensable to the mastery, even to the elementary demands, of any art, any craft, any cunning.

On the pistol range we spent many hours in "dry-firing," which is to say, practice with an unloaded gun, usually holding at "six-o'clock," then the simulated firing (or "let-off," as it's called). Dry-firing is a large part of the success of all good shooting. The muscles of the trigger finger must be so finely tuned to the demands of a gradually increased pressure that the shooter never quite knows the exact instant the hammer is going to hit.

I am aware of the gun controversy, and am not going to get into it beyond this observation: that in the 38 years I've lived in New York, I've never seen any plan—in the increasing semi-hysteria to disarm everybody—that will take these weapons away from criminals. Those who have a legal right to carry a gun will lose it. Those who have no right will continue to carry. The police know the former; no one knows who the others are. I am talking about hand-guns, not rifles.

The use of firearms is the least of the training for most Auxiliaries, but they do learn much else. Or they can if they wish to go after it. They learn how to make an arrest, how to hold evidence, how to hold a prisoner and how to present him in court; how to recognize wanted characters and what to do if they spot one. They learn how to cool off incipient fights and how to de-escalate them if they've started. They learn how to splint a fracture, how to put out a fire, and what techniques or equipment to use for what fire, whether oil, fireplace, or electric kitchen. They learn how to drag an unconscious person out of a smoke-filled room without losing consciousness themselves.

They learn (as "apprentice" police) how to take an insult without reacting. They learn a bit of law, too, and much about the new Code of Criminal Procedure. They learn your rights as a citizen and very early know them better than you do. And will instruct you in their meaning if you need this.

In a year, given two solid evenings a week and a tough training-sergeant (always one of the regulars), an Auxiliary Police officer is a valuable adjunct to any existing police facility, and a new and dependable reinforcement of public safety and private survival.

What's in it for an Auxiliary? Nothing at all. He's out there padding through the wet underbrush of a city park or cemetery for one reason only: to keep peace in his neighborhood. He is there to keep his family, and yours, safer than it is now.

What does it cost him? Auxiliaries have to buy everything they wear or carry. Their uniforms are the same as the regular police. And all Auxiliaries work without pay. If an Auxiliary is mounted, he must pay for the stabling of his horse. If he has a radio-equipped car, he has to maintain the equipment and buy the gas. But the tough profile of crime, pushing up behind every fence and peeking into every lobby, is beginning to bring in some new men.

The State Police, for many years and in many of our states, have recognized the supporting value of these volunteers. While touring the installations and stations of Connecticut a few years ago, I asked Commissioner Leo Mulcahy (now retired) how these "citizen police" were working out with him and with the regular troopers.

"We count on them. It's tough and they know it. One single unexplained absence and they're out. No appeal either. We don't lose many. They're as loyal as the regulars."

I spent many weeks with the New York State Police, sleeping in their dorms, eating with the Troopers, taking thirty or forty frightening rides, from the Canadian border to Lake Erie. Superior men in every way, hard-trained, fair, instant in their response to any emergency, any threat, whether lost child, killer-at-large, or forest fire.

I feel very sure that public service radio and television, were these outlets to be used for recruitment campaign purposes to bring in a new crop of Auxiliaries, would produce a new force in this land; a quality of response, gratifying where it now exists, that would reflect the inner resources and the basic courage of civilian populations everywhere. It's there but it's untapped, most not having been told what to do or where to go.

I doubt any citizen can get the "feel" of the police world unless he himself inhabits it, even tangentially. By inhabiting it, by sharing its drudgery—and make no mistake about the drudgery—and at times sharing a bit of the risk, a new quality of talk will begin to be heard at America's dinner-table conversations; a humanized understanding (being a participating one) of that special, misunderstood, and currently unpopular world. And a new, or a renewed, respect for it, brought into homes by one or another of its members through his being an honest part of it himself, however small.

Currently, there are signs that business is beginning to develop a susceptibility to the idea of getting into public problems; to the idea of releasing part of its office force for the relief of the crashing emergencies going on all about. The Xerox Company, a social-minded corporation, announced on September 8, 1971, that it was granting leaves of absence to many of its employees so that they may participate in such programs as drug-addiction aid, civil rights matters, and penal reform. Though there was no mention of police work, the announcement was strong indication of a deliberate reaching into community problems on a positive and a practical basis; and not, as we've so often had it before, on a committee or memo basis.

People respond when they're asked to. It is not illusory to expect that Americans, who generally behave well in any crisis, would respond, as boat-owners did, to one of the shortest commands in England's history:

"Your destination is Dunkirk."

Now we are there ourselves. Every American city is Dunkirk.

So is every prison.

GUN CONTROL AND GUN LAWS

Following are two editorials on gun control problems from the New York *Times.*

The Gun Menace

The criminal assault on Governor Wallace has once again spotlighted the nation's hideous crime against itself—its refusal to take effective measures to control the manufacture, sale and ownership of guns. The depressing aspect of recurrent flurries of public interest and Congressional response is that these all quickly evaporate in surrender to the gun lobby's powerful propaganda machine.

After each new outrage, the misguided defenders of the right to bear arms as a mark of free American manhood dust off their fatuous cliché that "people, not guns, kill people." It would be as logical to defend the uncontrolled and unregistered use of automobiles by arguing that "drivers, not cars, kill people."

The near-tragedy in Maryland speaks for itself. Police there made much of the fact that the Gun Control Act of 1968 enabled them to identify the source of the alleged assailant's gun within hours of the shooting. This small comfort merely points up what might have been accomplished had an effective control law been in force. In its absence, the suspect was able to buy a gun with no more difficulty than ordering a ham sandwich—even though he had recently been arrested on a concealed-weapons charge.

Entirely apart from the spreading terror of political assassination, the facts concerning the abuse of guns in the United States are appalling. During this century, civilian gunfire has killed over 800,000 Americans—more than all the military fatalities in all wars from the Revolutionary War through Vietnam. About 20,000

Americans are killed in this fashion annually; guns each year are used in over 120,000 robberies.

May 18, 1972

Illegal Guns

Federal gun-control legislation is an essential part of any effective response to the growing abuse of firearms that has reached epidemic proportions. But there is no reason to stand passively by and await Federal action which, if the past influence of the gun lobby on Congress is any indication, may not be taken until the bloodletting becomes even more appalling. There can be no excuse whatsoever for the continuing laxity in the enforcement of existing local and state statutes.

The recent gun play between rival underworld "families" is a case in point. It is difficult to understand, for example, why the police are so hesitant in moving toward the arrest of those members of the Mafia clans found in unauthorized possession of firearms.

The way to begin the process of domestic disarming is to move efficiently against all criminal elements, whether they are small-time muggers and burglars or the godchildren of organized crime, as well as against their illegal arms suppliers. A combination of effective law-enforcement by the police and imposition of maximum penalties by the courts is an absolute prerequisite to defeat those hoodlums, big and small, who try to terrorize and dominate the cities with deadly fire power.

June 10, 1972

APPENDIX 3

ATTICA REVISITED

THE FOLLOWING IS A PORTION OF AN ARTICLE FROM A SERIES ENTITLED "ATTICA REVISITED," BY BRIAN B. KING OF THE ASSOCIATED PRESS. THIS ARTICLE, CALLED "ROCKY & THE LEGISLATURE," APPEARED IN THE NEW YORK *Post* OF JUNE 8, 1972.

So what motion in terms of legislation the two bodies [Assembly and Senate] made this election year in the politically expendable area of prison reform revolved substantially around measures introduced in Rockefeller's influential name, if the record means anything. But the record at any level of government is written more with that basic political tool—the budget—than with the clerk's pens, recording debate and votes on individual bills.

For example, one line in the budget for the current fiscal year was virtually unheard of outside the hearing-and-hassle rooms: $100,000 for an "internal investigation staff," seven persons whose salaries would total $88,000. It is a basic development, as Oswald notes:

We got something that we wanted very badly . . . a new division of intelligence and investigation, to go out in these institutions, to make certain that our policies are carried out, to investigate complaints, to check into programs and to report directly back to "Executive Deputy Commissioner Walter Dunbar and me. It's a great thing . . ." . . . break the autonomy of years past of individual wardens and to open another communications channel, this one a combined ombudsman-inspector general.

An analysis of simply the dollars' columns in the budgets this year and last, either side of "Attica," told several other tales:

The $2.8-million deficiency appropriation for the department this January went mostly—$2.1 million of it—to pay for "Attica": over-

305

time for guards, $600,000; replacing destroyed food, clothing, household items and medical supplies, transferring half the inmates out and paying hospital bills, $700,000; buying protective equipment from the federal government because of "inadequacies," $800,000.

* * *

In January, 1971, blaming the deathless 1970 Auburn riots, Rockefeller asked for $2.2 million to increase prison security. In January, 1972, blaming the Attica uprising that left 43 men dead, Rockefeller asked for $2 million to increase security.

For 1970–71, total appropriations recommended from the state-purposes budget came to $89.8 million; $83.6 was appropriated.

For 1971–72, Rockefeller asked for $96.6 million; the fiscal committees cut back administration and inspection money, upped funds for rehabilitation slightly and made $97.5 million available. But $3 million of it was not appropriated. This year, after Attica, the request for state-purposes funds went from $94.5 [million] appropriated last year to $101 million. The committees cut it by $22 million, to a mid-1960s level, a cut the government later made irrelevant with two new measures.

Of the $93.4 million sought in the 1971–72 state-purposes budget for "rehabilitation and supervision of offenders," $69.2 million was earmarked for employes' salaries and other "personal services." For the budget after "Attica," $69.6 million out of $96.1 million was so earmarked.

Federal grants totalling $125,000 were expended for 1971–72; the actual total came to $3.6 million. Grants totalling almost $6 million are expected during this fiscal year.

The entire $1.1 million for "nonpersonal services" or programs under appropriations for rehabilitation and supervision from "other funds" in 1971–72 and the entire $3.1 million authorization of $10.3 million more ranged third among agencies in this "minus year," after a fiscal year with $2.5 million appropriated at the start and another $2.5 million deficiency item, to repair Attica. Only $4.1 million of the $10.3 million was to have been spent this year.

Last year, no capital-construction "first instance" money, or funds to be loaned rather than granted, went to corrections. This year, Rockefeller asked for $60 million, $3 million of it to come the first year. The fiscal committees were not responsive to this second-highest amount among agencies.

Last year, no "major projects" were under construction at 40-year-old Attica; the budget asked only for $7,750 to be reappropriated for furnishings, $50,000 in new funds to air-condition the hospital operating room, and a reappropriation of $97,500 to air-condition the administration building.

Attica did have a "major project" listed this year: "Restoration of damaged facilities." Out of the department's $60 million was to come $6 million over several years to alter and improve the entire compound and its kitchens.

At first glance, the regular budgets showed no overwhelming fistfuls of dollars to spend on prison reform over and beyond previous years, despite "Attica."

The supplemental budget, for example, contains a section creating a new funding base—to Oswald's eyes, the real source of hope for his programs—which is similar to that for the Mental Hygiene Dept.

Under the heading of the capital construction fund is a section for "Health and Mental Hygiene Facilities Improvement Corp. Correctional Services Expenditures," with that corporation empowered to act "as agent for the state dormitory authority."

A sum of $26.2 million is specified under the section, with the money Oswald sought—and lost at regular budget time—for community correction centers, adult camps, furnishings and equipment at new and existing facilities, a gymnasium at Attica and a new vocational shop building there, to replace the one burned down to structural unsoundness in the initial hours of the riot.

* * *

It is very hard for prison administrators to tell who gets what, when, or how much.—M. W.

Index